Companion to the Old Testament

Companion to the Old Testament

Introduction, Interpretation, Application

Edited by

Hywel Clifford

with Douglas Earl,

Ryan P. O'Dowd and

Lena-Sofia Tiemeyer

scm press

© Hywel Clifford, Douglas Earl, Ryan P. O'Dowd and Lena-Sofia Tiemeyer
2016

Published in 2016 by SCM Press
Editorial office
3rd Floor, Invicta House,
108–114 Golden Lane,
London EC1Y 0TG, UK

SCM Press is an imprint of Hymns Ancient & Modern Ltd
(a registered charity)
13A Hellesdon Park Road, Norwich,
Norfolk NR6 5DR, UK
www.scmpress.co.uk

Except where otherwise indicated, Scripture quotations are from the New
Revised Standard Version of the Bible, Anglicized Edition, copyright © 1989,
1995 by the Division of Christian Education of the National Council of the
Churches of Christ in the USA. Used by permission. All rights reserved.
Other versions used are:
The Authorized Version of the Bible (The King James Bible), the rights in
which are vested in the Crown, reproduced by permission of the Crown's
Patentee, Cambridge University Press.
The New International Version, Anglicised. Copyright © 1979, 1984, 2011
by Biblica (formerly International Bible Society). Used by permission of
Hodder & Stoughton Ltd, a member of the Hodder Headline Ltd.

British Library Cataloguing in Publication data

A catalogue record for this book is available
from the British Library

978 0 334 05393 4

Typeset by Regent Typesetting
Printed and bound by
CPI Group (UK) Ltd

Contents

Preface

This 'companion' is aimed at the student and general reader interested in understanding better the contents and the significance of the Old Testament. It proposes a fresh model for approaching the Old Testament, organized with reference to three key words: introduction, interpretation, and application. The second of these is the most important, and it occupies most space throughout the book. The model is explicitly Christian, in that all of the contributors focus the majority of their attention on tracing the history of the Christian interpretation of each of the canonical sections of the Old Testament, and they then seek to apply this to the life of the Christian Church. The reasons for this approach are given in the introductory chapter. This book should, nevertheless, serve the needs of a broad range of readers, the religious and the non-religious alike, who will find that it is not written in a religiously or denominationally partisan manner, but in a way that is accessible to all.

The book has chapters on the canonical sections of the Old Testament that are common to all major Christian denominations: the Pentateuch, the Historical Books, Poetry and Wisdom, and the Prophetic Books. There is a chapter on the Apocrypha/Deutero-Canon as well, although this chapter is written in such a way that does not presume its canonical authority for all Christian denominations. The book thereby contains five core chapters, topped and tailed by an introduction and a conclusion, which are substantial chapters in and of themselves. The book's breadth of coverage and contents place it somewhere between a textbook on the Old Testament texts and a collection of essays on their interpretation and use. Readers who do not find that it serves their specific interests and needs are invited to consult the concluding chapter, in particular, which recommends resources for further study.

The content of the chapters that I have contributed in this book has been 'tried and tested' in the classroom in the last few years; the chapter on the Apocrypha/Deutero-Canon is the most recent in this regard. I am grateful to the students that I have had the privilege of teaching for their thoughtful and perceptive questions and comments. The teaching has taken place at the University of Oxford, and at Ripon College Cuddesdon, the theological college where I am based. The straddling of the two worlds of university and seminary, with their respective expectations and discourses, is hugely stimulating and enriching for me, and I hope that something of the interests and needs of each are reflected sufficiently in the final product.

I would also like to thank my fellow contributors. Each of them has been a model of patience and promptness while this book gradually came to fruition, as well as being a delight to work with.

I am also grateful to SCM Press for their enthusiasm in taking on this project. In particular, I would like to thank Natalie Watson, and subsequently David Shervington, the commissioning editors, for their guidance and assistance along the way.

Finally, I would like to express my thanks to everyone not mentioned above – not forgetting the conscientious readers of pre-publication chapters – who have contributed, in one way or another, to the writing of this book about the Old Testament.

Hywel Clifford

Contributors

Dr Hywel Clifford (Oxford, UK) is the Senior Tutor, and the Tutor in Old Testament, at Ripon College Cuddesdon, Oxford, and also a member of the University of Oxford's Faculty of Theology and Religion. Hywel has published on Isaiah 40—55, Philo of Alexandria, and the prophet Amos. Hywel's areas of interest are monotheism, early Greek philosophy, biblical interpretation, and the archaeology of biblical lands.

Dr Douglas Earl (Durham, UK) did his PhD on the book of Joshua at the University of Durham, where he has also taught. Douglas is the author of *Reading Joshua as Christian Scripture, The Joshua Delusion?: Rethinking Genocide in the Bible*, and *Reading Old Testament Narrative as Christian Scripture*. Douglas's areas of interest are in the faithful interpretation of Scripture and theology and their relationship in the context of contemporary anthropology, philosophy, and science.

Dr Ryan P. O'Dowd (New York, USA) is the Senior Scholar, Chesterton House, at Cornell University and Adjunct Professor of Biblical Studies at Gordon College in Wenham, Massachusetts. Ryan is the author of *The Wisdom of Torah*, and co-author with Craig G. Bartholomew of *Old Testament Wisdom Literature*. His commentary on the book of Proverbs is in press. Ryan's areas of interest are poetry, wisdom literature, law, and matters related to the role and nature of food, work, ritual, sexuality, and knowledge (epistemology) in the Bible.

Dr Lena-Sofia Tiemeyer (Aberdeen, UK) is Reader in Hebrew Bible at the University of Aberdeen. Lena-Sofia is the author of *Priestly Rites and Prophetic Rage: Post-Exilic Prophetic Critique of the Priesthood* and *For the Comfort of Zion: The Geographical and Theological Location of Isaiah 40—55*, as well as two monographs on Zechariah 1—8. Lena-Sofia's areas of interest are the prophetic literature and the Bible in its later Jewish and Christian Reception History. She is currently writing a commentary on the book of Jonah.

Abbreviations

ABD	Freedman (ed.), *Anchor Bible Dictionary*
ACCS	Ancient Christian Commentary on Scripture
AD	Anno Domini (= CE)
ANEP	Pritchard (ed.), *Ancient Near Eastern Pictures Relating to the Old Testament*
ANET	Pritchard (ed.), *Ancient Near Eastern Texts Relating to the Old Testament*
AUSDDS	Andrews University Seminary Doctoral Dissertation Series
BAC	The Bible in Ancient Christianity
BAR	*Biblical Archaeology Review*
BBC	Blackwell Bible Commentaries
BBRS	Bulletin for Biblical Research Supplements
BC	Before Christ (= BCE)
BCE	Before the Common Era (= BC)
BS	Biblical Seminar
CBQ	*Catholic Biblical Quarterly*
CE	Common Era (= AD)
CEP	Centro de Estudios y Publicaciones
COS	Hallo and Lawson Younger (eds), *Context of Scripture*
DCLS	Deuterocanonical and Cognate Literature Studies
FAT	Forschungen zum Alten Testament
FOTC	Fathers of the Church
GSC	Geneva Series of Commentaries
HB	Hebrew Bible
HOTE	Handbooks for Old Testament Exegesis
JANER	*Journal of Ancient Near Eastern Religions*
JSNTS	*Journal for the Study of the New Testament Supplements*
JTI	*Journal of Theological Interpretation*
KJV	King James Version
LEC	Library of Early Christianity
LCC	Library of Christian Classics
LXX	Septuagint
MT	Masoretic Text
NRSV	New Revised Standard Version
OBT	Overtures to Biblical Theology

ABBREVIATIONS

OT	Old Testament
OTM	Old Testament Message
OWC	Oxford World's Classics
SBL	Society of Biblical Literature
SBLDS	Society of Biblical Literature Dissertation Series
SBLRBS	Society of Biblical Literature Resources for Biblical Study
SBLSS	Society of Biblical Literature Symposium Series
SHCT	Studies in the History of Christian Thought
STI	Studies in Theological Interpretation
Tg	Targum
Vg	Vulgate

Introduction: A Book about Books

HYWEL CLIFFORD

The sacred texts known as the 'Old Testament' have exercised an incalculable influence in the history of human society and culture. With that in view, this book inevitably joins a long list of literature whose authors have sought to explain and explore its significance for all kinds of readers, both religious and non-religious. In this book a fresh model is proposed and applied to this endeavour. The model is outlined in the closing section of this chapter, in answer to the question: 'What is in this book about the Old Testament?' It outlines the reasons for the choice of the word 'companion' in the book title, the design of the book, and the standpoint of the contributors. But there is also some groundwork that needs to be laid, especially for readers who are less familiar with the Old Testament as such. This chapter therefore opens with the question: 'What is in the Old Testament?' In this section, the contents of the Old Testament are discussed. The other question, at the centre of the chapter, is: 'What is the Old Testament?' This section is about the status of these sacred texts.

What is in the Old Testament?

Literature and sacredness

The Old Testament's opening – 'In the beginning God created the heavens and the earth' (Gen. 1.1) – is one of the best-known openings of any literature, ancient and modern. In this majestic proclamation we are invited to open our eyes to a cosmic perspective that gives us a context for human life; and the natural curiosity we have about our origins is satisfied through the confident presentation of God, the great divine protagonist, active in the time and space that we now inhabit. To understand this recital of creation we must try to imagine *nothing* and then *something* coming into existence, and watch as the cosmic picture is masterfully painted, stroke by stroke, colour by colour, so that the beauty of the parts and their purposeful whole – the world we experience – may be freshly envisaged and appreciated. The Old Testament also contains, however, something of the other extreme: what seems, momentarily, to be a comic moment in the early history of

Israel. Some boys from the ancient city of Bethel, north of Jerusalem, jeer at the prophet Elisha as he travels from Jericho towards their city: 'Go away, baldhead! Go away, baldhead!' But to mock a prophet of God, whose divine power is at hand, was beyond the pale; their comedy becomes their tragedy: turning to them, Elisha curses the boys 'in the name of the LORD', and two she-bears suddenly come out from the nearby woods and kill 42 of the unruly gang. The prophet continues on his travels (2 Kings 2.23–25).

The Old Testament has much else, in between the impressive and inspirational and the funny gone deadly. There are sacred laws that called on Israel, anticipating its settlement in the land of Canaan, to lend to those in the community in financial need even if the following year was when debts would be cancelled; or to care for the needy stranger who was to be treated as one of their own. Later, according to the historical narratives, the politics and geography of the settled Israel became such that it was often caught between the shifting power plays of kings, near and far: there are vivid scenes of military adventure – the successful and the disastrous – set in its own territories, and poignant allusions to violent crises in distant lands. Then again, the Old Testament contains much true-to-life poetry: crafted, pithy lines that scale the heights of praise and plumb the depths of depression. There are evocative metaphors that characterize the search for wisdom, a quest that is likened, in one instance, to miners who dangle perilously on ropes inside dark caves to find priceless jewels to make them rich. 'God understands the way to it', the poet responds. And not to be missed are the arresting criticisms of a society gone awry with wickedness, injustice, and suffering, alongside hopeful visions of renewal that promise a better world for all.[1]

These examples, selected to give a flavour of the variety of texts and ideas in the Old Testament, show that its texts are the literary legacy of an ancient culture, a textual testimony to Israel in its religious, political, and social development, with many twists and turns along the way. As its texts are usually thought to have been written over the span of about a thousand years (c. 1150–150 BC), it should not be any surprise that its contents are diverse in form and content. The same is true of the literature of other ancient cultures – Egyptian, Babylonian, and Greek – to name three examples with which many will be familiar, whether through digital media, holiday excursions, or their own reading. The texts of these and other ancient cultures, some of which have only been available in translation for the last 150 years or so – thanks to modern scholars' expertise in ancient languages – are nowadays routinely compared to those from ancient Israel. Here are excerpts from an ancient Babylonian creation account, whose broad similarities (e.g. cosmology, geography, calendar) and differences (e.g. one God vs many gods) to Genesis 1—2 are both visible:

Babylonian *Enuma Elish* Tablet V

(late second millennium BC)

He [Marduk] made the position(s) for the great gods, he established (in) constellations the stars, their likenesses. He marked the year, described its boundaries, he set up twelve months of three stars each ... To raise the wind, to cause rainfall, to make mists steam, to pile up her [Tiamat] spittle (as snow?), he assigned himself, put under his control ... From her eyes he undammed the Euph[rates] and Tigris ... Below the firmament, whose grounding I made firm, a house I shall build ... I shall call [its] name Babylon, (meaning) 'Houses of the Great Gods' ...[2]

Professors and other teachers typically encourage their students to read these texts to learn about the widespread literary conventions of antiquity, so as to be attentive, through comparison, to the 'genres' or forms of literature in the Old Testament (e.g. story, law, hymn, lament, proverb, oracle). This approach enables the effective interpretation of the biblical texts: to know what to expect from them as ancient texts – even if the biblical writers, as with writers of any period, frequently show themselves capable of surprising and provoking the reader in their creative use of those conventions.[3]

But the Old Testament texts are not only literary in quality, composition, and effect; they are explicitly and distinctly religious in content: in their inspiration, their formation, and their influence. Indeed, it is primarily as religious texts that the Old Testament texts were written, copied and transmitted to subsequent generations in antiquity. Already in the ancient period these texts were used, compiled and collected to serve the religious communities of ancient Israel; and they went on to exercise a key part in the Jewish matrix of temple and synagogue, at home and abroad, out of which both ancient Judaism and Christianity emerged. In other words, the Old Testament became known, in due course, as a sacred canon. This classification of these ancient texts is traditional – from the Latin *traditio*, 'delivered, passed over, handed down' – and that is still how most people tend to encounter them today, whether in church or synagogue, and theological college or seminary. That sacredness is not taken for granted (or it is rejected) in the more neutral or secular environment of the university and the public square of ideas, at least in the liberal democracies of Western countries. But their rich influence is, in fact, in plentiful evidence there too, in countries where these texts have played a formative role in shaping a culture, alongside others from antiquity, such as Greek and Roman texts. This book about the Old Testament is, for at least these ancient, traditional, and cultural reasons, organized along canonical lines, an aspect that is discussed further below.

History and reality

Another way of making sense of what is in the Old Testament is to grasp in broad outline the historical periods and episodes presented in the texts. The Old Testament, viewed as a whole, begins not only 'in the beginning' and has apocalyptic visions that look towards the climax of history, but it also contains a joined-up account of the history of Israel in its ancient Near Eastern setting. This may be understood in terms of seven major periods and episodes: (1) Primeval; (2) Ancestral; (3) Exodus; (4) Conquest; (5) United Monarchy; (6) Divided Monarchy; (7) Exile and Return. That same narrative may be understood in another way: life in the land of Israel, set between the Exodus (entrance into the land) and the Exile (exit from the land). These approaches are not merely modern impositions on an anthology of ancient texts. In the Old Testament itself, there are already markers of periodization and the memory of key episodes and events in the Old Testament (e.g. Isa. 52.4; Jer. 50.18; 1 Macc. 1.1–4). Indeed, the construction of a more detailed chronology – to assign dates to what is described – is another way in which this narrative may be charted and articulated; again, the biblical writers encourage this (e.g. Judg. 11.26; 1 Kings 6.1; Sir. Prologue). Some of the dates (BC) that serve as useful reference points are as follows: c. 1450 (Exodus); c. 1000 (King David); 722 (the destruction of Samaria, the capital of the exiled northern kingdom of Israel); 586 (the destruction of Jerusalem, the capital of the exiled southern kingdom of Judah); and 539 (the return of the exiles to the land of Israel).[4]

The ancient Israelite religion that gave rise to ancient Judaism and then to Christianity was not a 'philosophy' (i.e. a systematic collection of ideas with varying degrees of abstraction or real-life application) but it was, after all, a historical religion, rooted in episodes, events, customs, and practices that gained long-lasting significance for the communities that inherited its religious traditions. That it is possible to speak of the 'historical' in such straightforward terms has been, however, one of the most contentious issues in Biblical and Theological Studies in the modern era. What evidence or proof is available, in both ancient texts and archaeology, for what is described in the Old Testament? Aren't its texts, rather, a collection of religious myths, fables and legends, with historical reminiscence lying only somewhere in the background? And could we ever even answer such questions satisfactorily? The positions scholars have taken on this have been many and varied. In scholarly studies published towards the end of the twentieth century, for instance, there is frequent mention of 'maximalists' who hold that the Old Testament provides accurate history; 'minimalists' for whom there is very little, if any, reliable history in its texts; to which may be added the 'centrists' who detect both strengths and weaknesses in these opposed standpoints: the former claim too much; the latter too little.[5] Each of these positions has often been unfairly caricatured, in turn, as fundamentalist, nihilist, or fence-sitting; and the scholars themselves have often refused this kind of labelling, both the formal and the informal. There are many reasons for the emergence of this complicated and controverted landscape; and some of the core chapters in this book treat it, because it is an important part of the history of the interpretation of the Old Testament.

What may be said, by way of introduction, about this? The extent to which the Old Testament reflects the religious, political, and social realities of the ancient Near East is striking; that is a relatively uncontroversial claim. The successive influence of regional powers – Egypt, Assyria, Babylonia, Persia, and Greece – whose extant artefacts are now the treasured possessions of major museums, is seen throughout its pages. The varying impact of Israel's nearer neighbours, whose names are less well known, but whose texts and archaeology have also survived, is also visible: Aram, Phoenicia, Philistia, Ammon, Moab, and Edom. Indeed, it is possible to build up a rich picture of the 'world of ancient Israel', both at the level of daily life, and at the level of empire. At the level of daily life: the call to 'Tell it not in Gath, proclaim it not in the streets of Ashkelon; or the daughters of the Philistines will rejoice, the daughters of the uncircumcised will exult' (2 Sam. 1.20) mentions *huzot*, 'streets, bazaars', where market trade took place, as excavations in the Philistine city of Ashkelon have uncovered. This was where, for the biblical narrator, gossip and mockery about the downfall of King Saul, and his son Jonathan, could easily spread. At the level of empire: the all-conquering Cyrus, the king of Persia, whose policy to restore Babylonian sanctuaries, according to the *Cyrus Cylinder* (which is usually on display in the British Museum, London), echoes the authorized return of the exiles to restore national institutions back home in Judah; indeed, Aramaic correspondence with the Persians is quoted in the book of Ezra.[6]

The attentive reader is likely, quite rightly, to probe and question: what is meant by the 'realities of the ancient Near East', if those realities are no longer accessible, and that world appears to be so very different from the world of today? After all, the past lies dormant in the past. That world, though, is not as asleep as we might think. Scholars and students of ancient history – whether Philistine, Assyrian, Israelite, or Roman – are all engaged in the imaginative reconstruction of the realities that the evidence reflects, a task that requires openness to evidence, and whose exciting discoveries are on-going – as news outlets are often quick to report (albeit sometimes too sensationally). Those for whom this task is daily diet are frequently energized by what they see: ancient peoples whose outlooks, in both story and saying, are often similar to ours, even if the Old Testament texts come to us along with particular religious content. Imaginative reconstruction must, of course, be done intelligently (i.e. critically) and not naively. After all, there are things that we cannot investigate: all texts contain perspectives, or biases, that both include and exclude detail; and the imaginative aspect of any reconstruction might turn out to be our own face looking back at us, unwittingly imposed on the past. But this explains why scholars and students are often part of educational communities open to vigorous questioning and inquiry, to ensure that there are checks and balances on what is proposed, contested, and believed. This also characterizes communities for whom the theological and spiritual dimensions of the Old Testament in particular are not just antique but alive; and which continue to be discerned so as to be imitated with wisdom in the present: church and synagogue, and theological college and seminary. In other words, an openness not only to material evidence but also to divine reality, or at least to an acknowledgement of its claimed influence, is also integral to making sense of what is in the Old Testament.[7]

Religion and theology

Religious belief and practice – however the general terms 'religious' or 'religion' are defined and understood – is one of the most abiding hallmarks of human history and behaviour. The study of ancient history is frequently concerned with the religious, so much so that it cannot be treated separately when investigating what may be known of any ancient culture. The similarly general and widely used term 'culture', which in modernity is often used of the arts or sciences for that which develops or is tended (i.e. cultivated), also requires attention to the religious (i.e. the 'cultic') when applied to ancient history. Atheism and agnosticism were attested in antiquity, in varying types and degrees, even if not dominantly so – but not, thereby, insignificantly so, it should be added. The writers of the Old Testament were, in these respects, not very different from their contemporaries: Israel, in its ancient Near Eastern setting, is frequently portrayed in the Old Testament as an actively and a self-consciously religious culture, like elsewhere. But its writers acknowledged a full range of human responses to the divine (e.g. radical trust, customary acceptance, questioning doubt, defiance, and rejection). Its texts, incidentally, do not contain arguments for the existence of God in any extended philosophical form, even if they have traditionally been deployed as containing the impetus for such arguments (e.g. Ps. 19.1–6; Wisd. 13.1–9; cf. Ps. 14.1; 53.1).[8]

Taking account of the religious content of the Old Testament is therefore essential. An especially fruitful approach is the analysis of ancient Israelite religion in comparative perspective. While it would be wrong to suppose an overly fixed notion of what a religion includes, whether ancient or modern, it becomes quickly apparent that beliefs and practices in antiquity were similar and widespread: gods, temples, priests, sacrifices, festivals, prophets, and sages – to name some of the obvious. A passage in the Old Testament such as Exodus 24, about the establishment of the covenant between God and Israel at Mt Sinai, illustrates this well. That Israel forms a covenant with God, marked by sacrificial and festal rite, and solemnized by communal legal contract (24.3–8), recalls the treaty texts and rites of ancient Near Eastern cultures (e.g. Hittite, Aramean, Assyrian). That God is envisaged sitting on a throne in a heavenly palace or court (24.10), as in other Israelite texts (Gen. 1.26; 3.22; 11.7; 1 Kings 22.19–23; Job 1.6–12; 2.1–6; Ps. 82; Isa. 6.1–8), recalls other ancient portrayals of the gods in divine council (e.g. the Babylonian *Enuma Elish*, the Canaanite *Ba'lu Myth*, and the Homeric *Iliad* from Greece).[9] What is described in Exodus 24 also generated resonances in later Old Testament texts: the encounter with God on another mountain, again in priestly and communal service, on Mt Zion, at the temple in Jerusalem (e.g. Ps. 132); and in overwhelming and almost inexpressible prophetic visions of God (e.g. Ezek. 1) – resonances much like, for instance, the way that archaic Homeric traditions about the gods were later invoked in classical Greek religion.

That this example from Exodus points to a sacred tradition that developed in ancient Israel is a reminder that the Old Testament primarily makes sense in its own ancient context. In other words, its texts provide religious testimony – variously labelled Hebrew, Israelite, Judean, Jewish – to the activity of the God of Israel, who is also the God of the world, its creator and its redeemer. The comparative approach is hugely illuminating, but it ends up highlighting distinctiveness: that Israelite religion was in important respects untypical in the ancient Near East. The area where this is strongest is the understanding of God, for which the conventional modern label is 'monotheism': the belief that there is one true God. The Old Testament is dominantly about one God – called 'LORD' (YHWH) and 'God' (Elohim, El), who has unrivalled power and authority in the divine council – to whom alone worship must be directed (Deut. 6.4–6). The worship of other gods ('polytheism') is idolatrous and damaging. That this expectation – motivated by God's jealous love for Israel, and the people's willing assent to the covenant at Mt Sinai – did not sit easily in ancient Israel, let alone in the ancient Near East, is apparent in the Old Testament (e.g. Judg. 17; 1 Kings 17—18; Jer. 2–3). It is also confirmed by archaeological evidence (e.g. figurines, inscriptions) which, along with the biblical texts, attest a complex religious history of contest and struggle. But that makes its religious testimony all the more valuable: it helps to explain how distinctive religious perspectives, though hard won, became established, and shaped what followed later, in both the Judaism and the Christianity of later antiquity.[10]

Scholarly accounts of the religious or theological ideas in the Old Testament tend to show due recognition of what was distinctive about Israelite religion, both in its ancient context and also in terms of getting to grips with what lies at the heart of its texts. This has been be done in various ways. As already mentioned, the religious and theological content of the Old Testament may be analysed in terms of its institutions and practices (e.g. temple, priesthood, sacrifice). It may also be recast in more theological terms: divine *hesed*, or the 'mercy' or 'loyal love' of God – revealed at Mt Sinai, and regularly invoked in ancient Israelite texts (Ex. 34.6–7; Num. 14.13–19; Neh. 9.17; Ps. 103.8; Jonah 4.2 etc.) – is that on which Israel's life depended. Alternatively, themes may be drawn out for their structural importance or frequency; themes such as creation, covenant, promise, redemption, glory, law, and messiah. There are well-established scholarly genres for all of these approaches – such as 'The Religion of Ancient Israel' or 'The Theology of the Old Testament'. But there is always another dimension at play: what is held to be distinctive is often influenced by other factors, such as a scholar's prior religious commitments (e.g. Jewish, Christian) or modern attempts to analyse the same texts in solely historical terms. These dimensions often operate in concert because the Old Testament texts arose in ancient Israel, a heritage and legacy shared, albeit in different ways, in Judaism and Christianity.[11]

What is the Old Testament?

Nomenclature

The 'Old Testament' is the title for the first and the longest part of the sacred texts of Christianity that include the New Testament; together they form the Bible. The origins of the title are found in early Christianity: it translates the Greek *ho palaia diathēkē* ('the old covenant'), and more closely the Latin *vetus testamentum*. It is a hugely significant title, in that in traditional Christianity the 'Old' is typically understood in relation to the 'New', signifying at root the impact of Jesus Christ in his first-century Jewish religious and Roman imperial context that eventually led to this nomenclature (i.e. a system of names or terminology). The titles are an important way of capturing the revolutionary change that was brought about by his influence; and the legacy (cf. 'will and testament') that he left. This is readily seen in the pages of the New Testament, where aspects of ancient Israelite religious institutions, practices, and beliefs – Passover, Law, Covenant – are viewed in this new way (Luke 22.20; 1 Cor. 11.25; 2 Cor. 3.14; Heb. 8.8–12; 9.15). This terminology carries with it the senses of both renewal (faithful continuity with the past), and newness (radical development for the future). In consequence, in traditional Christianity the 'Old' and the 'New' are always combined when making sense of that trajectory and development: together they form a united anthology and sacred canon, and both are needed for their mutual illumination.[12]

There was, of course, a time when the title 'Old Testament' did not yet exist. Before the first century, and while the New Testament texts were still emerging, other terms described these texts. The word 'Bible' has been traced to the name of the ancient coastal city of Byblos (in modern-day Lebanon), whose trade included the papyrus used for writing in antiquity; and it is attested as a collective term for biblical texts before the New Testament era (*Let. Aris.* 316; cf. 2 *Clem.* 14.2). Alternative expressions were the plural Greek *hai graphai*, 'the writings', and its equivalent Latin *scripturae* (Matt. 21.42; Mark 12.10; 2 Tim. 3.16; 2 Pet. 3.16). In the pages of the Old

Testament, the usual word for a text or book (i.e. a scroll) is the Hebrew *sepher* (Greek *biblos*, Latin *liber*), which in Jewish tradition has been used for book titles (e.g. *sepher yehoshua*, 'The Book of Joshua'). It is important to recognize that the Christian title 'Old Testament' is not accepted in traditional Judaism, in which there is no 'New Testament' that assigns the more ancient biblical texts to the status of 'Old'. Rather, the mnemonic 'Tanak' (derived from the first Hebrew letters of *Torah*, 'law', *Nevi'im*, 'prophets', and *Ketuvim*, 'writings') is the convention. An alternative is 'Hebrew Bible' (HB), which identifies the original language of the majority of its texts. The latter is influential and popular in universities, given the more neutral or secular environment of the academy and the public square of ideas – even though some of the biblical texts were written in Aramaic, and the texts themselves attest varieties of ancient Hebrew.[13]

Thus, while there are general or neutral words for a text or book, both singular and collective, the religious expressions are weighted in a specific way. They indicate committed religious standpoints: specifically, that decisions and judgements were made, in time, about their sacred status. Recent attempts to find yet more neutral alternatives, which are motivated by the reluctance to denigrate others' religious standpoints – e.g. 'First Testament' and 'Second Testament' – are still weighted, however lightly or otherwise. The desire to use suitable terminology is entirely understandable, and in certain open contexts (e.g. interfaith dialogues) may well be appropriate and welcome. There is, nevertheless, a danger that should be acknowledged: the reasons these texts are read and stimulate on-going interest can become obscured. Above all, this is to do with the global impact of religions – primarily Christianity (the world's most populous), but also Judaism, and Islam (though the Qur'an has a different literary relationship to the Old Testament) – whose distinctive discourses are largely based on these sacred texts. This is not for one moment to deny that these texts are available to and owned by everyone, as a part of the cultural heritage of humankind – just as an organization such as UNESCO might categorize a text or an artefact. But these texts, in terms of those who originally wrote them, and those who have mainly read and interpreted them since, are part of a religious tradition: its representatives have been, and are, their most frequent spokespersons. It should be added that this leaves no room for presumption on their part; quite the opposite: it raises the bar extremely high for their advocacy of the importance of that religious continuity and its global impact.[14]

Canon

Another important aspect of the Old Testament is its size and limits: the 'canon'; that is, a definitive or fixed list of texts that includes some but excludes others. The Old Testament indicates that its texts were organized into collections in the ancient period: laws (Ex. 21—23), royal archives (1 Kings 11.41), pilgrim poetry (Ps. 120—134), wisdom sayings (Prov. 25.1), and prophetic oracles (Jer. 36.16–21) – to name some clear examples. There is evidence to imply the more self-conscious collection of texts whose sacred status had become recognized and accepted. This took place after the return from exile (2 Esd. 14.44–48; 2 Macc. 2.13; cf. Zech. 13.2–6; 1 Macc. 9.27), when the first five books – the Law ('Torah' in Judaism, or 'Pentateuch' in Christianity) – gained pre-eminence in religious matters, even if other Old Testament texts were already in circulation or still being composed. The categories of the canon with which readers are nowadays familiar, such as 'the Law and the Prophets', are attested by the second century BC (Sir. Prologue; cf. 2 Macc. 15.9) and the first century AD (e.g. Josephus C. Ap. 1.37–43; Luke 24.44; Rom. 3.21). What was held to be canonical in these later centuries is indicated by how the texts were used: not only their quotation, paraphrase and allusion in writings composed at the turn of the era, but also in commentary on them (e.g. Dead Sea Scrolls, Pseudepigrapha, Philo, Josephus, New Testament).[15]

Just as the title Old Testament is a marker of difference between Judaism and Christianity, so too are their biblical canons, beyond the obvious difference over the New Testament. That is to say: not all ancient Jewish religious texts that may be labelled 'scriptural' (i.e. a written text) are deemed 'canonical' (i.e. in a definitive list). This difference stems from antiquity. There is a broad distinction to be drawn between the Hebrew texts of ancient Judaism (recognized as canonical by the second century, according to rabbinic texts) and the Greek texts of early Christianity (for which discussions of the canon, in the first few centuries of the Church, are likewise attested). That said, the matrix from which this difference emerged was complex. The originally Hebrew (with some Aramaic) biblical texts were translated into Greek by Jews in Alexandria; but the medieval manuscripts, which include books that the rabbis did not recognize as canonical (i.e. the Apocrypha), were largely transmitted by Christians in early and medieval Christianity. Moreover, the Latin translation by Jerome followed the contents of the Greek canon, but where possible was translated from Hebrew texts. The canon of Ethiopic Orthodox Christianity includes, interestingly, *Enoch* and *Jubilees*, which neither Jews nor most Christians have deemed canonical. Then again, Protestants later reverted, during and after the European Reformation, to just the Hebrew canon that the rabbis had earlier recognized, while maintaining a traditional Christian order of the books of the Old Testament.

In spite of this complexity, the order of books that are held in common in the biblical canons of Judaism and Christianity have usually been understood to reflect distinctive standpoints – even if, again, salient caveats could be mentioned.[16] In Judaism, it is traditional to believe that the Torah has primary status as direct revelation, followed by the Prophets as the mediators of revelation, and then the Writings as human reflection on revelation. The Christian canon is organized by literary type and an overarching temporal framework: the Pentateuch and Historical Books are about the past; Poetry and Wisdom concern the present; and the Prophets prepare for the future. It is a Christian canonical approach that has been adopted in this book, as follows:

Pentateuch	Genesis, Exodus, Leviticus, Numbers, Deuteronomy
Historical Books	Joshua, Judges, Ruth, 1 and 2 Samuel, 1 and 2 Kings, 1 and 2 Chronicles, Ezra, Nehemiah, Esther
Poetry and Wisdom	Job, Psalms, Proverbs, Ecclesiastes, Song of Songs
Prophetic Books	Isaiah, Jeremiah, Lamentations, Ezekiel, Daniel, Hosea, Joel, Amos, Obadiah, Jonah, Micah, Nahum, Habakkuk, Zephaniah, Haggai, Zechariah, Malachi
Apocrypha/ Deutero-Canon	Tobit, Judith, Additions to Esther, Wisdom of Solomon, Sirach (Ecclesiasticus), Baruch, Letter of Jeremiah, Additions to Daniel (The Prayer of Azariah and the Song of the Three Jews, Susanna, Bel and the Dragon), 1 Maccabees, 2 Maccabees, 1 Esdras, Prayer of Manasseh, Psalm 151, 3 Maccabees, 2 Esdras, 4 Maccabees

The texts of the Apocrypha do not obviously fit into that scheme of past, present, and future (although their contents may easily be read in that way). But their discussion has been included in this book for various reasons. An awareness of them helps to fill out the broader picture of the ancient Jewish matrix from which Christianity emerged, given that they were written largely between the Old and New Testaments; they were quoted by many early Church writers as canonical Scripture; and their use or otherwise in later Christian history is a part of the history of the interpretation of the Old Testament in Christianity – and this is the central concern of this book. Their contested status is nevertheless a key question in the chapter on the Apocrypha (Chapter 6).

The latter issue, concerning the canonical status of specific books, is often discussed in terms of the 'criteria' of the canon. This issue is frequently broached through the popular question: who decided what should be in the canon? The criteria for qualification as a scriptural and sacred canonical text were, broadly speaking, as follows: (1) authorship; (2) use; and (3) orthodoxy. That is to say, a text had to have ancient and authentic origins (prophetic, apostolic; inspired, reliable, etc.); universal recognition and use in suitable church settings (e.g. doctrine, liturgy, catechesis, discipline); and conform to widely accepted Christian teaching and practice (i.e. the 'rule of faith'). In answer to the popular question, it seems as if the early Church was as much, if not more, a passive recipient of a diverse collection of earlier texts as it was an active player in making sense of them by an already agreed standard or obvious formula, theological or otherwise. These 'criteria', whether mutually complementary or not, were often applied flexibly, such that discussions of the canon in the writings of the early Church and beyond is best seen in terms of centre (e.g. Genesis, Isaiah) and periphery (e.g. Song of Songs, Sirach) – as was also the case with the New Testament.[17]

Translation

The aspects of language and translation were mentioned above regarding nomenclature and canon. More should be said about this because the Old Testament is read by most people in translation. A little knowledge that the Old Testament texts were written in ancient Hebrew might lead to the idea that during divine revelation, whether of the Law or through the prophets, Hebrew is the language that God spoke! It is, for this reason, no surprise that Hebrew came to be treasured as a 'sacred tongue' – whether in Judaism or by anyone interested in the biblical texts and their background. However, a lazy assumption may be made in collapsing together into one potent mix the realities of revelation, inspiration, composition, language, and then translation: that a familiar and beloved translation in any language gives direct and immediate access to the primal 'Word of God' of revelation and inspiration. After all, there are no extant original manuscripts with which to test such claims (as if they somehow could be tested!); and the biblical manuscripts that are extant attest variations in content (many minor, some major). Moreover, their Hebrew points to the development of that language over time; and some parts are not in Hebrew but in Aramaic (notably Ezra 4.8—6.18; Dan. 2.4b—7.28). These observations need not be invoked to question revelation and inspiration. Rather, they highlight that the believed reality and its textual evidence are different sides of a coin that makes the 'Holy Bible' both divine and human in developing historical circumstances.[18]

The oldest known manuscripts of the Old Testament are the Dead Sea Scrolls, which date from the third century BC to the first century AD; they were discovered in 1947. This is not the oldest textual evidence; there are more ancient inscriptions. A fine example is a silver scroll of the 'Priestly Blessing' (Num. 6.24–6), discovered in Jerusalem in 1979. It has been dated to c. 600 BC – although this date is debated.[19] Prior to these modern discoveries the oldest known manuscripts were medieval: the Leningrad Codex (dated 1008), and the older but incomplete Aleppo Codex, both of the Masoretic Text (MT) tradition, produced by medieval Jewish scribes. These now included vowels, and other annotations, added to the older consonantal Hebrew text.[20] This MT text type has underlain modern Protestant Bibles, and recent Catholic Bibles. However, already in the post-exilic era of biblical times, Hebrew had largely become the language of worship. Translations were needed into Aramaic: the diplomatic *lingua franca* since the late

Assyrian, Babylonian, and Persian periods, and the language later spoken in Palestine, including by Jesus (e.g. Mark 5.41; John 20.16).[21] According to later rabbinic texts (*m. Meg.* 3.2), the Hebrew read in synagogues was translated into Aramaic, but written translations were prohibited. Nevertheless, a series of Aramaic translations, known as the Targums ('translations, renditions'), emerged as early as the first century AD. Their expansive and explanatory character are valuable evidence for biblical interpretation in antiquity, in some cases being very similar to what is found in the New Testament.[22]

The Hebrew was also translated into Greek, from the third to the first centuries BC. This translation is known as the Septuagint (LXX), referring to the 'seventy' (or seventy-two) Jewish scribes commissioned to translate the Hebrew into Greek for the great library at Alexandria, where there was a Greek-speaking Jewish community. Remarkably, their translations agreed. The process had enjoyed divine oversight: it was inspired. The 'Letter of Aristeas' that claims this agreement shows, once again, not only the immense value attached to sacred texts, but it also raises the question of the difficulty and even the legitimacy of rendering religious texts faithfully into another language (cf. Sir. Prologue).[23] The New Testament writers typically quoted from the LXX, which is still used in Orthodox Christianity; it also underlies the Coptic Bibles of Ethiopic Orthodox Christianity.[24] However, the translation whose influence lasted longest in Western Europe, until the early 1500s, was in Latin, by Jerome (*c.* 347–420), who lived in a hermit's cell in Bethlehem near to the traditional site of Jesus' birth. Commissioned by Pope Damasus I (366–84), and known as the Latin Vulgate (Vg), it superseded the 'Old Latin' translations (of Greek versions) in circulation from the second century AD onwards. Yet another important translation was made into Syriac (a dialect of Aramaic). Known as the 'Peshitta' (Syriac for 'simple', given its lack of textual apparatus in manuscripts), it is still used in some denominations of the 'Church of the East' (i.e. in Asia).[25]

The history of Bible translation is as much a history of mission, doctrine, and politics in the Church, as it is of language. In Europe, the medieval period witnessed the call for vernacular translations. For instance, the Wycliffe Bible (1382–95) refers to translations from the Vulgate into the Middle English of the pre-Reformation Lollard movement that rejected many medieval church beliefs and practices. Critical editions, too: the turning to Greek manuscripts (for the New Testament), rather than following the Vulgate, is represented by the work of the Renaissance humanist Desiderius Erasmus (1466–1536). But it is William Tyndale (d. 1536) who is credited with initiating the first translation of the Bible into English, of the Old and New Testaments, from Hebrew and Greek manuscripts. Many translations into other languages followed in similar fashion. Among the most important in English are the Coverdale (1535), the Great (1539), the Geneva (1560), the Bishops (1568), the Douay-Rheims (1610), and of course the King

James Bible or Authorized Version (1611), whose memorable expressions, like those of Shakespeare, still roll off the tongue today.[26]

Later centuries have proved just as industrious. Among the best-known Bibles in English translation of recent decades are the RSV (1952), the Jerusalem (1966), the NIV (1978), the NKJV (1982), the NRSV (1989) and the ESV (2001) – not forgetting popular idiomatic translations such as *The Message* (1993–2002).[27] It is important to emphasize, however, that the greatest developments in modern Old Testament translation were made possible by the discovery of the Dead Sea Scrolls in the late 1940s: around 800 manuscripts, of which about 40 per cent are biblical. Among these, the *Great Isaiah Scroll* (housed in the Shrine of the Book museum in Jerusalem) is similar in broad measure to medieval manuscripts, whereas the manuscripts of Jeremiah attest a shorter version (like LXX) and longer version (like MT). Their discovery signalled a huge advance in the knowledge of ancient manuscripts of about 1,000 years. This explains their use by specialists in Old Testament translation since the middle of the twentieth century.[28]

Christianity has thrived on the translation of its sacred texts. This was a hallmark of the early Church, it having grown out of the linguistic mix of the Mediterranean, well represented by the inscription Pilate commissioned for the cross: 'Jesus, of Nazareth, King of the Jews', written in 'Hebrew [*hebraisti*, i.e. Aramaic], in Latin [*rōmaisti*], and in Greek [*hellēnisti*]' (John 19.20, 21). Translation was pragmatic, as it was for Aramaic- and Greek-speaking Jews, but it was also missional. Translation met the needs of the Church as it spread into the Roman Empire and beyond. This continued in the push for vernacular translations in the eras of Medieval and Reformation Christianity, and in the pioneering missions of the past two centuries or so. Organizations such as the United Bible Societies, and Wycliffe Bible Translators, have this missional impetus as their *raison d'être*; their distribution of Bibles in Arabic and in Chinese, to name two increasingly prominent global languages, are part of that on-going mission. Another key point is that translation is both a science and an art. It requires knowledge of biblical languages and manuscripts ('Textual Criticism') to answer the following key question: 'What are the most likely original words and meaning?' It also requires the wise use of that knowledge in view of other factors at play; such as: the audience's receptor language (whether it has equivalent vocabulary, grammar, and syntax), and the ecclesiastical translation policy (i.e. the way that specific Christian beliefs and practices are conveyed in new contexts). There are many examples of the controversial and the successful in the history of translation. Debates about gender-neutral language (e.g. Dan. 7.13, 'the Son of Man' in the KJV, or 'one like a human being' in the NRSV) is but a recent example of this. In other words, translation is to a large extent about interpretation, and all that is implied by that word.[29]

What is in this Book about the Old Testament?

Companion: a book about books

Isn't the New Testament the 'companion' to the Old Testament? After all, most readers of the Bible read the Old Testament in the light of Jesus Christ as portrayed in the New Testament: he is the lens through which it is viewed. Indeed, he is the person through whom all Christian theological understanding is traditionally directed, nourished, and inspired. The word 'companion' in the title of this book is not meant to question any of this as a 'given' of Christian discourse. Rather, the choice of this word signals a response to a perceived lack of understanding as to what the Old Testament has to offer. Too often, views of the Old Testament are either superficial or caught up in controversy. The response aimed at here is to provide intelligent enrichment for readers, so that their understanding of its texts might be broadened and deepened. Another aim is to respond to what is often felt by some to be the confusing pluralism of the contemporary world: the ever-increasing range of outlooks and opinions on daily view via the media and in human experience, and how these can easily impact on biblical interpretation. With this in view, the core of each chapter is, in effect, a sampling of what is now called the reception of the Old Testament, but from the perspective of the history of Christianity. The other main aim is to offer a model of reading that is educational, insightful, and useful: to illustrate how the Old Testament remains relevant today. Before outlining these three aims in a little more detail, some comments about the book's front cover are in order.

The cover provides another way of thinking about how this book may serve as a 'companion' to the Old Testament. It is from the series of frescos on the ceiling of the Sistine Chapel, in the Apostolic Palace of the Vatican, painted by Michelangelo between 1508 and 1512. The ceiling is commonly judged to be one of the finest examples of High Renaissance art. The fresco depicts a dynamic Daniel, reading a large open book, and writing his own with charcoal.[30] The prophet Daniel is reading an older book, perhaps that of the lamenting prophet Jeremiah, whom Daniel sits opposite on the ceiling. If this is the case, then the fresco recalls the vision of Daniel 9, which states that he read Jeremiah's prophecies about the 70 years of exile (Jer. 25.11–12; Dan. 9.1–2), which were then explained to him by the angel Gabriel to mean 70 'weeks' of years (490 years). This enabled Daniel to be a visionary of a later time, when the Jerusalem temple would be desecrated by Antiochus IV (Epiphanes) through his installation of an altar to the Greek god Zeus. This kind of interpretation, in which an old oracle is seen to encode a message for new situations, has parallels in apocalyptic and messianic texts of the Second Temple Jewish era (e.g. *Pesher Habakkuk*; 2 Esdras), including the New Testament (e.g. Matt. 1.23; Acts 13.41; Gal. 3.16), whose writers often quoted from the book of Daniel with similar outlooks (e.g. Matt. 16.27–28; cf. Mark 8.38—39.1; Luke 9.26–27). What this book contains is not, in principle, different. The reading and re-reading of the Old Testament in the history of Christianity follows ancient forebears: it began in the Old, was developed in the New, and those footsteps have been followed ever since.

Design: how this book is structured

It is now time to explain how the five core chapters (Chapters 2 to 6) of this book about the Old Testament are designed and structured. For ease of use and comprehension, each of the contributors of the chapters has followed the same general format or model indicated by the book's title. This model, in three developing and interlocking parts, is as follows: (1) introduction; (2) interpretation; and (3) application. A few words about each of these three areas will explain what the reader will find in each chapter.

The introduction to each chapter contains basic information about the general significance of each canonical section of the Old Testament. This first part includes discursive comments about its position within the Old Testament, the content and shape of that section, and what is often held to be distinctive about each canonical section in its ancient and later contexts. There is then a table about the books of each canonical section in overview. This is followed by discursive summaries of the books, or major themes within them. It is naturally a challenge to capture in such general, overview, and summary formats what might be said about each canonical section and each book, especially what is held to be significant about them. Readers may well be struck by different features, themes, and details, in their own encounters with the Old Testament. That is to be fully expected. This first part simply offers these different starting points, to help readers gain more confidence in understanding these biblical books – especially those that are less familiar – both in and of themselves, and as a necessary prelude to their interpretation.

The second and most extensive part of each chapter, on interpretation, is the heart of the book. Each of the canonical sections of the Old Testament are approached according to how thinkers, past and present, have read, understood, and used these sacred texts in Christianity. Primary sources (over 60 excerpts) are contextualized, presented, and analysed for the ways that they illustrate major trends in the history of the interpretation of the Old Testament. That history comprises Early (AD c. 0–500), Medieval (c. 600–1500), Reformation (c. 1500–1700), Modern (c. 1700–present), and Global Christianity.[31] These categories might seem rather Western or Eurocentric, and that might be somewhat inevitable given the contributors' backgrounds. But that is neither the intention nor is it in fact the result. The contributors wrote in full recognition of the limitations of any categories, and that others could have been used. In taking this approach, which is deliberately broad, both chronologically and contextually, each contributor has selected primary sources that not only illustrate the history of interpretation, but which are also likely to challenge any reader's views about the role and significance of the Old Testament. In other words, the purpose in this part is to offer an entrée into the history of the interpretation of the Old Testament that will encourage the virtue of humility, given that readers of its texts have always sought to interpret them with a Christian framework, and in so doing to encourage a contemporary reader to be self-aware and reflective about how that might be done today.

The third part of each chapter is about application; that is, application to the life of faith in view of what is presented in the previous parts. This part, like the first, is not as extensive as the second. It focuses, however, on two main areas: ministry and mission. For the sake of convenience, 'ministry' is taken to refer to applications of the Old Testament in worship and pastoralia, and 'mission' is taken to refer to applications of the Old Testament in society and culture – even though these areas are at root integrated and often intersect in practice. The leading question in this part is, in effect, as follows: 'What do each of the canonical sections of the Old Testament offer in ministry and mission?' The word 'application' should not be taken to mean that there is a simple and linear progression that begins with basic understanding, moves through interpretation, and is then finally embedded in real life. After all, the Old Testament texts themselves emerged out of the lived realities of ancient Israelite life, and their interpretation has always arisen out of the lived realities of subsequent contexts. Rather, application here signifies a concern by each of the contributors to be sufficiently informed by a representative understanding of the texts, and the history of their interpretation and use. This is so that any recommended applications to the life of faith are respectful of that history, faithful to what is distinctively Christian in that history, and wise about the possibilities and the limits of applications to ministry and mission in the contemporary world.

It will be clear to the reader that the general format or model used in the five core chapters of this book is intentionally integrative and synthetic; that the approach taken draws together the aspects of introduction, interpretation, and application in a purposeful way. This approach is intended to ensure that a reader's on-going encounter with the Old Testament texts does not quickly become unnecessarily fragmented or piecemeal, whether by getting lost in the details of their ancient context, or by becoming distracted by the more controversial issues that are often attached to these texts. There are, of course, many other ways in which the Christian use of the Old Testament may be approached and articulated. The hope is that readers of the Old Testament will nevertheless find in this book a holistic model that is clear, accessible, and easy to use. The experienced reader will recognize that the three components are not original in a strong sense, nor even their combination. But it may be claimed that the selection and the configuration of the content is new. However the fresh presentation of the past and its impact on the present is done, that it is done at all is crucial.

Each and every generation must assimilate and respond in appropriate ways to the sacred texts that lie at the foundations of many of our inherited and living patterns and practices.

Standpoint: approaches and attitudes

The contributors to this volume have written with the knowledge of, and a commitment to, the heritage of classical Christian orthodoxy, as is typically expressed week by week in the recitation of a creed or confession in church services. The Christian approach taken here is not, however, especially denominational, even if the contributors have been nurtured in specific church settings. The sources about the Old Testament selected for comment in part two of each chapter are diverse, from various times and places, but they are all from authors who have self-identified as Christian. The contributors are fully aware, at the same time, that these sacred texts (apart from the Apocrypha) are also canonical in Judaism. That recognition is reflected sensitively throughout the book. The other approach to the Old Testament that has influenced the contributors is that of the university or academy where they have learnt and been enriched by its more neutral or secular environment. The critical distance it prizes has meant taking account of the impact of both ecclesiastical change (e.g. the European Reformation) and intellectual change (e.g. the European Enlightenment). The complex legacy of the former highlights the importance of what is core to Christianity, while allowing for the necessity of historic disputes. The latter is about the use of critical methods: to read and analyse the Old Testament 'like any other book'. These are not, in principle, inimical to one another. These may be brought together, in an approach to sacred texts that is both 'faithful', from the perspective of believing commitment, and 'critical' – that is, characterized by open, rigorous investigation in a community of accountable commentators.

Of course, there can always be unexpected fruits and unintended consequences for which no explanation or guidance offered by an editor or a contributor could prepare readers: they will gain or discover new vistas of their own concerning the Old Testament, or they will realize that there are other, if not better, ways to proceed. Whatever readers come away with, from one or more of the chapters, it is hoped that the reading experience will prove to be educative and enriching. Finally, with respect to the sacred texts of the Old Testament as such, quite apart from what any modern book might present by way of commentary and analysis, the following ancient words have been germane to the contributors' approaches and attitudes, in terms of their own growth in understanding and current outlook. While these words arose as part of an early Christian pastoral response to a specific first-century scenario, their standpoint remain instructive for the future.

Paul: Romans 15.4–6

(mid–late 50s AD)

For whatever was written in former days was written for our instruction, so that by steadfastness and by the encouragement of the scriptures we might have hope. May the God of steadfastness and encouragement grant you to live in harmony with one another, in accordance with Christ Jesus, so that together you may with one voice glorify the God and Father of our Lord Jesus Christ.

Notes

1 These ideas may be found in the following Old Testament books and passages: Deut. 10.19; 15.7–11; Judg. 7; 1 Sam. 31; 2 Kings 19.35–37; Ps. 8; 88; Job 28; Isa. 5; Isa. 65.17–25. All biblical references and quotations are taken from the NRSV translation, unless otherwise stated.

2 Foster, B. R. (tr.), 2003, 'Epic of Creation (*Enūma Elish*)', in Hallo, W. H. and Lawson Younger, K. (eds), 1997–2003, *The Context of Scripture [COS]*, 3 vols, Leiden; Boston: Brill, vol. 1 (1.111), pp. 399, 400. For an analysis of the Babylonian text, see Seri, A., 2012, 'The Role of Creation in Enūma eliš', *JANER*, 12/1, pp. 4–29. The following places ancient thinking about creation in a broader intellectual context: Burkert, W., 1999, 'The Logic of Cosmogony', in Buxton, R. (ed.), *From Myth to Reason. Studies in the Development of Greek Thought*, Oxford: Oxford University Press, pp. 87–106. The genre category 'myth' was of contested use in Jewish and Christian antiquity (Sir. 20.19; 1 Tim. 1.4; 4.7; 2 Tim. 4.4; Titus 1.14; 2 Pet. 1.16). For a constructive modern understanding of it, see Rogerson, J. W., 1990, 'Myth', in Coggins, R. J. and Houlden, J. L. (eds) *A Dictionary of Biblical Interpretation*, London: SCM Press, pp. 479–82; and, for its on-going avoidance, see Wenham, G. J., 2015, 'Genesis 1—11 as Protohistory', in Halton, C. (ed.), *Genesis: History, Fiction, or Neither*, Grand Rapids, MI: Zondervan, pp. 73–97.

3 For a range of ancient Near Eastern texts, see Hallo and Lawson Younger (eds), *COS*. The older modern 'classic' is Pritchard, J. B. (ed.), 1969, *Ancient Near Eastern Texts Relating to the Old Testament [ANET]*, 3rd edn, Princeton, NJ: Princeton University Press, although this has in many cases been superseded by *COS*. See also Sparks, K. L., 2005, *Ancient Texts for the Study of the Hebrew Bible: A Guide to the Background Literature*, Peabody, MA: Hendrickson. This comparative literary approach may be complemented by ancient iconography: Pritchard, J. B. (ed.), 1969, *Ancient Near Eastern Pictures Relating to the Old Testament [ANEP]*, 3rd edn, Princeton, NJ: Princeton University Press; and Keel, O., 1978, *The Symbolism of the Biblical World: Ancient Near Eastern Iconography and the Book of Psalms*, London: SPCK (original 1972).

4 Tables and charts of historical periods and chronologies are standard in introductory books about Israel in its ancient Near Eastern setting. Some examples from recent decades are: Anderson, B. W., 1975, *The Living World of the Old Testament*, 4th edn, Harlow: Longman, pp. 645–51; Charpentier, E., 1981, *How to Read the Old Testament*, London: SCM Press, p. 17; McConville, J. G., 1996, *The Old Testament*, London: Hodder & Stoughton, pp. 36–7; Coogan, M. D. (ed.), 1988, *The Oxford History of the*

Biblical World, New York and Oxford: Oxford University Press, pp. 597–601; Collins, J. J., 2004, *Introduction to the Hebrew Bible, with CD Rom*, Minneapolis, MN: Fortress Press, pp. 11–14; Arnold, B. T., 2014, *Introduction to the Old Testament*, Cambridge: Cambridge University Press, pp. 40–50. See also Finegan, J., 2015, *Handbook of Biblical Chronology*, Peabody, MA: Hendrickson.

5 These three positions are represented, broadly speaking, by the following: Kitchen, K. A., 2003, *On the Reliability of the Old Testament*, Grand Rapids, MI: Eerdmans; Davies, P. R., 1992, *In Search of Ancient Israel*, Sheffield: JSOT Press; and, from a previous generation, Hayes, J. H. and Maxwell Miller, J. (eds), 1977, *Israelite and Judean History*, London: SCM Press.

6 The best atlas, which amounts to a history of ancient Israel, remains: Aharoni, Y. et al., 2002, *The Carta Bible Atlas*, 4th edn, Jerusalem: Carta. A readable primer on the ancient Near East that includes discussion of Israel is Van De Mierop, M., 2004, *A History of the Ancient Near East, ca. 3000–323 BC*, Oxford: Blackwell. See also Snell, D. C., 1997, *Life in the Ancient Near East, 3100–332 B.C.E.*, New Haven, CT; London: Yale University Press; a more detailed account is Kuhrt, A., 1995, *The Ancient Near East, c. 3000–330 BC*, London: Routledge. For the text of the *Cyrus Cylinder* in translation, see Cogan, M. (tr.), 2002, *COS*, vol. 2 (2.124), pp. 314–16. The details about *huzot*, 'streets, bazaars' may be explored further in King, P. J. and Stager, L. E., 2001, *Life in Biblical Israel*, Louisville, KY: Westminster John Knox, p. 191.

7 On the critical method and its historical background, see Barton, J., 2007, *The Nature of Biblical Criticism*, Louisville, KY; London: Westminster John Knox; and Legaspi, M. C., 2010, *The Death of Scripture and the Rise of Biblical Studies*, Oxford: Oxford University Press. For discussions about the relationship between the intellect and faith, see Migliore, D. L., 2014, *Faith Seeking Understanding: An Introduction to Christian Theology*, 3rd edn, Grand Rapids, MI: Eerdmans. In the area of biblical studies, in particular, see, for instance, Byron, J. and Lohr, J. N. (eds), 2015, *I (Still) Believe: Leading Bible Scholars Share Their Stories of Faith and Scholarship*, Grand Rapids, MI: Zondervan.

8 The breadth of human responses to God is explored in Janowski, B., 2013, *Arguing with God: A Theological Anthropology of the Psalms*, Louisville, KY: Westminster John Knox. On the relationship of the Old Testament texts to philosophical traditions, see Barr, J., 1993, *Biblical Faith and Natural Theology*, Oxford: Clarendon; and now especially Gericke, J., 2012, *The Hebrew Bible and Philosophy of Religion*, SBLRBS, 70; Atlanta: SBL. Varieties of atheism or scepticism in ancient Israel are discussed in Gericke, *The Hebrew Bible*, pp. 351–9; and briefly, regarding ancient Greece, by way of comparison, in Hoffman, C. A., 2006, 'Atheism', in Wilson, N. (ed.), *Encyclopedia of Ancient Greece*, New York and London: Routledge, pp. 108–9.

9 The ancient Near Eastern texts are translated in *COS*, vol. 1 (1.111; 1.86), pp. 390–402, 241–74. Homer's *Iliad* has often been translated; a recent example is Powell, B. P., 2015, *Homer's Iliad and Odyssey: The Essential Books; Translation, Introduction, and Notes*, New York: Oxford University Press. For an introduction to ancient Near Eastern religion, see Beckman, G., 2005, 'How Religion Was Done', in Snell, D. C. (ed.), *The Companion to the Ancient Near East*, Oxford: Blackwell, pp. 343–53; and Holland, G. S., 2009, *Gods in the Desert: Religions of the Ancient Near East*, Lanham, MD; Plymouth: Rowman & Littlefield.

10 For a modern account of ancient Israelite monotheism, see Smith, M. S., 2001, *The Origins of Biblical Monotheism: Israel's Polytheistic Background and the Ugaritic Texts*, New York: Oxford University Press. The term 'monotheism' has come under heavy scrutiny in recent years. See Petersen, D. L., 1988, 'Israel and Monotheism: The Unfinished Agenda', in Tucker, G. M., Petersen, D. L. and Wilson, R. R. (eds), *Canon*,

Theology, and Old Testament Interpretation: Essays in Honor of Brevard S. Childs, Philadelphia, PA: Fortress Press, pp. 92–107; and Moberly, R. W. L., 'How Appropriate is "Monotheism" as a Category for Biblical Interpretation?' in Stuckenbruck, L. T. and North, W. E. S. (eds), 2004, *Early Jewish and Christian Monotheism*, London: T&T Clark, pp. 216–34. For a flavour of the diversity of Israelite religious practices, against which the prophets often inveighed, see Stern, E., 2001, 'Pagan Yahwism: The Folk Religion of Ancient Israel', *BAR*, 27, pp. 20–30; and, more recently, Stavrakopoulou, F. and Barton, J. (eds), 2010, *Religious Diversity in Ancient Israel and Judah*, London: T&T Clark.

11 The following are useful primers: Albertz, R., 1992–4, *A History of Israelite Religion in the Old Testament Period*, 2 vols, London: SCM Press (original 1992); Niditch, S., 1997, *Ancient Israelite Religion*, New York and Oxford: Oxford University Press; Miller, P. D., 2000, *The Religion of Ancient Israel*, Louisville, KY: Westminster John Knox; London: SPCK. For Jewish accounts, an older, influential study is Kaufmann, Y., 1960, *The Religion of Israel: From its Beginnings to the Babylonian Exile*, Chicago: University of Chicago Press; a more recent study is Levenson, J. D., 1993, *The Old Testament, the Hebrew Bible, and Historical Criticism: Jews and Christians in Biblical Studies*, Louisville, KY: Westminster John Knox. An informative analysis of Exodus 34.6–7 is Lane, N. C., 2000, *The Compassionate but Punishing God: A Canonical Analysis of Exodus 34:6–7*, Eugene, OR: Pickwick. Two modern 'classics' of theological ideas are Eichrodt, W., 1961–7, *Theology of the Old Testament*, 2 vols, London: SCM Press (original 1933–9), and Von Rad, G., 1962–5, *Old Testament Theology*, 2 vols, Edinburgh: Oliver & Boyd (original 1957–60). More recent offerings are Preuss, H. D, 1995–6, *Old Testament Theology*, 2 vols, Edinburgh: T&T Clark (original 1991–2); Moberly, R. W. L., 2013, *Old Testament Theology: Reading the Hebrew Bible as Christian Scripture*, Grand Rapids, MI: Baker. For an incisive analysis of various approaches, see Barr, J., 1999, *The Concept of Biblical Theology: An Old Testament Perspective*, London: SCM Press.

12 This is captured well in the title of the following, which explores the relationship between the testaments: Baker, D. L., 2010, *Two Testaments, One Bible*, 4th edn, Nottingham: Inter-Varsity Press. This 'testamental togetherness' has been the dominant understanding in the history of Christianity. It is implicit in the ecumenical creeds (e.g. Apostles' Creed, Creed of Nicaea), and it is explicit in later confessions and catechisms (Catholic, Orthodox, Protestant). The following are examples: *Catechism of the Catholic Church* §§121–3; *The Longer Catechism of The Orthodox, Catholic, Eastern Church* §§25–43; the Protestant *Belgic Confession* §§3–7; the Anglican *Articles of Religion* §§6–7. These are all available online.

13 On the writing and the composition of the Old Testament in its ancient setting, these introductory surveys are useful starting points: Kratz, R. G., 2006, 'The Growth of the Old Testament', and Millard, A. R., 2006, 'Authors, Books and Readers in the Ancient World', in Rogerson, J. W. and Lieu, J. (eds), *The Oxford Handbook of Biblical Studies*, Oxford: Oxford University Press, pp. 459–88, 544–64; and, more recently, Schniedewind, W. M., 2013, 'Writing and Book Production in the Ancient Near East', in Carleton Paget, J. and Schaper, J. (eds), *The New Cambridge History of The Bible: From the Beginnings to 600*, Cambridge: Cambridge University Press, pp. 46–62.

14 On nomenclature, see Brooks, R. and Collins, J. J. (eds), 1990, *Hebrew Bible or Old Testament? Studying the Bible in Judaism and Christianity*, Notre Dame, IN: University of Notre Dame Press. For a defence of the traditional title, see Seitz, C. R., 1996, 'Old Testament or Hebrew Bible? Some Theological Considerations', *Pro Ecclesia*, 5/3, pp. 292–303.

15 For an introduction to canonical matters, see McDonald, L. M., 2011, *The Origin of the Bible: A Guide for the Perplexed*, London: T&T Clark; and Barton, J., 2013, 'The

Old Testament Canons', in Carleton Paget and Schaper, *The New Cambridge History*, pp. 145–64. Another recent study is Lim, T. H., 2014, *The Formation of the Jewish Canon*, New Haven, CT: Yale University Press. On the broader literary setting at the turn of the era, see Kugel, J., 1998, *The Bible As It Was*, Cambridge, MA: The Belknap Press of Harvard University Press; Kugel, J. L., 1998, *Traditions of the Bible: A Guide to the Bible As It Was at the Start of the Common Era*, Cambridge, MA; London: Harvard University Press; Nickelsburg, G., 2005, *Jewish Literature between the Bible and the Mishnah: A Historical and Literary Introduction*, 2nd edn, Minneapolis, MN: Fortress Press; and Docherty, S. E., 2014, *The Jewish Pseudepigrapha: An Introduction to the Literature of the Second Temple Period*, London: SPCK.

16 See Barton, 'Canons', pp. 162–4.

17 See further, Ludlow, M., 2003, '"Criteria of Canonicity" and the Early Church', in Barton, J. and Wolter, M. (eds), *The Unity of Scripture and the Diversity of the Canon = Die Einheit der Schrift und die Vielfalt des Kanons*, Berlin: de Gruyter, pp. 69–93. A useful book-length study is Bruce, F. F., 1988, *The Canon of Scripture*, Glasgow: Chapter House. For discussions of the idea of Sacred Scripture in antiquity, see Kugel, J. L. and Greer, R. A., 1986, *Early Biblical Interpretation*, Philadelphia, PA: Westminster John Knox; and, more recently, Xeravits, G. G., Nicklas, T. and Kalimi, I. (eds), 2013, *Scriptural Authority in Early Judaism and Ancient Christianity*, DCLS, 16, Berlin: de Gruyter.

18 On biblical Hebrew and biblical Aramaic, see Schniedewind, W. M., 2013, *A Social History of Hebrew: Its Origins through the Rabbinic Period*, New Haven, CT: Yale University Press; and Kahn, G., 2013, 'The Languages of the Old Testament', in Carleton Paget and Schaper, *The New Cambridge History*, pp. 3–21. On inspiration, in particular, see Abraham, W. J., 1981, *The Divine Inspiration of Holy Scripture*, Oxford: Oxford University Press; Trembath, K. R., 1987, *Evangelical Theories of Biblical Inspiration: A Review and Proposal*, New York and Oxford: Oxford University Press; and Farkasfalvy, D. M., 2010, *Inspiration and Interpretation: A Theological Introduction to Sacred Scripture*, Washington, DC: Catholic University of America Press.

19 For an introduction to the Dead Sea Scrolls, see VanderKam, J. C., 2010, *The Dead Sea Scrolls Today*, 2nd edn, Grand Rapids, MI; Cambridge: Eerdmans. Many of the extant Hebrew inscriptions are collated in Davies, G. I., 1991–2004, *Ancient Hebrew Inscriptions: Corpus and Concordance*, 2 vols, Cambridge: Cambridge University Press; see also the summary essay: Davies, G. I., 2002, 'Hebrew Inscriptions', in Barton, J. (ed.), *The Biblical World*, New York and London: Routledge, vol. 1, pp. 270–86. On the silver scroll in particular, see McCarter, P. K., 2000, 'The Ketef Hinnom Amulets', in COS, vol. 2 (2.83), p. 221; and the detailed study: Smoak, J. D., 2015, *The Priestly Blessing in Inscription and Scripture: The Early History of Numbers 6:24–26*, New York: Oxford University Press.

20 See further, Würthwein, E., 2014, revised and expanded by Fischer, A. A., *The Text of the Old Testament: An Introduction to the Biblia Hebraica*, 2nd edn, Grand Rapids, MI: Eerdmans (original 1988); and Kelley, P. H., Mynatt, D. S. and Crawford, T. G., 1998, *The Masorah of Biblia Hebraica Stuttgartensia: Introduction and Annotated Glossary*, Grand Rapids, MI: Eerdmans.

21 The reconstruction of the Aramaic of Jesus by William Fulco SJ that featured in Mel Gibson's film *The Passion of the Christ* (2004) was based on ancient Aramaic texts, biblical Aramaic (e.g. Daniel), Syriac and Hebrew. See Shepherd, D., 2015, 'From Gospel to Gibson: An Interview with the Writers behind Mel Gibson's *The Passion of the Christ*', *Religion and the Arts*, 9/3–4, pp. 321–31.

22 See further, Beyer, K., 1986, *The Aramaic Language: Its Distribution and Subdivisions*, Gottingen: Vandenhoeck & Ruprecht; and McNamara, M., 2010, *Targum and*

Testament Revisited: Aramaic Paraphrases of the Hebrew Bible: A Light on the New Testament, new edn, Grand Rapids, MI: Eerdmans.

23 See further, Schutt, R. J. H., 1985, 'The Letter of Aristeas', in Charlesworth, J. H. (ed.), *The Old Testament Pseudepigrapha: Expansions of the 'Old Testament' and Legends, Wisdom and Philosophical Literature, Prayers, Psalms, and Odes, Fragments of Lost Judeo-Hellenistic Works*, London: Darton, Longman and Todd, vol. 2, pp. 7–34. For an introduction to Septuagint studies, see Aitken, J. K. (ed.), 2015, *The T&T Clark Companion to the Septuagint*, London: Bloomsbury; and Law, T. M., 2013, *When God Spoke Greek: The Septuagint and the Making of the Christian Bible*, New York: Oxford University Press.

24 The 'four great uncials', the oldest biblical manuscripts in Greek that include the Old and New Testaments, albeit with varying levels of completeness, were transmitted by Christians: i.e. codices Sinaiticus, Vaticanus, Alexandrinus, and Ephraemi Rescriptus.

25 Many of these and other textual matters may be pursued in Danker, F. W., 2003, *Multipurpose Tools for Bible Study with CD-ROM*, 3rd edn, Minneapolis, MN: Fortress Press.

26 For the latter in particular, see Campbell, G., 2010, *Bible: The Story of the King James Bible, 1611–2011*, Oxford: Oxford University Press.

27 See further, Danker, *Multipurpose Tools*, pp. 177–95.

28 Note in particular Abegg, M., Flint, P. and Ulrich, E., 1999, *The Dead Sea Scrolls Bible*, Edinburgh: T&T Clark.

29 For an introductory survey of translation, which ranges both historically and globally, see Nida, E. A. and others, 1993, 'Translations', in Metzger, B. M. and Coogan, M. D. (eds), *The Oxford Companion to the Bible*, New York and Oxford: Oxford University Press, pp. 749–78.

30 The figures represent the faculties of the human soul: Daniel is 'reason' (*intellectus*), 'will' (*volontas*) supports the book, and 'memory' (*memoria*) hovers behind Daniel. For further details, see Wind, E., 2000, *The Religious Symbolism of Michelangelo: The Sistine Ceiling*, ed. by Sears, E., Oxford: Oxford University Press, pp. 127–8; and Pfeiffer, H., 2007, *The Sistine Chapel: A New Vision*, New York; London: Abbeville, pp. 162–7.

31 These categorical distinctions are, of course, crudely general. It is impossible to assign precise dates to each because of the continuity and overlap between them; and 'global' is not a chronological but a geographical designation. Nevertheless, to the extent that each has identifiable patterns and trends, they serve as a useful and convenient framework. Please note: for clarity's sake, some of the older spellings in some sources have been modernized.

2

Pentateuch

HYWEL CLIFFORD

Part 1: Introduction

In Judaism the first canonical section of the Bible is called the Torah. In Christianity it is known as the Pentateuch. Its sacred texts have provided the biblical foundations of these faiths ever since their emergence in antiquity as distinctive religious communities. In the contemporary world, Jews and Christians continue to draw guidance and inspiration from them. The five books that make up this collection – Genesis, Exodus, Leviticus, Numbers, and Deuteronomy – contain a narrative framework that stretches from the creation of the world through to the formation of the nation of Israel prior to its entry into the land of Canaan, promised by God to their ancestors. When compared with texts from other ancient cultures (e.g. Egyptian, Babylonian, Greek) that treat equivalent foundational topics, it becomes apparent that the Pentateuch has similar content (e.g. origins, laws, customs, history). But it also has distinctive theological and ethical content that helps to account for the unique and hugely influential contribution to world history and culture by the religious communities formed and nurtured by its texts.

The Pentateuch's internal chronology explains why the books were initially referred to by the Hebrew word *torah*, 'law'. Genesis covers more than 2,000 years in 50 chapters. But the approximately 40 years that follow in the other four books concern the Law in 137 chapters: its revelation by God to Israel through Moses at Mt Sinai, the testing of the people's loyalty to the Law during the wilderness wanderings, and the fresh exposition of the Law by Moses before entrance to the land of Canaan. This focus, especially in the context of its narrative framework, suggests that *torah* means not only 'law' (i.e. commandments, decrees, statutes, ordinances), but also instruction, teaching, custom, even wisdom. In other words, when read together, the narrative and the law are found to be mutually informative. The early forms of the texts were variously called 'the (book of the) Law of Moses/ the LORD' (e.g. Josh. 1.7–8; 1 Kings 2.3; 2 Chron. 25.4; Ezra 6.18). These expressions were translated in the New Testament with the Greek word *nomos*, 'law, custom' (John 7.23; Acts 13.39; 1 Cor. 9.9; Heb. 10.28). The Hebrew and Greek words, *torah* and *nomos*, thereby passed into ancient Judaism and Christianity as shorthand for this collection of books.

The Greek word *pentateuchos*, 'five books/scrolls', is attested among second- to third-century writers of the early Church (e.g. Origen of Alexandria, Tertullian of Carthage), although their fivefold division was already known by Jewish writers of the first centuries BC and AD (e.g. Philo of Alexandria, Flavius Josephus). Scribes had earlier copied and transmitted the ancient texts on scrolls, typically made of animal skin or reed papyrus – examples may be seen among the Dead Sea Scrolls discovered at Qumran. Scrolls continue to be used and read in synagogues today. The early Christians, however, went on to use the codex: sheets bound together, much like modern books in church use today. Either way, the narrative framework, from creation to the verge of the conquest of Canaan, linked the fivefold collection together in an obvious way. The conventional names of each book in Jewish and Christian use come from ancient biblical manuscripts and early tradition. The names were chosen either on the basis of the very opening word (e.g. Hebrew *bereshit*, 'in the beginning') or the content of each book (e.g. Greek *genesis*, 'origin, beginning').

Pentateuch in overview

Genesis	The creation of the world and humankind; the beginnings of human civilization; stories of the ancestors of Israel; the descent into Egypt for food due to famine in Canaan; the story of Joseph.
Exodus 1—18	The escape of the Hebrews from slavery in Egypt by miraculous liberation and the leadership of Moses; the plagues inflicted on Egypt; the Passover; the Hebrews' escape; journeys in the wilderness towards Mt Sinai; Israel's complaints; divine provision.
Exodus 19—40, Leviticus, Numbers 1—10	The vision of God at Mt Sinai; the establishment of the sacred covenant between God and Israel; the revelation of the Law to Israel through Moses; Israelite apostasy and covenant renewal; the tabernacle for centralized worship; laws about religion and society administered by priests; a census of the people; preparation for journeying.
Numbers 10—36	The wilderness wanderings towards Canaan, interspersed with laws; the testing of the covenant relationship between God and Israel; Israel's apostasy and purification; preparations for conquest.
Deuteronomy	Moses' review of the wilderness wanderings, and exhortations to the people to obey the laws in the land God promised to the ancestors; a developed recapitulation of the Law; the songs of Moses; the death of Moses.

Pentateuch in summary

Genesis

Genesis attributes to God both the creation of the world and the calling and appointing of the ancestors of Israel (Abraham, Isaac, and Jacob) as the means of blessing to all nations. Containing mostly narrative and genealogy, the book is structured by the Hebrew word *toledoth*, 'generations', regarding creation (2.4) and mainly human offspring (5.1; 6.9; 10.1; 11.10, 27; 25.12, 19; 36.1, 9; 37.2). The first part (chs 1—11) is universal in scope: the creation of the world, the first human pair (Adam and Eve) and their expulsion from the Garden of Eden for disobedience, and the ancestors of civilization, nations, and languages. The flood was sent as a punishment for human wickedness, but this was overcome by the rescue of righteous Noah and his family in a boat, followed by the divine promise in a covenant to preserve life, marked by the sign of the rainbow. The world was repopulated by their descendants, including those who built the Tower of Babel.

The second part (chs 12—50) is more national in scope. Abraham was promised, in a covenant with God, the land of Canaan, descendants, prosperity, and honour, but that he would also be a blessing to all nations. The episodes that follow describe his semi-nomadic family travels, and various tests of faith that climaxed in the divine command to sacrifice his son Isaac, who survived by angelic intervention once Abraham showed himself to be obedient. The promises to Abraham, now fulfilled through Isaac, passed by trickery from his son Esau to his other son Jacob who, in an encounter with God, was renamed 'Israel' (32.28); he eventually became reconciled with his brother. The young dreamer Joseph, one of Jacob's sons, was sold by his jealous brothers to local traders who took him to Egypt, but God looked after him and the family was eventually reconciled in Egypt. Jacob foresaw blessings for his twelve sons, who formed the nation of Israel.

Exodus

Exodus (Greek for 'way out') describes the redemption of the Hebrews from slavery in Egypt, and their formation as a worshipping community in covenant with God at Mt Sinai. The first part (chs 1—18) begins with Jacob and his sons in Egypt – whence the book's Hebrew name: *shemot*, 'names' (1.1) – they having earlier left Canaan due to famine (see Gen. 42.1–5). They multiplied in Egypt, and were seen as a military threat by the Egyptians who enslaved them, and tried to kill all their firstborn sons. But the child Moses was hidden, delivered, and grew up safely with royal privilege in Egypt. After killing an Egyptian whom he saw beating a fellow Hebrew, Moses escaped into the wilderness where he encountered God, who revealed to him the personal divine name YHWH ('Lord') (3.13–15). With Aaron as his spokesperson, Moses, equipped by God to work wonders, called for the

Hebrews' freedom from slavery. Faced with Pharaoh's refusal, God inflicted ten plagues on Egypt, which culminated in the death of the firstborn of the Egyptians, who pleaded that the Hebrews leave. The Hebrews celebrated the Passover, and the angelic destroyer did not kill their firstborn but 'passed over' their homes (12.27). They then escaped from Egypt. They journeyed to the 'Red Sea' (this translation follows the LXX; the Hebrew *yam suph* means 'sea of reeds') where they crossed over in safety and victory, and the pursuing Egyptian army was drowned. The Hebrews continued on their travels.

The second part (chs 19—40) opens with their arrival at Mt Sinai, and their careful ritual preparations, as a nation, to encounter God. There, God declared the Ten Commandments (also known as the Decalogue), but as the people were overwhelmed by the divine presence at Mt Sinai the people requested that Moses be the lawgiver on their behalf. A national covenant was established: a sacred relationship of mutually binding and beneficial legal obligations between God and Israel. God gave Moses plans for the tabernacle – a portable sanctuary – overseen by consecrated priests. But while Moses was up on the mountain, the people down below lost faith and worshipped an idol in the form of a golden calf instead. God was provoked to anger, but Moses interceded: after a special glimpse of God's glory was granted to him, God's merciful character was revealed, and the covenant was renewed. The last section describes the construction of the tabernacle, where Moses met with God and the priests led worship. Israel was thereafter favoured with God's protective presence during their wilderness wanderings towards Canaan, appearing as a cloud over the tabernacle by day and as fire by night.

Leviticus

Leviticus contains laws about worship, led by the Levites, priestly descendants of Levi (one of Jacob's sons) – which gave rise to the book's familiar name – and laws about life in community, given to Israel through Moses at Mt Sinai. Its Hebrew name is *wayyiqra*, 'and he (= the LORD) summoned (Moses)' (see 1.1). The key theme is holiness, expressed through ritual, the priesthood, and purity (e.g. 11.44). The first part (chs 1—16) begins with the rituals of sacrifice. Laws about sacrifice by individuals (e.g. burnt offering, grain offering) are followed by the duties of priests during sacrifices. The foundations for a consecrated priesthood are then established: the ordination, by Moses, of Aaron and his sons (themselves Levites), and the sacrifices they offered as they took office. They were instructed: 'You are to distinguish between the holy and the common, and between the unclean and the clean; and you are to teach Israel all the statutes that the LORD has spoken to them through Moses' (10.10–11). The next section of laws concern purity (e.g. diet, childbirth, skin disease), which culminated in the Day of Atonement when the whole community was ritually cleansed of its impurities through sacrifice.

The second part (chs 17—27) starts with rituals about animal slaughter and the proper treatment of blood. Next is a range of laws about purity in community (e.g. family relationships, social justice), including penalties for their violation. Special attention is given to priestly holiness, and then the offerings made by the community. An annual calendar of sacred festivals is outlined: the Sabbath, Passover, Unleavened Bread, First Fruits, Weeks, Trumpets, the Day of Atonement, and Booths. Two items in the tabernacle are mentioned (an ever-burning lamp, and twelve loaves of bread on the Table of the Presence), and then the serious case of blasphemy. Two kinds of year are indicated: the Sabbath Year to enable rest for the land, and the Year of Jubilee about property rights. The book draws to a close with a stark choice for Israel: the promise of peace and plenty for obedience, but for disobedience the threat of disease, famine, a ravaged land, and war. The book ends with instructions about vows and dedicatory gifts.

Numbers

Numbers contains narratives about the Israelites' wilderness wanderings, based at three encampments (Sinai, Kadesh, Moab), and more laws to regulate their life together. The book's Hebrew name is *bemidbar*, 'in the wilderness' (see 1.1). The first part (chs 1—10) begins at Mt Sinai with a census of the people – which, again, gave rise to the book's familiar name – to prepare for their march towards Canaan in a twelve-tribe arrangement. The Levites were responsible, in tribal clans, for worship at the tabernacle at the encampment's centre; they were specially designated 'Israel's firstborn'. The encampment had to be kept pure, so each of the tribes' leaders made sacrificial offerings to God. Two silver trumpets were blown by the priests: to summon all Israel to the tabernacle, for festivals, and before travel or warfare.

The second part (chs 10—21) includes laws about worship and narratives about the wilderness wanderings: complaints about living conditions, and rebellion against Israel's leaders. In response, God provided food and water, and favoured Moses and Aaron. But that faithless generation, who had seen God's wonders, would not be allowed to enter the land of Canaan, though they tried, and had to wander for 40 more years. Joshua and Caleb were faithful exceptions, but even Moses would forfeit that privilege for not obeying God completely.

The third part (chs 22—36) is set in the Plains of Moab by the River Jordan, in view of the Promised Land. The Moabite king Balak called on the seer Balaam to curse Israel, but through revelation and a confrontation with an angel, while riding his donkey, Balaam blessed Israel instead. But the people apostatized: they mixed sexually and religiously with the Moabites so God purged them with a plague, aided by the zealous priest Phineas. A fresh census indicated that the nation was still as large, but of the thousands who had left Egypt, only Moses, Joshua, and Caleb remained. After Midian and the Transjordan were conquered, Moses gave Israel directions for the conquest of Canaan itself.

Deuteronomy

Deuteronomy (Greek for 'second law') presents the final words of Moses: a repetition of the Law, with exhortation and expansion, in the form of three addresses and an epilogue. The book's Hebrew name is *debarim*, 'words' (see 1.1). The first part (chs 1—4) introduces Moses as the Law's expositor and interpreter; after reviewing Israel's wilderness wanderings from Horeb (the name for Mt Sinai in Deuteronomy) to the Plains of Moab, he calls for Israel's obedience in response to God's faithful actions on their behalf.

The second part (chs 5—28) begins with the Decalogue, and Moses' giving of the Law to Israel. In view of their recent history, they needed plenty of exhortation – promise and threat – about the life expected of them in the Promised Land. The book's central legal content instructed Israel about the worship of one God (see 6.4–6), leadership in religion, society, and many other matters (e.g. sacrifice, festivals, land use, warfare, inheritance), to guide and shape the exclusive covenant relationship between God and Israel. To ratify the covenant, Moses and the elders called on the people to inscribe the laws on large stones when they entered the land, and then to make sacrifices; a list of curses are included as warnings, followed by promises of blessing for obedience, and further warnings against disobedience.

The third part (chs 29—30) starts with covenant renewal in the Plains of Moab. The people were assured of God's faithfulness even if they failed, but they were exhorted to choose the way of life, rather than death. According to the epilogue (chs 31—34), Joshua became Moses' successor, the Law's regular reading every seventh year was instituted, and Moses and Joshua were called and encouraged by God to be courageous. Two poems from Moses, including warnings and blessings for the tribes of Israel that climax in praise to God, are sandwiched by the foretelling and the description of Moses' death. A tribute to Moses concludes the book of Deuteronomy – and the Pentateuch.

Part 2: Interpretation

Early Christianity

The first Christians were Jewish so the Torah, later called the Pentateuch in Christianity, informed their religious life in a foundational manner: explicitly and implicitly. Its sacred texts were interpreted by them in ways that were often similar to near-contemporary Jewish groups but the texts were also seen through distinctively Christian eyes in the first-century AD setting of the Roman Empire. This approach helped to articulate and nurture the identity, hopes and practices of the early Christian community. For example, among the various pastoral issues addressed by Paul in 1 Corinthians, the propriety of eating meat sacrificed to idols in local pagan temples (8.10; 10.21, 25) was just the kind of issue that Gentile Christians faced at Corinth in Greece, given the theological principles of inherited Jewish dietary strictures. The excerpt below shows Paul using the Pentateuch to frame his response, through an interweaving of texts about ancient Israel that addressed a church that included both Jews and Greeks:

Paul: 1 Corinthians 10

(mid-50s AD)

[1] I do not want you to be unaware, brothers and sisters, that our ancestors were all under the cloud, and all passed through the sea, [2] and all were baptized into Moses in the cloud and in the sea, [3] and all ate the same spiritual food, [4] and all drank the same spiritual drink. For they drank from the spiritual rock that followed them, and the rock was Christ. [5] Nevertheless, God was not pleased with most of them, and they were struck down in the wilderness.

[6] Now these things occurred as examples for us, so that we might not desire evil as they did. [7] Do not become idolaters as some of them did; as it is written, 'The people sat down to eat and drink, and they rose up to play.' [8] We must not indulge in sexual immorality as some of them did, and twenty-three thousand fell in a single day. [9] We must not put Christ to the test, as some of them did, and were destroyed by serpents. [10] And do not complain as some of them did, and were destroyed by the destroyer. [11] These things happened to them to serve as an example, and they were written down to instruct us, on whom the ends of the ages have come. [12] So if you think you are standing, watch out that you do not fall. [13] No testing has overtaken you that is not common to everyone. God is faithful, and he will not let you be tested beyond your strength, but with the testing he will also provide the way out so that you may be able to endure it.

[14] Therefore, my dear friends, flee from the worship of idols. [15] I speak as to sensible people; judge for yourselves what I say. [16] The cup of blessing that we bless, is it not a sharing in the blood of Christ? The bread that we break, is it not a sharing in the body of Christ? [17] Because there is one bread, we who are many are one body, for we all partake of the one bread.

The early Christians knew the biblical texts in Greek translation, as did some of their Greek-speaking Jewish contemporaries. The translation available to Paul is quoted directly (Ex. 32.6 at 10.7) alongside allusions to various Pentateuchal episodes. The number 23,000 (10.8) differs from the expected 24,000 (Num. 25.9), although it is not clear why, and at what stage in the transmission of texts, this difference arose. Perhaps the lower number was already present in the Greek Bible available to Paul, or it was triggered for the translator of that Greek Bible, or for Paul, by the memory of other passages (e.g. Num. 26.62). There is also some textual variation in theological detail: the reference to 'Christ' (10.9), which associates it with an earlier verse (10.4), is what most ancient New Testament manuscripts state; but some have 'Lord' and a few have 'God', which reflects more closely the literal sense of the Pentateuchal passage (Num. 21). These differences, as with the numerical variation mentioned above, make little interpretative difference overall.

Israel's past is made relevant by Paul to the contemporary Christians in rich and specific ways. The dramatic deliverance through the sea is likened to baptism, and God's provision of food and drink in the wilderness is likened to the eucharistic meal (10.2–4, 16–17). The claim that 'the spiritual rock that followed them ... was Christ' (10.4) is an early Christian equivalent of very similar ancient Jewish interpretations of the desert rock that issued water for a thirsty people; this widely interpreted narrative detail could symbolize divine wisdom (Wisd. 11.4; Philo *Leg.* 2.86), or signify that God provided miraculously for Israel as they travelled through the arid wilderness (Ps.-Philo *L.A.B.* 10.7; *Tg. Onq. Num.* 21.16–20; *t. Suk.* 3.11). The Christian claim that the rock 'was Christ' also contains a significant aspect later highlighted and developed in Christian doctrine: that Israel's ancient past had known the divine activity of the pre-incarnate Christ – that is, centuries before Jesus was born.

The failings of Israel in their wilderness wanderings, as described in Numbers, which had provoked God to anger, are here mentioned as *tupoi*, 'examples, patterns, types' (10.6), and *tupikos*, 'as an example' (10.11). Invoked as salutary examples, because their behaviour was damaging and destructive, Paul warns his contemporary audience of Jewish and Gentile Christians not to fall into similar transgressions: to not 'put Christ to the test' (10.7–10; i.e. to provoke divine anger). That Paul refers to 'our ancestors' (10.1) indicates this was no mere example that provides a general moral lesson, but he identifies his Christian audience with an ancient and on-going community and tradition, whose identification with it carries similar religious responsibilities. But encouragement follows as well: God helps the faithful during their trials by providing an *ekbasis*, 'way out, outcome' (10.13). The initially unifying 'all' of the redeemed (10.1–4) contrasts, therefore, with the 'most' or 'some' who fell (10.5–10), but that unity should now be the hallmark of the redeemed Christian community: the 'all' and 'many' who commune in the 'one' eucharistic meal (10.16–17).

The religious dining practices of the early Christians have often been linked to the implied biblical precedent of the Jewish Passover meal, and with reference to other ancient Jewish texts. This is hinted at here in the phrase 'the cup of blessing' (10.16; cf. *B. Pesach.* 119a; *Jos. Asen.* 8.5). Participation in this meal ruled out the Gentile 'cup of demons' (10.21), which risked spiritual contamination and invited divine anger – as had happened to disastrous effect during the wilderness wanderings (e.g. Num. 25). This concern for purity in worship follows ancient Levitical thinking on the close identity of the worshipper and the offering, which was especially vivid in the consumption of the body and blood of Christ for the early Christian worshipper – a practice that followed the initially controversial teaching of Jesus himself (John 6.22–71). This richly symbolic notion defined spiritual communion with God through Christ, and was integral to the worshipping practices of the early Christians.

The early Christians also believed that their community had a major role to play in the fulfilment of God's activity in the history of salvation. As the texts of many ancient Jewish groups indicate, this was a hallmark of a widely attested Jewish and Christian apocalyptic outlook, typically concerned with reassuring the people of God with the knowledge of God's sovereign and decisive rule in the world. This meant viewing Old Testament history in stages of developing significance, in which the most recent was the most significant to date. It is implied in the words of the excerpt: 'to instruct us, on whom the ends of the ages have come' (10.11; cf. *1 En.* 91.12–17; 1 *QpHab.* 7.1–9; 2 Esd. 6.7–10). For the early Christians, the person of Christ was the unique agent of that activity of divine rule and salvation (10.4, 9, 16; cf. John 1.17; Heb. 1.1–3).

Beyond the often occasion-bound settings of the New Testament texts, biblical interpretation developed a more systematic character as distinctively Christian doctrine and spirituality emerged in the early Church – although the writers of the canonical New Testament texts, such as Paul, had already set a direction of Christian doctrinal and spiritual travel in motion. The *Homilies on Genesis* by Origen (AD 184–254), begun in Alexandria in Egypt where he was educated, and continued in Caesarea Maritima (in the Judea Province of the Roman Empire) where he encountered its Jewish rabbinic centre, illustrate these trends well. The following excerpt is from his commentary on Genesis 22, the narrative episode about God's command to Abraham to sacrifice his son Isaac, the child of promise:

Origen of Alexandria: *Homilies on Genesis*

(third century AD)

We said above, I think, that Isaac represented Christ. But this ram no less also seems to represent Christ. Now it is worthwhile to know how both are appropriate to Christ, both Isaac, who is not slain, and the ram, which is slain. Christ is 'the Word of God', but 'the Word was made flesh'. One aspect of Christ therefore is from above; the other is received from human nature and the womb of the Virgin. Christ suffered, therefore, but in the flesh; and he endured

---

death, but it was the flesh, of which this ram is a type, as John also said: 'Behold the Lamb of God, behold him who takes away the sin of the world.' But the Word continued 'in incorruption', which is Christ according to the spirit, of which Isaac is the image. For this reason he is both victim and priest. For truly according to the spirit he offers the victim to the Father, but according to the flesh he himself is offered on the altar of the cross. And it is said of him, 'Behold the Lamb of God, who takes away the sin of the world', so it is said of him, 'You are a priest forever according to the order of Melchizedek'.[1]

Origen learnt his textual skills in Alexandria: manuscript study, literary analysis, and interpretative decision-making. This skill is evident in his comments that highlight the severe testing of Abraham: the repetition 'Abraham, Abraham'– not the earlier 'Abram' but his new name meaning 'the father of many' (Gen. 17.5) that signified his role in the now uncertain fulfilment of the promises; the horrible precision of 'your son, your only son Isaac whom you love' which made the divine expectations unavoidably clear; and that Abraham had to endure a number of days of travel without a dutiful Isaac knowing what would be required of them both. The ancient Jewish rabbinic commentary *Genesis Rabbah* (*c.* fourth to fifth centuries AD) shows striking similarity with Origen on the pertinence and pathos of these narrative details.[2]

But a strong and distinctively Christian typological tradition developed among second- to third-century texts and commentators (e.g. *Epistle of Barnabas*, Clement of Alexandria, Melito of Sardis): Abraham as God the Father, Sarah as Mary, the wood carried by Isaac as the cross, and the mountain they ascended as Calvary. In the excerpt Origen offers an elaborate version of this interpretative approach: Christ is like both Isaac (figuratively resurrected) and the ram (actually killed) because the incarnated *logos* was Christ 'in the spirit' as the High Priest, and Christ 'in the flesh' was the ram or lamb as the sacrificial victim. These typological links continued to develop in the early Church. According to Jerusalem's fourth-century Old Armenian Lectionary, Genesis 22 was read on the Thursday before Easter, coupled with Isaiah 61, a 'servant' passage quoted in Luke 4.[3] The same links are visually evident in the impressive sixth-century Byzantine mosaics of the San Vitale Church in Ravenna, Italy.[4]

If the literal sense of a text proved problematic for Origen he would often propose an allegorical sense, an approach that discerned deeper meaning beneath the plain surface of the text: 'precious jewels of the mysteries that lie hidden where they are not esteemed'.[5] For Origen this meant following Paul (Rom. 7.14; 2 Cor. 3.14–16) in a further 'unveiling' of the meaning of the sacred text. Abraham's belief in resurrection – 'the Word continued "in corruption" … of which Isaac is the image' (cf. Heb. 11.9) – is a case in point: he did not lie to Isaac about their return (Gen. 22.8). Similarly, as Origen later comments, that Abraham later called the place of sacrifice 'The Lord saw' (22.14 LXX) does not literally mean that God has eyes like a human being. Rather, God, who is incorporeal, saw 'in the spirit'. And again, just as Sarah bore Isaac beyond a normal child-bearing age so it is the advanced soul that produces joy, gladness, virtue and wisdom – offerings of the soul that lead to God's final gift: eternal life.

The distinction in the excerpt between the literal and the spiritual, or body and soul, reflects the influence on Origen of Platonism, whose categories he used to construct a coherent Christian philosophy alongside alternative pagan worldviews in antiquity. This philosophical influence is seen at the start of these homilies on Genesis, where Origen argues for a non-temporal understanding of creation in view of John 1, which presents the divine *logos*, 'word', as Jesus Christ. All things were created through the pre-existent Christ: 'in the beginning' (Gen. 1.1; John 1.1) thus means 'in' the eternal being and activity of the *logos*. Similarly, 'in our image, according to our likeness' (Gen. 1.26) concerns the inner person: likeness to God is likeness to an incorporeal being so Christians should contemplate Christ who is one with an incorporeal God. These more philosophically minded approaches were also typical of early Christian discourse about the inter-related topics of the Trinity, anthropology, and salvation (e.g. Athanasius of Alexandria, Augustine of Hippo). Genesis, given its initially universal scope, played a prominent role as a rich source for these doctrinal and spiritual discourses in an increasingly international Christianity.[6]

Medieval Christianity

Christian spirituality was nourished by the texts of the Pentateuch from the early Church onwards. Moses' wondrous ascent of Mt Sinai to encounter God in worship inspired contemplative praise and prayer (e.g. John Cassian, Caesarius of Arles, Gregory of Nyssa). The narratives of the wilderness wanderings about the opposition to the consecrated leadership of Moses and Aaron were taken to be warnings about troublesome schism that threatened the unity, order, and hierarchy of the Church. Concerning worship in particular, the Pentateuch's influence on the practices of medieval Christianity is illustrated very well by the writings of Richard of St Victor (d. 1173), in his 'Some allegories of the tabernacle of the covenant'. This summarizes *The Mystical Ark*, a detailed and systematic account of six stages of contemplation of God: from the known with the imagination, via reason, to that which is beyond reason.

Richard read the plan of the tabernacle (Ex. 25—30) as an extended allegory. The altar of burnt offering in the courtyard outside is the human body under strict discipline, whereas the tabernacle itself is the habitation of God: the state of perfection. The soul's ascent towards perfection begins inside the tabernacle: the candelabrum is meditation, the table is sacred reading, and the altar of incense is prayer. The soul then moves into the tabernacle's interior, which contained the Ark of the Covenant. From its 'lower' wood box through to its 'higher' golden cherubim, the details of its construction provide a literal guide to the spiritual contemplation of the visible, the invisible, and finally the divine. In this way, Richard's allegory on the ark (Ex. 25.10–22) situated the soul's ascent in a Christian view of knowledge that reflects Aristotelian influence: from the known through to the unknown. The journey climaxes with the cherubim, whose wings suggest flight to the divine. And they face each other: their mutual gaze is the agreement of divine Unity and Trinity. The following excerpt, his allegory on a piece of tabernacle furniture called the Table of the Showbread (literally, 'the bread of the presence', Ex. 25.23–30), where bread for Israel's twelve tribes was offered weekly, shows biblical interpretation at work in this mystical landscape:

Richard of St Victor: 'Some Allegories of the Tabernacle of the Covenant'

(pre-AD 1150)

The table of the shew bread is made from wood, covered over with gold, encircled by a lip, embellished by two crowns. By the work of wood we under-stand the historical sense; by the lip, the tropological; by the two crowns, the allegorical and anagogical. The table is made of pieces of Setim wood [NRSV 'acacia'], which is said to be very incorruptible. Sacred history, alien from all falsity and foolishness, pertains to incorruptible wood. The gilding of the table itself is the subtle and wise exposition of the letter. Beautiful gilding is the com-mendation of prophetic divine judgements. Surely it ought to be noted that the first work is of pieces of wood, but it is gilded. But the other three works are not gilded; they are of gold. That difference which is between wood and gold is the difference between the historical and spiritual senses of Scripture. History holds first place in Sacred Scripture. But mystical understanding is tripartite. Tropology holds the lowest place; allegory holds the middle; anagogy holds the highest ... Tropology treats of those things which everyone understands easily, and for this reason it remains in the lowest place ... A crown worked in low relief is placed upon the lip because allegory is engaged with more subtle and sublime things ... By the aureole crown [NRSV 'moulding of gold'], as has been said, we understand anagogical teaching. This concerns supreme things, hence its large representation occupies the highest place ... It should be noted that only Sacred Scripture uses allegorical and anagogical senses mystically, and among all the senses, it is crowned by this supereminent pair.[7]

This is an excellent example of medieval biblical interpretation. The key feature is Richard's methodical discussion of the four senses of Sacred Scripture: the wood signifies the historical or literal sense; and the gold signifies the three spiritual senses of the tropological (how to live: ethics), the allegorical (what to believe: doctrine), and the anagogical (where hope is directed: the afterlife). This may be understood alternatively as follows: the literal refers to the plain sense, and the spiritual refers to faith (allegory), hope (anagogy) and love (tropology) – to invoke the famous New Testament list. This fourfold approach, known as the Quadriga (from the classical idea of a chariot drawn by four horses), was standard in the medieval period: it provided a ready 'rule of thumb' for the exegesis, or drawing out, of meaning from the sacred text. Albeit detailed and florid in manner and approach, this shows how a seemingly obscure biblical detail could bear significance for a later Christian audience.[8]

In these *Allegories* Richard thus commended a rigorous yet sensitive allegorical model ('subtle and wise exposition'), as well as a hierarchy of spiritual insight in which reason serves a preparatory but limited role in contemplation. Richard goes on to exhort 'holy teachers' to study the table's four rings at its four corners: the proof of truth, the reproof of falsehood, exhortation to justice, and opposition to injustice. Any doubt and hesitation about what Sacred Scripture proposes are represented by the four corners – sharper obstacles that need to be navigated – but this is where rings are placed for poles so that the table may be carried around. Its four legs ('feet') are divine commands: precepts, prohibitions, admonitions, and concessions, whose observance or disregard will lead to either merit or guilt. Thus, the true preacher will use its two poles (again, made of wood and gold) – keenness in instruction for truth, and keenness in exhortation to virtue – to be able to carry 'the doctrinal table' from one heart to another heart.

As well as providing nourishment for Christian spirituality, the Pentateuch was also at the heart of late-medieval scholastic debates about its divine Law: which of its commands, if any, are binding on Christians? That was an obvious question to ask given that their initial and primary audience was the ancient Israelite community. The indicators of a distinctively Christian attitude to the Law were already present in the New Testament and early Church writings, but the analysis of this question was given magisterial expression by Thomas Aquinas in his *Summa Theologica* ('Compendium of Theology'). Aquinas' work was written with an awareness of the Jewish philosopher Moses Maimonides' *Guide to the Perplexed* (*c.* 1190). Both defended the rationality of the laws of Sinai under Aristotelian influence, though Aquinas' philosophical reflection is characterized by a more thorough appeal to natural law, and a conviction that Christ is the fulfilment of the Torah is of course central to his Christian faith. Maimonides was to Jewish thought what Aquinas was to Christian thought.

Aquinas' analysis of the Law is set within an overarching framework. The 'eternal law' is that by which God governs all things. The 'natural law', grounded in the former, is reflected in the general moral structures of good and evil that all humans recognize (cf. Rom. 2.14–15). The 'human law' of different societies is (or should be) derived from natural law; it promotes the common good, but its scope is limited: it only treats serious acts (e.g. murder, adultery, theft), not the interior self or conscience, so a more comprehensive divine law is required to reorder the human self in society. The 'Old Law' of the Pentateuch was a 'divine law', a law given by God, in ancient Israel which helped reform the human habit of sinfulness, though of itself it could not justify by imparting the gift of the Holy Spirit. The 'New Law' of the gospel is, most basically, this divine gift of the Holy Spirit, by whom humankind is 'graced' to direct them by laws being inscribed on their hearts, leading them through divine transformation to everlasting happiness. This is the framework for Aquinas' division of the 'Old Law' into moral, ceremonial, and judicial (civil) precepts, as expressed in the excerpt below:

Thomas Aquinas: 'The Precepts of the Old Law' in *Summa Theologica*

(1265–74)

As has been said above, it is the function of the divine law to regulate relationships between men, and the relationship of men to God ... it is necessary to divide the precepts of the Old Law into three classes: the moral precepts, arising from the dictates of natural law, the ceremonial precepts, which are concrete applications of the principle of divine worship, and judicial precepts, which are the concrete application of the principle that justice has to be observed among men. This is why when St. Paul has said that the law is holy he goes on to say that the commandment is just, and holy and good: just in the judicial precepts which it contains, holy in the ceremonial ones (for that which is consecrated to God is said to be holy), good, that is conducive to virtue, in its moral precepts.

Hence:
1 Both the moral and the judicial precepts have the function of directing human life ...
2 Judgement imports the carrying out of what is just, and this is effected by applying reason so as to arrive at a decision on particular cases in the concrete. Hence the judicial precepts have something in common with the moral ones, to the extent that they have their source in reason. They also have something in common with the ceremonial precepts to the extent that they represent specific applications of general principles. It is for this reason that sometimes both the judicial and the moral precepts are included under the heading of judgements as in the passage, *Hear, O,*

Israel, the ceremonies and the judgements. But sometimes it is the judicial and the ceremonial precepts which are grouped together in this way, as in the passage, *You shall do my judgements and shall observe my precepts,* where *precepts* refers to the moral precepts, while *judgements* refer to the judicial and the ceremonial ones.

3 The exercise of justice in general falls under the moral precepts, but its application in specific cases falls under the judicial precepts.[9]

The 'moral law' is binding for all time since it is basically equivalent to the natural law, whose general principles are known universally. Its most basic precepts are the Decalogue. According to Exodus and Deuteronomy, this was spoken directly by God, which indicates that these precepts arise from 'the dictates of natural law', and may be derived directly by rational deduction, although they had to be revealed because human sinfulness and corrupt customs can obscure them. The less basic natural law precepts are presented as given through Moses because, although derived from the natural law, they can only be discovered by rational reflection on the part of the wise ('they have their source in reason'). The ceremonial and judicial laws, however, are not now binding. The former both regulated worship well, and pointed forward to Christ's fulfilment of them; he replaced them with a small number of new sacraments that point back to his sacrifice. The judicial precepts were a particular *determinatio* ('determination') of the natural law to suit the conditions of ancient Israel, and seem to serve as an exemplar for how human lawgivers should fulfil their task in their own places and times. For this threefold division of the Law, Aquinas followed early Christian thinkers (e.g. Clement of Alexandria, Hippolytus of Rome, Augustine of Hippo) whose views followed on from their exegeses of the sacred texts. Aquinas here quotes from Paul (Rom. 7.1 the law is 'holy [= ceremonial] and just [= judicial] and good [= moral]' and the original Law itself (Deut. 5.1; Lev. 18.4).[10]

This approach has not convinced all readers: the biblical texts do not present a systematic let alone philosophical account of the Law; and a particular law might not fall neatly into one division alone: the Sabbath could be assigned to all three. Moreover, this threefold division should not blind the reader to the importance of the laws in their detail and their entirety, if indeed Jesus Christ embodied, modelled, and fulfilled them all. Aquinas did not dispute these points. Nevertheless, Aquinas, his predecessors, and his successors, detected statements and tendencies in Sacred Scripture that they believed justified this division for interpretative and practical purposes. Not only the Law's content, but the biblical refrain about God's preference for (moral) mercy rather than (ceremonial) sacrifice (e.g. 1 Sam. 15.22; Prov. 21.3; Hos. 6.6), coupled with New Testament ideas (e.g. Matt. 23.23; Luke 11.42; Acts 11.1–9; 1

Cor. 7.19), had all pointed in this direction. It also is worth noting that, in this excerpt, Aquinas appeals broadly to Scripture, tradition, and reason – an approach that became a guide to all matters theological, associated in particular with Richard Hooker (1554–1600), an Anglican churchman of the Protestant Reformation era, to which we now turn.

Reformation Christianity

The Protestant Reformation in Europe was driven by the recovery of the power and radical simplicity of the Christian gospel through close study of the Bible. The Sacred Scriptures of Christianity have supreme authority in doctrine and practice: *Sola Scriptura*, 'Scripture Alone', became one of the movement's slogans. Complex and divisive political events and currents also attached themselves to this religious and social revolution. This was a reaction against the accumulated traditions, structures, and institutional corruption of the late-medieval Christianity. The experience in sixteenth-century Europe is the best-known example of a series of radical renewals in Christian history; in other words, other reforms had taken place before, and have taken place since. The strongest early personality in this movement was undoubtedly the German monk, Martin Luther (1483–1546), whose new outlook influenced his treatment of the Pentateuch, as well as the rest of the Bible. It may be understood through what became, for him, a thematic contrast between law and gospel, rather than arbitrarily between the Old and the New Testaments.

For Luther, the Law brings to the fore the plight of humanity. Laws address obvious sins, but they also expose the darkness of the human heart. Moreover, Moses presented a religious life that humankind could not achieve: the wilderness wanderings had illustrated this all too well. And the repetition of laws in the Pentateuch shows that obedience had to be called for repeatedly: it does not come naturally. With this plight in view, Luther discovered, when reading Paul's Letter to the Romans, that salvation is about accepting righteousness as a gift of God, regardless of a person's good works: it is this that enables justification and acceptance by God. This new outlook is seen in Luther's *Lectures on Deuteronomy* (1525). On the laws that prohibit a woman bearing the weapons of a man and a man from wearing female clothing (Deut. 22.5), Luther affirms traditional male and female roles (while observing this law does not apply 'to cases where this is necessary to avoid danger or to playing a game or to deceive the enemy'). But Luther's new outlook was still influenced by late-medieval thought, as seen in his allegorical interpretation of these laws: just as male and female roles must not be confused, so faith and trust in God must not be confused with good works for human masters.[11] How, then, did Luther answer the broader question posed above about the Law: which of its commands, if any, are binding on Christians?

Martin Luther: 'How Christians Should Regard Moses'

(1525)

Moses is dead. His rule ended when Christ came. He is of no further service ...

Now this is the first thing that I ought to see in Moses, namely, the commandments to which I am not bound except insofar as they are [implanted in everyone] by nature [and written in everyone's heart] ... In the second place I find something in Moses that I do not have from nature: the promises and pledges of God about Christ. This is the best thing. It is something not written naturally into the heart but comes from heaven ... In the third place we read Moses for the beautiful examples of faith, of love, and of the cross, as shown in the fathers, Adam, Abel, Noah, Abraham, Isaac, Jacob, Moses, and all the rest.

I have stated that all Christians, and especially those who handle the word of God and attempt to teach others, should take heed and learn Moses aright. Thus where he gives the commandments, we are not to follow him except so far as he agrees with the natural law. Moses is a teacher and doctor of the Jews. We have our own master, Christ, and he has set before us what we are to know, observe, do, and leave undone ...

Many great and outstanding people have missed it ... they rage and fume, chattering to people 'God's word, God's word!' All the while they mislead the poor people and drive them to destruction.[12]

Luther resisted the popular Protestant tendency to make too much of the laws of Moses just because they are in the Bible. Luther criticized enthusiastic reformers such as Thomas Müntzer who, in his *Sermons to the Princes* (1524), called on Saxon leaders to enact iconoclasm inspired by Deuteronomy, or to abolish the taxes not mentioned in the Bible. This criticism is evident at the end of the excerpt ('they rage and fume'). But the excerpt also shows that Luther's stance, though traditional and sharply expressed, cannot be characterized as that of the categorical rejection of the Law: the books of Moses given originally to the ancient Jews are to be followed in so far as they agree with the natural law implanted in the human person and the teachings of Christ, and for their examples of faith. Thus, laws such as those in the Decalogue are still valid for Christians. But not all of them in equal measure: while political leaders may learn from Moses, they are not bound by the judicial (civil) laws, and the ceremonial laws have been dispensed with – as Aquinas and others had already argued.

But Luther saw in the Pentateuch, and the Old Testament generally, the basis for a robust faith, and also the grounds for opposition to late-medieval Church practices that easily distracted believers from faith in Christ alone. The biblical texts present a transcendent God who is strict yet faithful; they affirm creation and history with a realism that discourages ascetic withdrawal from reality; and they contain critiques of worldly power (e.g. Moses against Pharaoh) that Luther turned against the medieval papacy in his *Sermons on the Second Book of Moses* (1524–7). Luther still used medieval approaches to Scripture that he had learnt, but he modified them in the service of his new outlook. For instance, on Deuteronomy 22.5 (above), Luther urged that tropology (from the Greek *tropos*, 'way, path') is not about moral or ethical prescription in the narrow sense, but the way or path to the Christ of faith. This gave Luther's interpretations a radical simplicity, unlike the complexity of some medieval writing – a tendency that may be seen above in the excerpt from Richard of St Victor.

The Frenchman John Calvin (1509–64), another of the magisterial reformers of the Protestant Reformation, also affirmed traditional Christian views of the Law. The conventional explanation was that its larger and higher purposes are understood from New Testament perspectives. In general, Calvin held that human beings, in their fallen nature and condition – including their natural reason (unlike Aquinas) – are directed by the Law towards God in order to receive the grace that guides and restores them. But, unlike Luther, who more typically emphasized the condemning function of the Law (which is an undoubted strand of the biblical texts), Calvin argued that it retains a positive purpose for the believer. This gave the Law an even more integral place in his outlook.

John Calvin: *Institutes of the Christian Religion*

(1559)

... because we need not only teaching but also exhortation, the servant of God will also avail himself of this benefit of the law: by frequent meditation upon it to be aroused to obedience, be strengthened in it, and be drawn back from the slippery path of transgression. In this way the saints must press on; for, however eagerly they may in accordance with the Spirit drive toward God's righteousness, the listless flesh always so burdens them that they do not proceed with due readiness ... Doubtless David was referring to this use when he sang the praises of the law [Ps. 19.7–8; 119.105] ... These do not contradict Paul's statements, which show not what use the law serves for the regenerate ... He lays hold not only of the precepts, but the accompanying promise of grace, which alone sweetens what is bitter. For what would be less lovable than the law if, with importuning and threatening alone, it troubled souls through fear, and distressed them through fright? David especially shows that in the law he apprehended the Mediator, without whom there is no delight or sweetness.[13]

Calvin saw deep continuity between the people of God in Old Testament times and the Christians of his own day who, likewise, experienced joys and sorrows, blessing and chastisement, success and opposition. For Calvin, this continuity is expressed in the idea of covenant: the bond between the people and God, who remains faithful to them. This was an important way in which a Christian could have a sense of self, since, when human beings gain a proper knowledge of God, they then understand themselves – the opening theme of his *Institutes*. This led Calvin to teach that spiritual nourishment can be derived from the Law: it directs and disciplines believers in the sovereign will of the God of the covenant. In the excerpt, Calvin moves from the Law as a prompt for obedience, via the Psalms of David on the Law's spiritual qualities, to the importance of divine grace as an encouragement that sweetens the Law's discipline – as David perceived – and, through this, it anticipates Christ's mediating role as High Priest.

To help Christians understand the Law, Calvin also analysed its texts with systematic clarity in his *Harmony of the Law* (1563) – modelled on Gospel harmonies – the result of weekly Bible studies by Calvin and other local pastors in Geneva. It is an explanation of the Pentateuch's laws organized according to the topics of the Decalogue, which also provide a framework for understanding them: its moral law is the basis of the ceremonial and the civil – an approach with ancient antecedents (i.e. Philo, Augustine). The aim was that readers would profit from the Law in an integrated way, since Calvin observed that its laws are spread throughout the biblical texts and its doctrinal teaching is thereby unconnected. For example, the Decalogue's second commandment, which prohibits the worship of idols, is a synecdoche (a part that represents the whole) about worship, which presents an opportunity to discuss ceremonial laws (e.g. priesthood, sacrifice), followed by civil laws that relate to idolatry (e.g. the removal of idols and altars to other gods). This had inevitable implications, in the hands of Calvin, for Reformation era disputes about the use of icons and images in worship.

This Renaissance literary skill and a reforming agenda were hallmarks of his outlook. For the line, 'For I, the Lord your God, am a jealous God' (Ex. 20.5; Deut. 5.9), Calvin suggests that Moses' double-use of *elohim* and then *el*, different Hebrew words for 'God', magnified divine power so that God might be feared respectfully. In exploring the term for 'jealous' in Hebrew, and in Greek and Latin translation, Calvin explained that this is not unhealthy envy, a 'guilty rivalry', but it is like that of a husband who rightfully 'suffers no rival' in his marriage, itself an allusion to the danger of the violation of the covenant between God and Israel: 'this spiritual marriage'.[14] While Calvin mentions New Testament texts that paved the way for typological, if not allegorical, interpretations of a law (e.g. the Day of Atonement prefigured Christ's sacrifice), he sometimes avoided these approaches, preferring, as in the excerpt, to focus on the plain sense of the biblical text. But Calvin also urged a reformation of Christian practice: that the Levites were set apart for the sanctuary, with Aaron as High Priest, justifies neither the primacy of the Roman See nor a hierarchy of bishops and elders, which easily leads to ambition and tyranny. Rather, Christ, as Aaron's true successor, is the head of all pastors, who should behave with modesty and mutuality; although natural reason still shows that some degree of leadership is needed to prevent confusion. And regarding the civil commands that Israel should drive idolaters from the land, and not make covenants with them, Calvin argues that the Church in each country no longer exists in geographical separation, but the principle remains: the Church must guard itself from all corrupting influences.

Modern Christianity

In his *Preface to the Law* (1523), Luther had suggested that the seeming untidiness of the laws of Moses is like life itself: duties and concerns are mixed in together. In his *Harmony of the Law* (1563), Calvin presented the laws and their doctrine systematically to overcome this disparateness. These approaches reflected a Renaissance ethos: *ad fontes*, 'back to the sources'; but these churchmen still treated the Law as Sacred Scripture. However, the critical inclination that is, to varying extents, evident in their comments grew significantly in the modern period. Commentators, Christian or otherwise, saw themselves as increasingly unconstrained by Church teaching. They were guided more by reason, and less by Christian tradition, with regard to literary and historical questions concerning the biblical texts, which began to be treated more and more like any other ancient anthology of writings. The modern approach to the Pentateuch is probably the best example of this trend.

In late antiquity, and much pre-modern commentary that followed thereafter, Moses was held to be the author of the Pentateuch, due to references to him writing (e.g. Ex. 24.4; Num. 33.1–2; Deut. 31.9). He was also promoted by Jews and Christians as an intellectual sage in the author-conscious Greek and Roman cultures of late antiquity. But those biblical references concern only discrete biblical sections; and Moses is most often spoken about by an anonymous narrator, including mention of his unrivalled humility (Num. 12.3), and his death (Deut. 34). Moreover, in the New Testament, 'Moses says' is a shorthand for the Law – much like David is for the Psalms, even though he did not compose all of them. Accordingly, in addition to some medieval commentators who argued that Moses had not authored the entire Pentateuch, various seventeenth- and eighteenth-century thinkers (e.g. Thomas Hobbes, Richard Simon, Baruch Spinoza, Jean Astruc) contributed to a developing view that the Pentateuch had been composed over a much longer period by anonymous writers, whose later contexts are implied (e.g. Gen. 22.14; 36.31) – whatever Moses' original contribution had been. This view was fuelled by other observations: differences in theology, literary style and vocabulary that imply separate human authors at work (e.g.

creation in Gen. 1.1—2.4a and 2.4b—3.24). There also appear to be inconsistencies that require explanation: for instance, given the variations in the
Decalogue between Exodus 20 and Deuteronomy 5, what did God actually
command at Mt Sinai? These observations led to new hypotheses about the
Pentateuch's composition. The most influential in the modern period has
been the Documentary Hypothesis of the German Protestant scholar Julius
Wellhausen:

Julius Wellhausen: *Prolegomena to the History of Israel*

(1878)

We come then to the Law. Here, as for most parts of the Old Testament, we
have no express information as to the author and date of composition, and
to get even approximately at the truth we are shut up to the use of such data
as can be derived from an analysis of the contents, taken in conjunction with
what we may happen to know from other sources as to the course of Israel's
history ... The very idea of canonicity was originally associated with the Torah,
and was only afterwards extended to the other books, which slowly and by a
gradual process acquired a certain measure of validity given to the Torah by
a single public and formal act, through which it was introduced at once as
the Magna Charta of the Jewish communion (Neh. viii–x) ... the canonical
character is much more essential, and serious difficulties beset the assumption that the Law of Moses came into existence at a period long before the
exile ... In my early student days I was attracted by the stories of Saul and
David, Ahab and Elijah; the discourses of Amos and Isaiah laid a strong hold
on me, and I read myself well into the prophetic and historical books of the
Old Testament ... my enjoyment of the latter was marred by the Law ... Even
where there were points of contact between it and them, differences also
made themselves felt, and I found it impossible to give a candid decision in
favour of the priority of the Law. Dimly I began to perceive that throughout
there was between them all the difference that separates two wholly distinct
worlds ... I readily acknowledged to myself the possibility of understanding
Hebrew antiquity without the book of the Torah.[15]

The excerpt mentions the lack of definite knowledge about the Pentateuch's
composition, and the major consequence of it not being acknowledged
much in the earlier Historical Books – however important the Law certainly became in Judaism. Building on his nineteenth-century predecessors'
views, Wellhausen went on to propose that four sources, each with distinct
characteristics, underlay the Pentateuch, and were composed between the
tenth and fifth centuries BC in the order JEDP: J for Jahwist (from the
German for YHWH), E for Elohist, D for Deuteronomic, and P for Priestly

writers. These four sources were gradually compiled and edited into their more familiar form after the Babylonian Exile. Wellhausen's hypothesis also helped articulate his views about the religious history of ancient Israel: from joyous spontaneity at multiple sanctuaries (J and E), via the struggle for centralization (the mid-point: 'the book of the law' in D), through to the strict centralization of early Judaism (typified by P) after the Babylonian Exile. This hypothesis, a classic example of Source Criticism, is similar to modern proposals of a 'Q' source (from the German *Quelle*, 'source') of Jesus' sayings that are common to Matthew and Luke, but that are not shared by Mark. Responses to the Documentary Hypothesis about the Pentateuch have been various, both religious and critical.

While a text's composition, from its beginnings through to its final form, implies a process with many stages, traditional readers have often expressed concern that this type of hypothesis risks severing the link between sacred event and sacred text, if the literary sources were composed much later. Accordingly, there has since been a strong movement of using archaeo-logical discoveries to attempt to identify more securely the places and events that the Pentateuch describes in its ancient setting. The Egyptian *Merneptah Stele* (c. 1208 BC) contains the earliest known extra-biblical reference to 'Israel' in its period of settlement in Canaan; an Aramaic inscription from Deir 'Alla, in modern Jordan (c. 850 BC), has visions of the seer Balaam that bear comparison with Numbers 22—24; and a silver scroll found inside a tomb at Ketef Hinnom in Jerusalem contains the oldest known inscription of a biblical text (c. 600 BC): the Aaronic blessing (Num. 6.24–26).[16] As to the developmental picture Wellhausen proposed, both Jewish and Christian scholars have detected anti-Judaistic bias, but as a proxy for Protestant dis-putation with Roman Catholicism: from a free prophetic piety through to a formalistic priestly religion from which Jesus later liberated people. If this is indeed present, it raises questions about the neutrality and objectivity of modern critical study that Wellhausen has often been said to represent.[17]

Others have disputed the hypothesis on critical grounds. Biblical texts might have, embedded within them, literary 'genres' or forms of literature that preserve earlier content (e.g. story, hymn, ritual, custom). Form Criti-cism is the name given to the approach whereby these embedded genres or forms are detected. While its proposals have, at times, been criticized as speculative, this approach has the potential to reduce the chronological gap between sacred event and sacred text. As for the inconsistencies between texts, these may be explained in alternative ways. The variations in the texts of the Decalogue imply a primal revelation – a shorter *Urdekalog* ('original Decalogue') – that was put to different uses by the compilers and editors of Exodus and Deuteronomy respectively, such that its expansion and adap-tations only serve to reflect its great importance in ancient Israel (cf. Hos. 4.2; Jer. 7.9). From this perspective, apparent inconsistencies may be viewed quite differently. New hypotheses about the Pentateuch's composition have been proposed as well, even if many of them build on the critical approach typified by scholars such as Wellhausen. These critical counter-responses do not, however, automatically imply a return to the views of late antiquity and pre-modernity. Rather, they reflect the fact that the current scholarly situation concerning the Pentateuch's composition is in flux. There is also a growing recognition of the need to understand much better how the ancient biblical writers composed texts, sacred and otherwise.[18]

James K. Hoffmeier: *Ancient Israel in Sinai: The Evidence for the Authenticity of the Wilderness*

(2005)

When the Egyptian itineraries are examined, they compare very favourably to those in the Pentateuch. Pap. Anastasi I, dating to the reign of Ramesses II [c. 1303–1213 BC], contains the words of a bragging scribe to his colleague about his knowledge of travel to and in different parts of the Levant. He describes travel routes, names of forts, cities, water sources, the challenge of finding enough water, and the trials of having to deal with the Shashu-Bedouin. This is not unlike the accounts in the Israelite wilderness travels that identify sites, oases, wells, lack of water, and a hostile clash with the Amalekites. The similarities between the two suggest that the 'itinerary' genre and the nature of travel accounts, not the canons of the Priestly school, explain the style of the wilderness itineraries in the Pentateuch.[19]

This excerpt is an example of the traditionalist reaction to the impact of the modern source-critical approach to the Pentateuch. Hoffmeier is concerned to refute the claims of the 'critics' of the last 150 years or so who question that its texts preserve accurate historical knowledge. The itinerary texts are not merely the product of a 'Priestly school' who wrote almost a millennium after what is said to have happened in Exodus and Numbers; texts that often, according to modern source critics, both agree and disagree in their details. Hoffmeier's rebuttal is part of his broader discussion of modern attempts to identify the geographical location of Mt Sinai (where Israel encountered God), a location of sacred memory that went on to bear huge significance in the traditions of ancient Israel and beyond. The cultic symbolism of Mt Zion and its temple worship in Jerusalem were, to a large extent, modelled on the worship at Mt Sinai.

Hoffmeier's approach and reasoning may be seen as twofold: comparative and literary. The comparative aspect is the mention of Papyrus Anastasi I, a thirteenth-century BC satirical letter from ancient Egypt (now held in the British Museum in London) that has details similar to Exodus 12—19 and Numbers 33. It includes mention of the Shashu (Bedouin), an Egyptian term (Bedouin is an Arabic term) for pastoralists who posed a threat to those travelling through deserts; just as the fleeing Hebrews faced opposition, according to the Pentateuch. The literary aspect concerns a widespread itinerary genre that typically itemized the details of military campaigns. Identifying this genre implies that the Pentateuch contains content consistent with its ancient setting. This, for Hoffmeier, raises questions about some of the claims made by the modern critics about the apparent lateness of the sources that underlie the Pentateuch.

This response is legitimate in principle: there is no good reason to be overly sceptical about there being genuine historical knowledge in the Pentateuch, as an anthology of texts of an ancient Near Eastern nation. After all, the narrative episodes about the wilderness wanderings are realistic and true to life, given the threat of death that desert regions present to its inhabitants; and they describe the range of human responses that would understandably accompany arduous travel (e.g. faith and doubt). It is, however, important to recognize the challenges, logistic and financial, of identifying desert locations used by long-gone travellers, as Hoffmeier did in his role as director of the North Sinai Archaeological Project (1999–2008). Such observations about the Pentateuch's realism serve the traditional conviction that Judaism and Christianity are religions rooted in historical times and places; and any successful identifications of locations from ancient narratives may then bolster religious faith in their historical reality. This is attractive in its capacity to restore, against modern criticism, the link between sacred event and sacred text.

But some caveats need mentioning. The itineraries seemingly contain not only real place names (e.g. 'the wilderness of Zin': Ex. 16.1; Num. 33.11) but also aetiological place names, characteristic of folk memory that carry a moral lesson about faith. For instance, Marah (Ex. 15.23), meaning 'bitter', was the location of an episode about the Israelites' complaint over the lack of drinkable water in the desert, whose purpose was to display divine provision and to provide teaching about the testing of the relationship between God and the people. Focusing on the geographical details of this may well bring about an unintended consequence: distraction from the theological drama. In other words, the 'itinerary' genre is not merely a geographical map, but also a theological 'map'. This is important for other genres as well, such as hymn (e.g. Ex. 15) and law (e.g. Num. 36), whose content is concerned with praise and custom, respectively. This is another way of saying that biblical interpretation requires not only knowledge about facts but also intelligent and practical insight (i.e. wisdom). The Pentateuch contains a variety of genres, each with different hallmarks and purposes. What kind of historical knowledge they each contain is but one question among others in their interpretation.

John Barton: *Ethics and the Old Testament*

(2002)

Very often the book to which Christians, who are familiar with it, seems a comfort and an inspiration strikes others as thoroughly barbaric and alien; it seems to come from a world so remote from our own that it can have nothing to say to us. This is perhaps nowhere so obvious as when we speak of the Bible as a resource for Christian ethics. There is nothing easier than to produce a list of reasons why the ethicist might want to ignore the Old Testament in particular. Old Testament law lays down the death penalty for adultery (Lev. 20.10; Deut. 22.22), appears to envisage mutilation as a punishment for assault ('an eye for an eye ...', Ex. 21.23–24; Lev. 24.19–20; Deut. 19.21), forbids the taking of interests on loans (Deut. 23.19), which would cause severe difficulties to modern economies, and treats those with various skin diseases – *sara'at*, traditionally translated 'leprosy' – as social and religious outcasts (Lev. 13—14). And the law is only part of the story.[20]

Certain laws in the Pentateuch, when read with a concentrated focus on their ancient historical setting, are often said to be morally problematic for modern readers, as the excerpt expresses. Barton goes on to explain that, while some Christians may feel bound to its texts as Holy Scripture and seek to accommodate them in a 'coherent moral system', many other Christians, and non-Christians, consider this to be 'implausible at best and ridiculous or even immoral at worst'.[21] To avoid these rather contrasted stances, Barton goes on to approach the Old Testament as an ancient text, but highlights that, while modern readers might see its texts as patriarchal, sexist and racist, with huge internal variety and concepts that are strange to them, its texts still have much to teach us – just as readers might learn from the writings of other ancient cultures (e.g. Greek tragedy). Barton judiciously proposes, on the one hand, that their social vision, summarized in texts such as the Decalogue – duties towards God and neighbour – remain essential; but that, on the other hand, the content, which is time-bound, inconsistent, and alien, nevertheless ends up addressing contemporary life in its broken-ness and particularity. The latter point may well be surprising to modern readers, but this discerning approach proves beneficial. Taking a cue from this, what may be said about the four cases in the excerpt?

Understanding their ancient context helps illuminate them: either that these laws represented advanced thinking in their own day or were simply appropriate in their own immediate context. Laws on sexual activity priori-tized the purity and honour of the members of a community; hence, the death penalty for adultery, which was standard in ancient law, was a major deterrent to marital unfaithfulness – although there are no descriptions of its enforcement in ancient Israel. The expression 'an eye for an eye' meant that punishment had to be proportionate to the crime committed; it prevented the poor simply being bought off by the rich: all were meant to be equal under the law. It was not obviously applied literally: monetary compensation for bodily injury (Ex. 21.18–19) and the freeing of injured slaves (Ex. 21.26–27), which are unusual in ancient legislation, imply this. Not charging interest on loans to fellow Israelites assumes that the rich would assist the poor, and that economic stability for all Israelites was paramount in its emergence as a nation (cf. Ezek. 22.12). The term 'leprosy' covered various contagions on skin, clothing, and in houses, rather than leprosy proper (Hansen's disease). The laws on the removal of the leprous person (Lev. 13.45–46) preserved the purity and health of the community, and they also provided for that person's eventual reintegration.

Christian interpretations of these four cases are informed by Jesus' teaching, and through recognition of the Gentile contexts into which Christianity initially spread – just as interpretations from the early rabbinic period (until *c.* 600) became authoritative in medieval Judaism. Jesus exposed the hypocritical use of the law on adultery: people could not live by it in all honesty (John 8.1–11); and Gentile Christians were told that God had cleansed those guilty of this and other sins (1 Cor. 6.9–11). Jesus exhorted his hearers not to 'get even', even proportionately, but to overcome evil with good (Matt. 5.38–42); and Gentile Christians were challenged not to take out lawsuits against each other but to anticipate their vindicated status in the new heavens and new earth (1 Cor. 6.1–8). Jesus taught that financial generosity is part of the Kingdom of God (Luke 6.35), while allowing for the practices of bank deposits and interest (Matt. 25.27; Luke 19.23). Jesus showed compassion to lepers by touching and healing them (Mark 1.40–45), rising above the impulse to avoid them. These new attitudes to the interpretation and use of the Law in Jewish society of the Roman period, and in Gentile Christian communities to which the Law had not originally been given, thereby preserved and developed its principles and values: purity, forgiveness, generosity, and inclusion.

These kinds of observations may yet inspire the realistic, principled and hopeful use and influence of biblical law today, interpretation nonetheless guided by Christian ideals. These four laws again serve as examples. While adultery is no longer a capital offence in many contemporary societies, Christian hope encourages cleansing, repentance, and forgiveness – while acknowledging that the hugely damaging effects of adultery need treating with practical realism and pastoral care. The expression 'an eye for an eye' echoes the sentiment 'the punishment should fit the crime', avoiding both unjust leniency and harshness; even then, Christian notions of justice are not mechanical: forgiveness has the potential to break the cycle of recrimination. Governments nowadays regulate interest rates locally and internationally, and loyal commercial relationships are often rewarded. This is typically a neutral matter for Christians, provided that reward is not an opportunity for greed (e.g. gambling) – a criticism to which capitalist economic models are often vulnerable. The same goes for public health inspection and quarantine: these are modern equivalents of the ancient rule of exclusion for a set period. There are Pentateuchal laws whose contribution is welcome and obvious (e.g. the fair treatment of slaves, prisoners, debtors, the landless, the disabled). But even these four cases suggest that laws that initially seem wholly inapplicable may still yet speak to us with realism and hope, because the principles they enshrine still address the difficult practical realities of contemporary life in community.[22]

Global Christianity

Liberation Theology is a phrase coined by the Peruvian priest Gustavo Gutiérrez. He was part of a radical church movement in Latin American Roman Catholicism that arose in the 1950s–60s in response to endemic poverty. Grassroots organizers (i.e. priests, nuns, laypersons) developed a view of Christianity, expressed in terms of liberation from economic and political oppression, since injustice was at the root of hardship experienced by the poor. Guided by a conviction that the God of love is concerned with justice and equality for all, they urged that the Church should exercise a 'preferential option for the poor' – who, according to them, are the real subject of the Bible. Parish networks of 'Base Ecclesial Communities' were seen as the true Church involved in group struggle and solidarity. Their purposes were not just development in the conventional Western sense, but also liberation, even political revolution. Several theologians emerged as influential exponents of the movement: Gustavo Gutiérrez, Juan Luis Segundo, José Severino Croatto, and José Miguez Bonino. The following excerpt expresses their outlook well:

Gustavo Gutiérrez: *Theology of Liberation*

(1971)

The liberation of Israel is a political action. It is the breaking away from a situation of despoliation and misery and the beginning of the construction of a just and fraternal society ... The Exodus is the long march toward the promised land in which Israel can establish a society free of misery and alienation. Throughout the whole process, the religious event is not set apart. It is placed in the context of the entire narrative, or more precisely it is its deepest meaning. It is the root of the situation. In the last instance, it is in this event that the dislocation introduced by sin is resolved and justice and injustice, oppression and liberation, are determined ... By working, transform

---

ing the world, breaking out of servitude, building a just society, and assuming his destiny in history, man forges himself. In Egypt, work is alienated and, far from building a just society, contributes rather to increasing injustice and to widening the gap between exploiters and exploited ... The Exodus experience is paradigmatic. It remains vital and contemporary due to similar historical experiences which the People of God undergo ... In Christ, and through the Spirit, men are becoming one in the very heart of history, as they confront and struggle against all that divides and opposes them. But the true agents of this quest for unity are those who today are oppressed (economically, politically, culturally) and struggle to become free.[23]

Liberation theologians transfer the biblical story into their own context. The story of the Exodus provides the paradigmatic narrative of liberation from oppression: Israel's theology was a 'liberation theology'. But this is not confined to the Pentateuch: the prophets, too, were concerned for the poor and marginalized, and proclaimed a messianic vision of justice and hope. In the New Testament Gospels, Jesus preached good news to the poor and reintegrated social outcasts – often in confrontation with the established religious and political leaders. The book of Acts speaks of the ideal Christian community: just and free. And the book of Revelation condemns oppression by all monstrous potentates throughout history. In their reading of the Bible, Liberation theologians are influenced by a Marxist philosophy of historical progress via social and political class rivalry and struggle. It highlights what is, for them, already very evident in the Bible: the unjust relationship between rich and poor.

To sharpen this claim all the more, Liberation theologians argue that the Church and its priests have been complicit in this oppression. Its Western theologians and theologies are much too elitist and intellectualist; a certain strand of apocalyptic Christian pessimism about the world easily leads to an uncaring abdication of responsibility; and the self-interested legitimizing of the prevailing 'structures of sin' has often reinforced poverty and its effects. Thus, rather than indulge in an overly spiritualized theology, influenced by some of the dualistic strains of Greek philosophy that emphasize the importance of the soul at the expense of the body, Liberation theologians have called for orthopraxis, and not merely orthodoxy: not just 'God talk' but 'God walk'. Christian salvation is not just about the cure for sin and the afterlife, but it is all-encompassing: the breach between God and humanity needs to be seen in all forms of social misery, deprivation, and alienation. This is what Jesus, 'the liberator', came to deal with. The bodily and the spiritual go together.

Liberation Theology has faced criticism. Concerning its biblical interpretation, aspects of the Exodus narrative do not match its utopian view of progress towards justice and equality in the terms of the excerpt above. The Exodus was about departure from an oppressive society rather than liberation and revolution within; and the liberation of Israel out of slavery in Egypt led to the dispossession of other peoples, the Canaanites, when Israel entered the Promised Land. Another weakness is that its Marxist philosophy easily reduces salvation to economic concerns, and therefore Christianity to radical (and sometimes violent) political action. This prompted official Roman Catholic censure in the 1980s. In 1983, Pope John Paul II memorably reprimanded Fr Ernesto Cardenal SJ on the runway of the airport in Managua, Nicaragua, for his involvement in revolutionary politics; he was later dismissed from clerical office. After all, there are many kinds of oppression, in addition to poverty (e.g. against vulnerable women, racial minorities). While salvation is broad in scope, it is more fundamental than any of these different kinds of oppression put together: it is about reconciliation between God and a fallen humanity, a theology that identifies an even more profound starting point of liberation for all.[24]

And yet any legitimate criticisms should not distract from the valuable insights and influence of Liberation Theology. It offers an effective and vivid reminder that all biblical interpretation, wherever, whenever, and by whomever, is contextual: biblical texts gain fresh significance for different audiences, who always bring their own experiences to their Bible reading. Indeed, the Exodus narrative is a good example, not least because it was already being applied to new situations in the biblical period: the restoration of Israel after the Babylonian Exile was like a 'Second Exodus'; and the Jewish Passover meal lay in part behind the early Christian eucharistic meal. But most importantly, at its best, Liberation Theology presents an inspirational discourse about economic and social justice. In uniting theory and practice, it encourages a healthy view of the whole person, and reminds the Church of its prophetic responsibility to defend the defenceless. As a fruit of Christian salvation, its outlook and practice thereby sit within the long-standing tradition of compassionate Christian social involvement. Pope Francis overturned the ruling against Ernesto Cardenal in 2014.

Let us now turn east to the continent of Africa. The excerpt below is from a commentary on Genesis in the first-ever produced single-volume Bible commentary written by Africans for Africans. Over 70 English- and French-speaking African theologians from different Evangelical denominations contributed, although many of them were educated in Western as well as African universities and seminaries. The volume was produced to respond to the educational needs of African Christianity: phenomenal numerical Church growth, but a lack of solid biblical knowledge and understanding across its various groupings and denominations. But even more than this, it was intended to foster the study of the Bible to encourage not only knowledge and understanding of its texts, but the application of its ideas to the realities of African life and culture. This would then enable biblical ideas to operate as evaluators of culture, whether that means echoing and supporting helpful African customs or exposing and critiquing harmful practices.

Each biblical book is introduced (title, setting, themes, structure, etc.), and each section of text is explained; but it is then commented on in ways that speak to Africans directly. For instance, on Genesis 1—11, Barnabé Assohoto (Benin) and Samuel Ngewa (Kenya) observe that the God who said at creation 'let there be' (1.2, 6, etc.) can 'raise Africa to new heights'; they go on to challenge their readers to see Sabbath rest (2.2) not as an excuse for the widespread 'lazy rest', but as an opportunity to think and dream of new projects that will benefit individuals and society at large. The strife between Cain and Abel (4.1–16) is read as a reminder of the civil and tribal wars between Africans that curse the continent: 'we need to deal with these problems', they say. And the story of Babel (11.1–9) shows how not to undertake a project: to build Church unity not with grandiose ideas of self-promotion, but with the ideals of community in view.

The commentary on each book also contains short articles on selected topics. On Exodus 2, R. Pohor (Côte d'Ivoire) addresses slavery (child, prostitution, domestic) and calls for human dignity and love in action; and on Exodus 12, J. Milasi (Kenya) uses the Passover as an analogy for initiation rites that prepare young people for life (i.e. teaching on child-rearing, animal hunting) in contrast to those that are barbaric (e.g. Female Genital Mutilation). On Leviticus 18, E. Afriyie (Ghana) sees moral taboos in Africa and elsewhere (e.g. incest) as evidence for the universal knowledge of God, but advises that Christians should be delivered from superstitious fears (e.g. unnecessary dietary prohibitions). On Numbers, A. Boniface-Malle (Tanzania) envisages the wilderness wanderings as a picture of Africa in transition, facing major issues such as globalization, poverty, epidemics, disease, pluralism, interfaith, and denominationalism. On Deuteronomy, M. Douglas Carew (Sierra Leone) places Israel in its ancient Near Eastern context, but then reminds readers of the contribution of Africans to ancient progress: Egyptian hieroglyphic writing, medicine, and engineering (e.g. the pyramids). This following is illustrative of the hallmarks of the commentary:

Barnabé Assohoto and Samuel Ngewa: 'Genesis'

(2006)

This passage [Gen. 9.25–27] has sometimes been referred to as the 'curse of Ham' and used to justify the enslavement of black people and the material poverty of the African continent as natural results of divine punishments. But this interpretation is clearly wrong. For one thing, the curse was not pronounced on Ham but only on his son Canaan. The genealogy in 10.6–20 shows that Ham's other sons, who were not cursed, included *Cush* (the ancestor of the

Ethiopians, and the father of Nimrod, who is praised in 10.8), *Mizraim* (the ancestor of the Egyptians) and *Put* (the ancestor of the Libyans). It is not God who despises black people, but other people (see Song 1.5–6). Holy Scripture should not be used to justify all historical events. Rather, with faith and respect we should use the word of God to analyse, appreciate and judge events in our history.

So what effect did this curse on Canaan have? We do not know the whole picture. ... It is, however, possible that the words of rejection and exclusion pronounced by his grandfather aroused scorn and rebellion in Canaan, leading him and his descendants to become distanced from God. A profound moral degeneration would then be understandable, and hence, God's judgement.

Given this possibility, this incident is a reminder to us of the need to be patient and wise in our judgements. We need to be certain of our grounds for making judgements and to be aware of their possible consequences (Matt. 7.1–2). We should not allow anger to lead us into uttering curses on our parents or our children. We are not always aware of the devastating effects of such words.[25]

Assohoto and Ngewa offer an effective rebuttal of interpretations that have contributed to the dreadful practice and legacy of slavery. The commentators then go on to make a broader point: given that the curse was uttered on Canaan, not Ham, and given that divine punishment later fell on Canaan, this episode is a moral warning about the danger of rash words under alcoholic influence, which can have devastating long-term effects. The pertinence of this interpretation in certain African settings, where curses are believed to hold great psychological power, is not in doubt. However, while Assohoto and Ngewa rightly highlight communal and inter-generational responsibility, they make Noah overly responsible for the behaviour of Canaanites – which, according to biblical writers, was their own moral responsibility. It might be that modern Source Criticism helps at this juncture (see Wellhausen, above). Rather than supposing, as do Assohoto and Ngewa, that Genesis 9.25–27 was written by Moses well ahead of the Israelite settlement in the land of Canaan, and then speculating that the curse had a direct psychological influence, a later date of composition would suggest this episode was written when there was already hostility between Israel and Canaan. In other words, Genesis 9.25–27 is an aetiology (i.e. explanatory account) that traces existing ethnic division back to a primal episode, but in a way that is more about the contemporary situation of hostility than the original cause itself.

Finally, let us move farther east to Asia. The one God of the Pentateuch has many names in Hebrew: the personal name YHWH ('LORD') and the generic names Elohim and El ('God'), and Adonai ('Lord'). Each has different linguistic origins, even though they refer in the Pentateuch to the one God. But what happens when these biblical texts are read in a distant culture whose divine names imply both similar and different ideas in their own texts and religious practices? Which indigenous words should be used? And who decides which are the most appropriate? Moreover, what happens in a situation of mutual interaction and influence when the morality of the biblical texts is in conflict with the traditional ethical practices of that culture? These two issues – theology and ethics – have recurred in Chinese Christian history. According to the *Nestorian Stele* (781), the earliest missionary to China was Alopen (635), who brought sacred texts that were translated during the Tang Dynasty. Nestorian scholars, skilled in languages and dialogue, presented the Christian faith with an awareness of the different perspectives of the Chinese. Nestorians translated references to the biblical God with *Zhen Zhu*, 'true lord'. But a significant period of interaction occurred during the Jesuit missions to China in the late Ming/ early Qing Dynasties. This is the context for the following excerpt:

Tian Haihua: 'Confucian Catholics' appropriation of the Decalogue'

(2008)

When Confucian Catholics considered the first and fourth commandments they created a new word *da fumu* (... the Great Parent or Great Father and Mother), a word embedded in the Chinese cultural milieu and one which came to play an important role in the inculturation process of Christianity in China. They held Tianzhu to be the creator of all things. Tianzhu is precisely the same as the ancient Chinese expression, Shangdi or Tian, in the Confucian classics *The Book of Documents* (*Shangshu*) and the *Book of Odes* (*Shijing*), where it states 'heaven gives birth to human beings' (*tian sheng ren*). This was to be the source of later controversy among Protestant translators, concerning the question of whether or not the ancient Chinese had a sense of one, supreme, omnipotent deity.

In addition to the forces of inculturation which focus on the local culture, there is also a corresponding acculturation, where Christianity has exerted influence on, and to some extent transformed, Chinese culture. In the late Ming and early Qing period, the most obvious acculturation of the Decalogue into Chinese traditional morality is seen in the sixth commandment, 'You shall not commit adultery' ... we can see the conflict between the Decalogue and traditional morality in China, and the acculturation of the Decalogue into the Chinese social and moral order ... The moral notions of Christianity affected and changed their ways of life, and this was manifest in their attitudes to concubinage. In the sphere of moral practice, Christian culture did influence marriage practice in feudal China.[26]

Led by the impressive but controversial Matteo Ricci (1552–1610), the Chinese were introduced to Christianity with historical, apologetic, and catechetical literature. This included the Decalogue, which, in Catholic thought, is an expression of natural law and, therefore, as valid in China as anywhere else; thereby aspects of Confucian morality either complemented or could be accommodated with it. Christian converts understood 'the Lord your God' of the Decalogue in ways that echoed Confucian patriarchy. Hence, the biblical God was referred to with divine names used in the Confucian classics: *Tianzhu*, 'lord of heaven', or *Shangdi*, 'lord, emperor'. Ricci held that those texts had a notion of one God, and that ancestor veneration was not a religious rite, but a legitimate social practice. But Franciscan and Dominican missionaries disagreed, arguing that polytheistic Chinese religious practice was prohibited by the first commandment. A papal ruling in 1704 forbade ancestor veneration, and restricted the divine name to *Tianzhu* to avoid the associations with imperial and popular religion. Another point of conflict was that the sixth commandment on adultery ruled out Confucian concubinage: non-marital relationships had to be terminated, and monogamy insisted on, before the baptism of new converts could proceed.

Protestant missionaries of the nineteenth century, active from the late Qing Dynasty of semi-colonial rule, also had apologetic strategies. For instance, in view of Chinese accounts of the great flood, they traced the Han Dynasty (after which China's majority ethnic group still names itself) to Noah's tribal descendants who emigrated to China, just as they did the European people groups from Japheth – an ethnological explanation widespread in pre-modern Christianity. They were also keen Bible translators: the first complete Chinese Bible was completed by 1823. But their missionaries also disagreed over the translation of theological words, a debate known as the 'Term Question'. Some avoided the negative associations with traditional Chinese religion, and opted for the generic *shen*, 'spirit, god, awareness, consciousness' (e.g. R. Morrison, W. Boone). Others, such as the Scottish Congregationalist and Oxford University's first Professor of Chinese, James Legge (1815–97), whose reputation was built on his English translations of Chinese classics, argued for the traditional *Shangdi* of imperial and popular religion. Nevertheless, the variety of translations in circulation increased Chinese access to the Bible and Christian engagement with its local cultures.

The contemporary Christian scene in China is mixed: the persecution of religious groups under Communist Rule since 1949, invitations to dialogue from the Vatican and the World Council of Churches, and burgeoning growth in Evangelical churches. More recently, Archie Lee, based in Hong Kong, has articulated a 'cross-textual reading', in which indigenous Asian Christians are encouraged to take account of 'Text A' (Asian culture and religion) and 'Text B' (the Bible) so as to compare them without the weighty and complex legacy of Western colonial Christian activity (i.e. denominations).[27] Whether or not this proves successful, it is in some respects a continuation of previous Christian activity, and many of the issues are likely to be replayed. To what extent do biblical and Christian ideas complement or conflict with traditional or contemporary Asian thought and practice? What do human beings share naturally and universally, and what special light do Christian ministry and mission bring? These have been perennial questions since the spread of early Christianity, not only in more 'distant' cultures, but also in societies where Christians have frequently played a strong role. Due to the forces of secularization, they now find themselves making the case, once again, for Christianity without either the luxury or the burden of overfamiliarity with its claims.[28]

Part 3: Application

Pentateuch in ministry

Christians believe that the Church receives its ministry from the God described in the Pentateuch: the creator of the world, and the redeemer of Israel and the nations. This has often been articulated in terms of the major covenants of the Pentateuch. From an international perspective, God promised, in a covenant with Noah, to maintain the natural world and, in establishing a covenant with Abraham, promised that his descendants would be the means of blessing to all nations (Gen. 8.21–22; 12.1–3). These unconditional covenants remind us, in a world subject to change and instability, of God's commitment to all nations for their good. From a national perspective, at Mt Sinai God promised to the people of Israel *shalom*, 'peace', within their borders, provided that they played their role in a conditional covenant – in responsibilities summarized in the Decalogue (Ex. 20; Deut. 5). When they broke faith and worshipped other gods, they were restored through the mercy of God (Ex. 34.6–7; Num. 14.13–25). That national covenant also contains promises that the early Christians read as anticipating the ministry of Jesus Christ: he is the prophet, like Moses, that God would later 'raise up' (Deut. 18.15–22; 34.10–12; e.g. Acts 3.22; 7.37). Thus, through these major covenantal developments the Pentateuch sets up a framework: Israel is formed as a nation to be a beacon in the world as the people of God, a story that continues in the Church of God drawn from all nations. It is within this framework that both the narratives and laws of the Pentateuch exercised their influence in Christianity.

The narratives of the Pentateuch function as a means of revelation for Christian self-understanding. In the Pentateuch's primal, ancestral, and national episodes, Christians find the origin of their identity traced, and their faith is guided and nurtured by it. The primal episodes of Genesis prompt reflection on the human condition: the dignity of humankind created in the 'image of God' alongside the realism that mortal life comes 'from the dust'; lessons in wisdom when faced with trials and temptations and the need to learn from mistakes; and the ambiguity of the opportunities allocated to humans, in which work and family relationships produce occasions for gratitude or pride, joy or sorrow – as the story of Adam and Eve and their early descendants famously shows. Since New Testament times, the interpretation of these opening biblical chapters has been concerned with the transformation of this mixed human condition, with Christ as the agent of redemption and renewal. This is signalled by their retelling in New Testament books, whose opening chapters (e.g. John 1; Eph. 1; Col. 1) echo the primal episodes of Genesis. Later Christian thinkers, such as Origen, followed this trend.

The ancestral narratives are often read for their examples of faith – as Luther stated; not only because the divine promises to Abraham reassure, but precisely because the portrayal of dysfunctional families shows God creatively at work in relationships: Jacob wresting with an angel before facing his estranged brother Esau with whom he was then reconciled; and Joseph, all but dead to his family, providentially delivered from prison to exercise stewardship of the resources of Egypt for its benefit and that of his family in Canaan. Furthermore, Christians have often read the ancestral narratives as types and allegories of the sacrificial ministry of Jesus Christ – as Origen's interpretation of Genesis 22 illustrates. Similarly, the wilderness wanderings that follow the redemption out of slavery in Egypt, which were initially narratives of both success and failure, are seen in a new light: Jesus overcame his trials and temptations in the wilderness, and is now looked to as the dependable custodian of this new house of faith: the Church (Matt. 4.1–10; Heb. 3.1–6).

What about the laws of the Pentateuch? In revealing God's will for ancient Israel, they provide guidance for Christian action, but not in a simplistic way. The first Christians were Jewish so, as the Church emerged, its practices were informed by the Law; this is evident in Paul's letters. But since the early Church drew from Gentile nations to whom the Law had not been given, the Law gained a modified status and role. While it had been divine instruction for ancient Israel, it was now seen as a preparatory and interim means of revelation. In this respect, early Christian views of the Law differed quite sharply from those in Rabbinic Judaism, but this did not mean that they rejected the Law. Rather, its interpretation was guided by Jesus Christ: the model interpreter, perfect law-keeper, and fulfiller of its deeper purpose. This may be articulated as follows: to form and instruct a new community for the worship of God and to live according to the divine will – a dual focus the Decalogue enshrines. An interpretative sifting nevertheless took place, to determine how they remain binding on Christians, given their divine principles (e.g. holiness, justice). The traditional threefold division of the Law (moral, ceremonial, civil), as Aquinas and others have presented it, is an important touchstone and example of this interpretative approach, even if the laws originated in a society very different from that which modern readers encounter, as highlighted by Barton.

Accordingly, the moral law addresses matters common to humanity (e.g.

family honour, sexual fidelity, neighbourly respect). The civil laws, while informative about Israelite society (e.g. governance, crime, property), cease to be binding in Christ's new kingdom – although the call to good citizenship remains (cf. Rom. 13; 1 Tim. 1.8–11). The ceremonial laws, which are informative about sacred worship (e.g. priesthood, sacrifice), were fulfilled in Christ's life, death, and resurrection – although this does not imply their irrelevance (see below). Taken together, this all suggests that the Church, which represents the Kingdom of God on earth, should seek to live out and demonstrate what the Law pointed to: the love of God and neighbour. Such ideals are always tempered by realism: while God promises to write the divine laws on human hearts, and to renew their lives by the power of the Holy Spirit, they continue to need discipline and instruction – as Aquinas' and Calvin's outlooks both expressed. Christian communities, aided by both teaching and encouragement, should therefore strive to be a united body whose words and actions echo the ancient call of Deuteronomy: 'one Lord, one faith, one baptism' (Eph. 4.5; cf. Deut. 6.4–6).

The Pentateuch also plays a foundational role in the worship of the Church. Inheriting its lectionary cycles from the ancient Synagogue, the early Church included its more recently written New Testament texts in the on-going recounting of the story of the people of God. At its inception, the worshipping Church traced itself to the *ecclesia*, 'congregation', of the wilderness (Acts 7.38; cf. Heb. 11), but applied this to a people now spread around the diverse lands of the Mediterranean basin and beyond – the perfect picture of a pilgrim Church journeying through the world. The wilderness traditions were still referred to in Paul's letters as examples of the dangers of apostasy in pagan environments – just as Christians face the forces of secularization and rival worldviews in many societies today. The ceremonial laws of the Pentateuch, though they gave instructions about worship in ancient Israel, still present a potent challenge to the Church. Approaching God and imitating Christ with a holy attitude and disposition remains a precondition for divine presence and blessing – founded on a life of prayerful contemplation and active self-sacrificial service (Mark 10.45; Rom. 12.1; 1 Cor. 3.16). Such impulses have been expressed in many and diverse contexts in the history of Christianity, whether in the mystical aspirations of medieval monks and nuns (e.g. Richard of St Victor) or the 'God-walk' activism of Liberation Theology (e.g. Gutiérrez).

The sacramental rites of Christian baptism and the eucharistic meal conventionally signify initiation into, and participation within, the life of God; these, too, have their prefigurations in the Pentateuch – and their reconfigurations in the pages of the New Testament, and in later Christian writings. Indeed, more broadly, all the sacred rites and calendars of the Pentateuch (e.g. Ex. 12—13; Lev. 16; 23; Num. 28—29; Deut. 16) have been given fresh significance in the Church's practices and patterns, in its weekly, monthly, and annual dimensions. For example, the weekly Sabbath of Judaism became, in Christianity, the weekly 'Day of the Lord', when the resurrection of Jesus Christ is commemorated and celebrated. Another area of application to ministry is that of Church leadership. Different models of leadership have been traced to the Pentateuch: Catholic and Orthodox practice tends to follow the Pentateuchal portraits of a corporate and a specially consecrated priesthood, whereas Protestant practice typically aspires to the more corporate model of a 'holy nation' led by pastors. Either way, the governance of the Church requires responsible leadership to avoid confusion, and mutual collaboration to avoid power struggles for the health of all its members.

Pentateuch in mission

Christians also believe that the Church's mission begins with the action of God as described in the Pentateuch. While the grandeur of Genesis's opening has inspired many an artist (e.g. Joseph Haydn's oratorio Creation; William Blake's frontispiece The Ancient of Days), it is surely noteworthy that the accounts of creation are primarily preludes to human history. With no detail about the activity of God before creation, the interaction between God and humanity soon comes to the fore: in dialogue with the first couple in the Garden of Eden, in preferring the offerings of Abel rather than those of Cain (who is still granted divine protection), and in God's remembrance of righteous Noah during the Flood. This continued with Abraham, a Gentile called to be the ancestor of Israel, through whom God would bless all nations. While the promises to Abraham were fulfilled through Jacob and Isaac, God remained concerned for outsiders. Hagar, the mother of Ishmael (and ancestor of the Arabs in Jewish and Islamic tradition), was cast out into the wilderness by the matriarch Sarai, but Hagar was cared for by the angel of the LORD. Interestingly, her individual story anticipates the later wilderness wanderings of Israel. This is no mere myth, fable, or legend: there are sufficient grounds for confidence that the Exodus narratives contain genuine historical memory – as Hoffmeier argues – even if the analysis of its literary sources, as Wellhausen influentially argued, requires critical insight and judicious interpretation, given their varied genres and dates of composition.

The divine compassion shown to Hagar, and to others, is also reflected in the laws of the Pentateuch. The Decalogue required that everyone in Israel, including the outsider, was to be given weekly rest – because it is the pattern that was established by God at creation, and because the Hebrews, the ancestors of Israel, had known slavery and oppression in a foreign land. Other laws echo this compassion: strangers were invited to participate in Passover; they should be protected from abuse just like the widows and orphans of Israel; and, like the Israelite poor, they could take any remaining crops after harvest. Indeed, the Israelite was called to 'love the stranger', even to treat the alien as if he or she were a fellow Israelite, since there was meant to be one law for all (Lev. 19.18, 34; Num. 15.14–16; Deut. 1.16). Even though certain non-Israelites were excluded from aspects of Israelite life (e.g. Deut. 23.3–8), this compassionate concern exemplifies the dignity of humankind made in the image of God, and it prefigures the communal emphasis of early Christianity, in a Church of both Jews and Greeks drawn from all nations (e.g. Acts 2.42–47; Rom. 12.9–13).

The mission of the Church also includes the call to proclaim the action of God as described in the Pentateuch's narratives. In reviewing the wilderness wanderings, Moses reminded the people that they had been recipients of unique revelation: God spoke audibly to them out of the fire at Mt Sinai (just as Moses had experienced at the burning bush); and the people had enjoyed redemption from foreign slavery with mighty wonders so that they might acknowledge that there is no other god like this (Deut. 4.32–35). This grand narrative of struggle and liberation was portrayed memorably in Cecil B. DeMille's biblical epic *The Ten Commandments* (1956). But these blessings, proceeding from God's love and loyalty to the ancestral promises, were not due to Israel's greatness or goodness: quite the opposite (Deut. 7.6; 9.4–6). The uniqueness of Israel's experience, and their dependence on God, was meant to form them into a nation of priests to the world, a mission to which the early Church was later called (Ex. 19.6; 1 Pet. 2.9–20; Rev. 1.5–6). Christianity has since spread around the world. From its inception until today, the Church is a global missional community that proclaims a unique message of divine redemption.

The Church's mission and influence have been assisted by points of contact in recipient cultures, whether expressed through Greek philosophy during the Roman Empire (e.g. Origen) or through the social ethics of Confucianism in feudal China (see Haihua). This is usually understood as a consequence of the collective, natural wisdom that all human beings enjoy as a result of being made in the image of God. These are ideas that also influenced the later political idealism of modernity: 'all men are created equal… endowed by their Creator with certain unalienable rights' (the United States' *Declaration of Independence*, 1776).[29] This missional influence has often been an effective force for the good of society, whether in holding political authority to account – the authors of the Magna Carta (1215) drew on Israelite notions of royal responsibility under law (e.g. Deut. 17.14–20; cf. 1 Sam. 10.24–25) – or in challenging various forms of oppression, as seen above (e.g. Gutiérrez, Assohoto and Ngewa). The Pentateuch continues to inform this mission: Jubilee 2000, a worldwide movement in over 40 countries that called on rich governments to relieve the debt of poorer nations, drew on the Levitical laws about the Year of Jubilee (Lev. 25.1–55), which stipulated that people sold into slavery, or land lost through poverty, were to be redeemed. It is this kind of compassionate concern for justice that makes the Law a delight (cf. Ps. 19; 119).

What drives this missional activity? It is compassion, inspired by the character of God. It is also to do with the uniqueness of the message. The Church has a distinctive contribution to make to world history and culture, as the various examples mentioned above illustrate. Indeed, it is, at root, a vision for renewal and hope that makes both Christian ministry and mission a privilege for its participants and a benefit to humankind – even if Christians have often made many mistakes and caused much hurt, for which they should repent, seek forgiveness, and make amends. They, as much as any-one else, depend completely and entirely on a transformed view of human history, traced to the foundational ideas of the Pentateuch. Just as the image of God in humankind is defaced, so the redemptive work of God in Jesus Christ restores humankind to its godlikeness. In the earliest Christian texts, the image of God – that which sets humankind apart in the natural world – is always spoken of in terms of this promise of transformation (Rom. 8.29; 1 Cor. 15.45; Col. 3.10).

This message of renewal and hope, returning to what was signalled at the start of this third and final part, is set within a cosmic framework in the Christian worldview. That is to say, a new heavens and a new earth is anticipated. God and humankind will once more enjoy fellowship, as in Eden, with God as their eternal 'light' (Rev. 22.1–5). Christian faith and spirituality holds to the promise of a vision of God that, unlike Moses' vision, will not fade. Christians are granted a vision of a heavenly Jerusalem, and proclaim a kingdom that, unlike Mt Sinai, cannot be shaken (2 Cor. 3.1–18; Heb. 12.18–29). This should utterly transform life and behaviour in the present, both during life itself, and then when facing the end of mortal life. Meanwhile, the love of God and neighbour, which summarizes the Law, is meant to characterize this new community (Matt. 22.34–40; Rom. 13.8–10; James 2.8–13). This, then, is the ideal, which draws on Pentateuchal foundations: a 'holy nation', the Church, drawn from all nations, thankful for and responsive to the redemptive, purifying, and transformative work of God through Jesus Christ in the Holy Spirit. Just as the early Christians were routinely addressed as 'holy ones, saints' (e.g. Rom. 1.7; Phil. 1.1; Col. 3.12), they continue to be called and invited to imitate the love and mercy shown to them by God. In so doing, they seek to attract others to this wonderful vision of restoration for humankind.

Notes

1 Heine, R. E. (tr.), 1982, *Origen: Homilies on Genesis and Exodus*, 8.9, FOTC, 71, Washington, DC: Catholic University of America Press, p. 145.

2 See Hayward, C. T. R., 1990, 'The Sacrifice of Isaac and Jewish Polemic against Christianity', *CBQ*, 52, pp. 292–306; and Kalimi, I., 2010, '"Go, I beg you, take your beloved son and slay him!": The Binding of Isaac in Rabbinic Literature and Thought', *The Review of Rabbinic Judaism*, 13/1, pp. 1–29.

3 See Wilkinson, J., 1981, *Egeria's Travels to the Holy Land*, Jerusalem: Ariel/Warminster: Aris & Phillips, p. 267.

4 This, and near-contemporary Jewish mosaics, are discussed in Kessler, E., 2002, 'The Sacrifice of Isaac (the akedah) in Christian and Jewish Tradition: Artistic Representations', in O'Kane, M. (ed.), *Borders, Boundaries and the Bible*, Sheffield: Sheffield Academic Press, pp. 74–98.

5 Origen, *Homilies on Genesis*, 8.1. Heine, *Origen*, p. 136.

6 See further, Bouteneff, P. C., 2008, *Beginnings: Ancient Christian Readings of the Biblical Creation Narratives*, Grand Rapids, MI: Baker.

7 Zinn, G. A. (tr.), 1979, *Richard of St. Victor: The Twelve Patriarchs, The Mystical Ark, Book Three of the Trinity*, New York: Paulist Press, pp. 364–7.

8 For further discussion of this, see Lubac, H. de, 1998, *Medieval Exegesis: The Four Senses of Scripture*, vol. 1, Grand Rapids, MI: Eerdmans (original 1959).

9 1a2ae, 99, 4, ad 1–3. Bourke, D. (ed., tr.), 1969, *St Thomas Aquinas Summa Theologica: Latin Text and English Translation, Introductions, Notes, Appendices and Glossaries*, London: Eyre and Spottiswoode, vol. 29, p. 45.

10 See further, Davies, B., 1992, *The Thought of Thomas Aquinas*, Oxford: Oxford University Press, pp. 244–61.

11 See Caemmerer, R. R. (tr.), 1960, 'Lectures on Deuteronomy', in Pelikan, J. (ed.), *Luther's Works*, St Louis, MO: Concordia Publishing, vol. 9, pp. 219–20, 224.

12 Theodore Bachmann, E. (tr.), 1960, 'How Christians Should Regard Moses', in Theodore Bachmann, E. (ed.), Lehmann, H. T. (gen. ed.), *Luther's Works*, Philadelphia, PA: Muhlenberg Press, vol. 35, pp. 165, 168–9, 173–4.

13 2.7.12. McNeill, J. (ed.), Lewis Battles, F. (tr.), 1969, *Calvin: Institutes of the Christian Religion 1*, LCC 20, Philadelphia, PA: Westminster Press, vol. 1, pp. 360–1.

14 See Calvin, J. *Commentaries on the Last Four Books of Moses, Arranged in the Form of a Harmony*, Bingham, C. W. (tr.), 1853, Edinburgh: The Calvin Translation Society, vol. 2, pp. 110–11.

15 Wellhausen, J., 1878, *Geschichte Israels: In zwei Bänden. Erster Band*, Berlin: G. Reimer; 1883, *Prolegomena zur Geschichte Israels*, 2nd edn, Berlin: G. Reimer, in Sutherland Black, J. and Menzies, A. (tr.), 1885, *Prolegomena to the History of Israel*, Edinburgh: A&C Black, p. 3.

16 For translations of these texts, see *COS*, vol. 2 (2.6; 2.27; 2.83), pp. 40–1, 140–5, 221.

17 See further, Barton, J., 1995, 'Wellhausen's *Prolegomena to the History of Israel*: Influences and Effects', in Smith-Christopher, D. L. (ed.), *Text and Experience: Towards a Cultural Exegesis of the Bible*, BS, 35, Sheffield: Sheffield Academic Press, pp. 316–29.

18 See further, Davies, G. I., 2001, 'Introduction to the Pentateuch', in Barton, J. and Muddiman, J. (eds), *The Oxford Bible Commentary*, Oxford: Oxford University Press, pp. 12–38.

19 Hoffmeier, J. K., 2005, *Ancient Israel in Sinai: The Evidence for the Authenticity of the Wilderness Tradition*, Oxford: Oxford University Press, p. 117.

20 Barton, J., 2002, *Ethics and the Old Testament*, 2nd edn, London: SCM Press, p. 1.

21 Barton, *Ethics*, p. 2.

22 For another constructive Christian approach, see Wright, C. J. H., 2010, 'Preaching from the Law', in Kent, J. G. R., Kissling, P. J. and Turner, L. A. (eds), *He Began with Moses: Preaching the Old Testament Today*, Leicester: Inter-Varsity Press, pp. 47–63.

23 Gutiérrez, G. A., 1974, *Theology of Liberation: History, Politics and Salvation*, London: SCM Press, pp. 155, 157, 159 (original 1971).

24 For an analysis of Liberation Theology by Cardinal Joseph Ratzinger (later Pope Benedict XVI), in his capacity as Prefect of the Congregation for the Doctrine of the Faith ('Instruction on Certain Aspects of the "Theology of Liberation"', August 1984), see the Vatican website (www.vatican.va).

25 Assohoto, B. and Ngewa, S., 2006, 'Genesis', in Adeyamo, T. (ed.), *Africa Bible Commentary*, Grand Rapids, MI: Zondervan, pp. 25–6.

26 Haihua, T., 2008, 'Confucian Catholics' Appropriation of the Decalogue: A Case Study in Cross-textual Reading', in Starr, C. (ed.), *Reading the Christian Scriptures in China*, London and New York: T&T Clark, pp. 169, 172, 175.

27 For a recent essay on this approach, see Lee, A. C. C., 2014, 'Scriptural Translations and Cross-Textual Hermeneutics', in Wilfred, F. (ed.), *The Oxford Handbook of Christianity in Asia*, New York: Oxford University Press, pp. 121–33.

28 For an introduction to Christianity in China, see Berthrong, J., 2005, 'Chinese Religions and Christianity', in Bowker, J. (ed.), *Christianity: The Complete Guide*, London: Continuum, pp. 205–9.

29 *The Universal Declaration of Human Rights* (1948), formulated after the Second World War, does not refer to God or allude to the 'image of God'. Rather, it refers to 'religion', in articles 2 ('Everyone is entitled to all the rights and freedoms set forth in this Declaration, without distinction of any kind, such as race, colour, sex, language, religion, political or other opinion, national or social origin, property, birth or other status'), 16 ('Men and women of full age, without any limitation due to race, nationality or religion, have the right to marry and to found a family'), and 18 ('Everyone has the right to freedom of thought, conscience and religion; this right includes freedom to change his religion or belief, and freedom, either alone or in community with others and in public or private, to manifest his religion or belief in teaching, practice, worship and observance'). For the full text, see the UN website (www.un.org).

3

Historical Books

DOUGLAS EARL

Part 1: Introduction

The 'Historical Books' is the collective name that has been given to the books of the Old Testament outside the Pentateuch and the Prophets that depict Israel's history from the entrance to the Promised Land until the return from the Babylonian Exile. There are some differences between the Christian traditions as to which books might be included and thought of as 'Historical Books', and whether they are 'authoritative' or 'canonical' Scripture or simply 'profitable for reading'. Common to all Christian traditions are Joshua, Judges, Ruth, 1 and 2 Samuel, 1 and 2 Kings, 1 and 2 Chronicles, Esther, Ezra, and Nehemiah. Other books, which are also recognized in some Christian traditions as comprising the 'Historical Books of the Old Testament', extend into a later period. The Orthodox tradition recognizes 1 and 2 Maccabees as canonical, for example, books that the Roman Catholic Church recognizes as 'deutero-canonical', and the Anglican Church as 'profitable for reading'. Post-Reformation Evangelical traditions generally disregard these books altogether. The decisions to omit certain books in the Western traditions might be traced to Jerome and Luther.

Thus within the worldwide Church there are important differences regarding which books are taken as canonical within this collection. However, such debates are not new, for the canonical status of 1 and 2 Chronicles was debated in the early Church, with rather little interpretation of these books having occurred in that period. Differences also exist in the naming of the books. Owing to the division and naming in early Greek versions, 1 and 2 Samuel and 1 and 2 Kings are together referred to as 1—4 Kings in the Orthodox Church. Ezra and Nehemiah were regarded as a single book until the Middle Ages and, as with Chronicles, Christian interpretation of these books was rather sparse until the modern period.

Importantly, the decision to categorize these books as the 'Historical Books' is not as automatic as it might seem to us today, as can be seen by comparison with the arrangement of books in the Jewish Hebrew Bible. Rather than adopting the divisions that many Christians today take for granted of Law, History, Wisdom, and Prophets, the Hebrew Bible is divided into Law, Prophets, and Writings. The books that many Christians call 'historical' are divided between the Prophets and the Writings in the Hebrew Bible. For example, Joshua is placed in the same category as Isaiah, and Ruth in the same category as the Psalms. This suggests that there is an ancient tradition that understands the significance of these books as something other than 'history'. Indeed, as we shall see when we look at Origen's homilies on Joshua, for example, early Christian interpreters often did not read books such as Joshua as 'history' at all in the sense that we understand the term, with historical difficulties that trouble modern interpreters simply being seen as cues that point towards a 'spiritual' reading of the text.

However these books are classified and analysed, the Historical Books, as they are now collected and arranged, provide a powerful and coherent *story* of Israel. It is this story as it developed and emerged that constructed the identity, worldview and hopes of God's people Israel via a story of entrance to the Promised Land, through the establishment of the monarchy to the Exile, and finally the return from exile. This story was taken to be foundational for the Incarnation, and thus for the construction of the identity of the Christian Church when read through the lens of the Incarnation. Whether or not we have here 'history' writing in the modern sense, we have a powerful story that we may enter, inhabit, and meditate upon. It is a story that shapes our identity and worldview, both corporately and individually. It is a story that gives us glimpses of God's nature and his purposes for the whole of creation. In the process of reflecting on this story we are encouraged to praise and worship God. We come to know God better and how to respond to him more fully by seeing how he is portrayed as working with people, and how people have responded to him, faithfully or otherwise, in the ages past.

Historical Books in overview

Joshua	Narrates Israel entering and possessing the Promised Land under Joshua, focusing on various exceptional individuals or groups.
Judges	Evocative portraits of Israel's deterioration as people turn away from God. Successive leaders are appointed, but ultimately a king is shown to be required to bring order and proper worship.
Ruth	The story of an exceptional 'outsider' from the despised Moabites who becomes a part of Israel and ancestor of King David.
1 and 2 Samuel, 1 and 2 Kings, 1 and 2 Chronicles	Provide an account of the establishment of the monarchy and its subsequent history until the Exile. Kings are judged according to their faithfulness to God. Chronicles retells Samuel–Kings with different emphases.

Ezra, Nehemiah	Reports the return from the Exile and the rebuilding of Jerusalem.
Esther	The story of an exceptional Israelite who bravely saves the Israelites in exile.

Historical Books in summary

Joshua

The book of Joshua takes for its setting the conquest of the Promised Land, apparently representing the fulfilment of Deuteronomy 7. Troubling for modern readers is the central notion of 'utter destruction' (Hebrew *herem*) as a description of what is carried out in the conquest. It was introduced as a command in Deuteronomy 7.1–5 and is reported as being conducted in Joshua 6—11. It is a concept that is difficult to translate well from ancient Hebrew, but conjures up images of Holy War and total annihilation. However, closer reading of the book indicates that Joshua is not simply an account of conquest, nor is it simply the fulfilment of Deuteronomy 7.1–5. Much of the story is devoted to unusual people who do not fit well with an ideology of conquest and even some of the theology expressed in Deuteronomy. For example, Rahab, the Canaanite prostitute introduced in Joshua 2, is doomed to destruction according to Deuteronomy 7. But owing to her faith and faithfulness, she is spared in Joshua 6. However, Achan, the idealized Israelite, acts unfaithfully in Joshua 7 and is destroyed as a result. The Gibeonites trick Israel into a treaty (Josh. 10) and are spared as a result. None of these stories fit well with an ideology of conquest, or the somewhat exclusive picture of the nation of Israel that we find in Deuteronomy. In Joshua, the distinctions between 'Israelite' and 'non-Israelite' are blurred. Although the story is set in a context of conquest, the theology of Joshua is that of redefining or refining the nature of Israelite identity as the people of God. Identity – and the nature of the relationship with God – is shown in Joshua to be based on faith and faithfulness to God rather than ancestral or political origins. This is well expressed in Joshua 5.13–15 where it seems that God will not take political sides. However, when read in the context of the whole Old Testament, the book also functions as a significant part of God's 'salvation history', painting a picture of God's providential care and discipline for the people he chooses and loves. Perhaps this is a role that the book did not originally have, as indicated for example by the observation that the prologue to Judges was probably a late addition to the book to harmonize Joshua and Judges into a historical scheme. Read as a literary text, or in terms of the traditional Christian or Jewish understanding that scriptural texts have multiple senses or meanings, we need not think that we must choose one way of reading the story over the other. We can read it in both ways and learn from each reading.

Judges

The book of Judges is another often troubling book for contemporary Christians given the many descriptions of brutal violence and warfare at the hands of God's people. But perhaps part of the message of the book is that violence does not work – Israel will not succeed if she remains as a squabbling group of divided tribes who tend to fall into idolatry. The repeated refrain 'Israel had no king in those days' (e.g. Judg. 17.6; 18.1; 19.1) points to this, with an obvious implied solution – Israel needs a king. The main body of Judges focuses on a repeated cycle of events – Israel hits a crisis, God raises up a saviour, Israel is saved, Israel slides back into sin, and a new crisis develops. Judges indicates that Israel needs a king to break this cycle, keeping Israel safe and faithful to God. Within this scheme there are a number of well-known stories – the stories of Gideon and Samson, for example. Read in its canonical context, Judges develops the problems raised by living among the Canaanites and worshipping their gods. In terms of the story of 'salvation history' it looks back to the failure to fully possess the land and eradicate idolatry, and forward to the establishment of the monarchy in which order and the proper worship of God will be encouraged and restored.

Ruth

The book of Ruth is a delightful story about Ruth, a foreigner to Israel, who, through loyalty to various family bonds in the midst of times of adversity, romances and marries Boaz. One of their descendants is King David. There are several important themes in the book. First, Ruth is a foreigner to Israel, and not just any foreigner but a Moabite. The Israelites and Moabites were staunch enemies, and Israel generally had nothing to do with Moabites owing to their sinfulness and idolatry as a people (Deut. 23.3–4). Second, Ruth exemplifies 'steadfast love, faithfulness' (Hebrew *hesed*) towards what remains of her (Israelite, by marriage) family after death and famine, and so in this sense she acts and behaves just like the ideal Israelite. She is very similar to Rahab (in Joshua), being a foreigner from a sinful enemy nation who demonstrates *hesed* in the most demanding circumstances. With her exclamation 'your people shall be my people, and your God my God' (Ruth 1.16), she shows that it is possible to become an Israelite, and the sort of character traits that it requires (faith and faithfulness). Finally, the closing section of the book traces her descendants to King David. As with Joshua and Judges, Ruth can be read at various levels. It can be read as part of the 'big picture' of Israel's national story, filling in some of the gaps between the time of Judges and Samuel. Or, like Joshua, it can also be seen as challenging narrow, nationalistic, or political definitions of the people of Israel, defining God's people in terms of faith, character, and faithfulness to God.

Samuel and Kings

The books of Samuel and Kings deal with the story of Israel in terms of the rise of the Davidic dynasty and God's promise to David, the division of the kingdom, and the subsequent judgement of the Exile as kings frequently turn away from God. The books relate to the politics of Israel's leadership, and its assessment by God, especially in terms of the theology of Deuteronomy. For this reason, Samuel–Kings (along with Joshua and Judges) has been termed the 'Deuteronomistic History' by modern scholars. Samuel–Kings reports the beginnings of the institution of kingship in the figure of Saul, whose 'house' or dynasty is soon replaced by that of David.

The books of Samuel and Kings understand and recount events that could be interpreted in political terms and in theological terms. A prophetic witness is often involved, notably Samuel, Elijah and Elisha. The result is, for example, stories about the ark (1 Sam. 4—6; 2 Sam. 6), the battle of David with Goliath (1 Sam. 17), God's covenant with David (2 Sam. 7), building the temple (1 Kings 5—8), Elijah's confrontation with Ahab and the priests of Baal (1 Kings 18—19), and Hezekiah's confrontation with Sennacherib (2 Kings 18—20). The account is generally told through reports on the reigns of the kings interwoven with theologically significant events. Their reigns are assessed according to their faithfulness to the Deuteronomic covenant. Subsequent kings turn away from God to idolatry, leading to exile, first in the north, and then in the south. Notable kings reversed the trend. Josiah (2 Kings 22.1—23.30) in particular led the people back into faithfulness to God through the renewal of the covenant and the eradication of idolatry.

Chronicles

The books of Chronicles appear very similar to Samuel–Kings on first reading – they appear to be an edited and shortened version. This is largely the case, and most scholars regard Chronicles as an edited version of Samuel–Kings. In modern scholarship they have been called the 'Chronicler's History'. What is important is the way in which they have been edited, and why. Whereas Samuel–Kings dealt with the northern kingdom of Israel and the southern kingdom (Judah), Chronicles focuses solely on Judah. Chronicles also portrays some of the kings in a different light. Notably, David is portrayed in a wholly positive light. Omitted are some of the more dubious episodes from his life, such as his adulterous relationship with Bathsheba (2 Sam. 11—12). Another important difference in portrayal is that of King Manasseh. He is one of the most wicked kings according to the book of Kings (2 Kings 21.1—18), but Chronicles supplies an account of his repentance (2 Chron. 33.1—20). Finally, in the census that David conducted that displeased God, Samuel–Kings reports that it is God who incited David to conduct it (2 Sam. 24.1), whereas in Chronicles it is Satan (1 Chron. 21.1).

These differences give us some insight into the distinctive concerns of Chronicles. Chronicles is only interested in the southern kingdom, and portrays David as the ideal king. Indeed, it generally portrays the kings more positively. It provides hope for the future by looking at the best of the past. Some theological elements of Samuel–Kings appear troubling to the chronicler. Attributing the problematic census to God in Samuel seems troublesome, and Chronicles offers another interpretation. The long reign of Manasseh – an evil king – needs some explanation within the framework of a reward–retribution theology, and so he is portrayed as, in the end, a penitent sinner (2 Chron. 33). Finally, unlike Kings, Chronicles ends on a note of hope with Cyrus' edict for the return of the Israelites to Jerusalem (2 Chron. 36.22–23). The book of Chronicles thus makes good sense as an edited, upbeat version of Israel's leadership in order to build a hopeful vision of the form of kingship that will be needed to rebuild the nation in Judah.

Ezra and Nehemiah

The books of Ezra and Nehemiah deal with the restoration of Israel at the end of the Exile, and are closely related to Chronicles. The return of groups of Israelites is reported, along with the rebuilding of the temple and Jerusalem through divine favour amid strong opposition. A new Israel is formed, with a strong emphasis on reform and purification so as to avoid a fall into idolatry again. Ezra is commissioned to teach God's Law, and both in Ezra and Nehemiah a strong condemnation of marriages with foreigners is to be found (Ezra 10; Neh. 13). This offers an interesting contrast to the book of Ruth. A major theme is thus that obedience to the Mosaic Law is required for Israel's restoration (Neh. 1.7). In this sense the identity of Israel that Ezra–Nehemiah is written to construct is closer to that found in the book of Deuteronomy (especially Deut. 7.1–5, which may be reflected in Ezra 10) than that found in the books of Joshua or Ruth. It is interesting to see then that the Historical Books do not present a uniform picture of what constitutes the identity of Israel. Central to each book, and thus Israel's identity, is the call to worship Yahweh faithfully through the covenant, and to avoid idols and idolatry. However, differences exist regarding the perception of foreigners, for instance, and whether they may form part of the people of Israel. Recall that in Genesis, Israel was originally formed as the descendants of Abraham.

Esther

Esther tells the story of how a seemingly powerless but courageous, intelligent and resourceful Israelite woman, assisted by her cousin Mordecai, saved the nation of Israel. Set in Persia under the rule of King Xerxes, Esther becomes queen, so gains access to the king and indirect political influence.

Together with Mordecai they outwit Haman, who had plotted to destroy the Israelites. As a result, a royal edict grants peace and rest to the Israelites. The book is bound up with the establishment and celebration of the festival of Purim (9.18–32), being a charming story of God's providential care of his people through unlikely people and circumstances, circumstances that might not seem at all 'supernatural'. The book exists in two forms – a short version, which is the version included in Protestant Bibles, and a significantly longer version often known as 'Greek Esther' since it is the version preserved in the Septuagint. Greek Esther includes a number of lengthy prayers at key moments in the story. Notably in the short version, God is not mentioned, although divine providence is perhaps implied throughout, especially when read in its canonical context. The longer version makes the role of God explicit. The story of Esther has been compared with that of Joseph in Genesis and Daniel in the Prophets. Each story explores in different ways the question of how an Israelite can faithfully live and worship within the corridors of power of a foreign land. Each story develops in different ways the sense in which assimilation to another culture can or cannot take place so as to benefit the life of Israel.

Part 2: Interpretation

Early Christianity

There is little interpretation or development of the stories from the Historical Books in the New Testament. References are generally made in passing and not developed. A number of the judges, and Rahab, are mentioned in a list as exemplars of faith in the book of Hebrews (Heb. 11.29–34), but here it is only the story of Rahab that is developed, and only briefly. In the book of James, Rahab's story is used to illustrate the point that genuine faith is accompanied by actions (James 2.18–26). In various places the idea that Jesus is a king in the line of David is developed (e.g. Matt. 1.1; 9.27; Rom. 1.3). Generally speaking, the use of the Historical Books as Christian literature was developed later, beyond the New Testament.

In the early Church it was commonplace to read the Old Testament in a typological or allegorical way, with characters like Joshua understood as 'types' or figures of Christ. As the name 'Joshua' is the same as 'Jesus' in Greek, which was the language in which the Old Testament was often read in this era, this led to a very natural typological identification of the two people, for names were thought to express something of the essence of who or what was named. The interpretation of the Historical Books in the early Church reflected the common practice of the era of reading ancient literature allegorically. This was coupled with a desire to understand the Old Testament as anticipating Christ, with Christ being the fulfilment (in some sense) of the Old Testament. What was recorded in an 'earthly' or 'literal' sense in the stories of the Old Testament anticipated greater 'spiritual' realities of the New. However, interpreters such as Origen in the Alexandrian tradition were more allegorical in their interpretation than interpreters in the Antiochene tradition, who were more concerned with the 'literal sense' of the stories.[1] But in general, early Christian interpreters wished to see the Old Testament as witnessing to the same God as the God revealed in Jesus Christ, with the Old Testament having on-going value in speaking through the Holy Spirit to guide the Christian life. Thus interpreters tried to discern ways in which the Old Testament witnessed to Jesus, the Church or to the spiritual life. So stories from the Historical Books were read as moral exemplars to teach about the Christian life, and the cultivation of virtue in particular.

Rahab's story (Josh. 2 and 6) was often developed, and Theodoret of Cyrus' (c. AD 393–466) reading in the excerpt below is typical, indicating some of the standard ways of reading the Historical Books in the early Church:

Theodoret: *Questions on Joshua*

(fifth century AD)

Our Joshua [Jesus] dispatched the apostles not only as spies but also as generals. As the spies sent by Joshua, the son of Nun, saved the faithful prostitute by giving her the crimson cord as a token of salvation [Josh 2.1–21], so the apostles of our Savior delivered from her former licentiousness her who had once been a prostitute, the Church devoted to competing idols, and accorded her eternal blessings. It was with no token of a crimson cord, but with the sacred blood, that they accomplished her salvation.

No one should imagine that Rahab was unworthy of being a type of the Church. ...

Furthermore, the pact made by the spies was very much in keeping with the reality: 'Whoever goes out of doors, will be responsible for his own fate, and, as you have agreed, we shall be guiltless' [Josh. 2.19]. Indeed, salvation comes to us through the Church, and those outside it do not enjoy eternal life.

This prefiguration of reality continues throughout the rest of the narrative.[2]

Early interpreters were careful readers of the text and well aware of some of the historical and ethical difficulties in the Historical Books. They took such difficulties as indications that the real meaning of the text is to be found in a spiritual and not literal sense – historical and ethical criticism is in one sense nothing new! The 'rule of faith' guided interpretation. So, for example, because Jesus taught about loving one's neighbour, texts that spoke of violence often were not interpreted in a literal way as this would go against the 'rule of faith', and not be worthy of the Holy Spirit. But all of Scripture was thought to edify the Christian, so the difficult texts were thus read spiritually. Origen of Alexandria (c. AD 185–254) was a master of this form of interpretation, as we see here in his sermon on a morally problematic text in Joshua (10.20–26). Here, he dismisses the approach of a group who were considered heretics by the early Church, criticizing them for wishing to treat the text as a literal historical report. In the following excerpt Origen proposes a different and more fruitful reading for the Christian who wants life guidance from the text:

Origen: *Homilies on Joshua*

(third century AD)

But Marcion and Valentinus and Basilides and the other heretics with them, since they refuse to understand these things [Josh. 10] in a manner worthy of the Holy Spirit, 'deviated from the faith and became devoted to many impieties,' [1 Tim. 6.10] bringing forth another God of the Law, both creator and judge of the world, who teaches a certain cruelty through these things that are written. For example, they are ordered to trample upon the necks of their enemies and to suspend from wood the kings of that land that they violently invade.

And yet, if only my Lord Jesus the Son of God would grant that to me and order me to crush the spirit of fornication with my feet and trample upon the necks of the spirit of wrath and rage, to trample on the demon of avarice, to trample down boasting, to crush the spirit of arrogance with my feet, and, when I have done all these things, not to hang the most exalted of these exploits upon myself but upon his cross. Thereby I imitate Paul, who says, 'the world is crucified to me' [Gal. 6.14] and, that which we have already related above, 'Not I, but the grace of God that is in me' [1 Cor. 15.10].

But if I deserve to act thus, I shall be blessed and what Jesus [Joshua] said to the ancients will also be said to me, 'Go courageously and be strengthened; do not be afraid nor be awed by their appearance, because the Lord God has delivered all your enemies into your hands' [Josh. 10.25]. If we understand these things spiritually and manage wars of this type spiritually and if we drive out all those spiritual iniquities from heaven, then we shall be able at last to receive from Jesus as a share of the inheritance even those places and kingdoms that are the kingdoms of heaven, bestowed by our Lord and Savior Jesus Christ, 'to whom is the glory and the dominion forever and ever'. Amen! [1 Pet. 4.11].[3]

Elsewhere in his *Homilies on Joshua*, Origen reads Joshua through Ephesians 6 (*Hom.* 12.1), since for Origen the book of Joshua is really about the spiritual battle that the Christian faces in Christ. Thus symbolically Joshua teaches something about the nature of the Christian life and the battles with sin that it involves. The book of Joshua prefigures such battles, and Joshua's conquest of the land is understood to prefigure Jesus' spiritual conquest of the world in which Christians participate.

The spiritual approach to reading the Historical Books was an approach taken by many interpreters. It was applied widely and not just to the book of Joshua, where there was the linkage between the names of Joshua and Jesus. One can see a similar approach in a theological work of Ambrose of Milan (*c.* AD 333–97), in the excerpt below, when he refers to an incident from Judges 6.19–21:

Ambrose of Milan: *On the Holy Spirit*

(fourth century AD)

Gideon, moved by that message, when he heard that though thousands of the people failed, God would deliver his own from their enemies by means of one man, offered a kid, and according to the word of the angel, laid its flesh and the unleavened cakes upon the rock and poured the broth upon them. And as soon as the angel touched them with the end of the staff which he bore, fire burst forth out of the rock, and so the sacrifice which he was offering was consumed. By which it seems clear that that rock was a figure of the body of Christ, for it is written: 'They drank of that rock that followed them, and that rock was Christ.' [1 Cor. 10.4] This certainly refers not to his Godhead but to his flesh, which watered the hearts of the thirsting people with the perpetual stream of his blood.

Even at that time was it declared in a mystery that the Lord Jesus in his flesh would, when crucified, do away the sins of the whole world, and not only the deeds of the body but the desires of the soul. For the flesh of the kid refers to sins of deed, the broth to the enticements of desire, as it is written: 'For the people greedily lusted, and said, "Who shall give us flesh to eat?"' [Num. 11.4] That the angel then stretched forth his staff and touched the rock, from which fire went out, shows that the flesh of the Lord, being filled with the divine Spirit, would burn away all the sins of human frailty. Wherefore, also, the Lord says, 'I have come to send fire upon the earth.' [Luke 12.49][4]

Again, we can see how the events narrated in the ancient text are, through New Testament Scripture, brought directly into the life of the Church.

Not all interpreters in this era read the texts in quite this way though. For example, unlike Origen, Augustine (AD 354–430) seemed to understand some parts of the stories in Joshua in a more literal, historical way (e.g. *Questions on Joshua* 16), even if Augustine also read spiritually. Augustine was perhaps more concerned than Origen with what we would call today 'apologetics'. Augustine offered reasoned accounts for the reliability of various parts of the biblical narrative in a way that did not concern Origen (e.g. *City of God* 15.9). Other interpreters such as Chrysostom (*c.* AD 349–407) or Theodoret often offered more literal readings of Old Testament narratives. They were more concerned for the development of the plot and the background to the story at hand. They read the story more 'on its own terms' than was the case for Origen. But, to take the interpretation of Joshua, while both Augustine and Origen were extremely influential figures in the history of the Church, it was Origen's approach to Joshua rather than Augustine's that was generally adopted until the rise of interest in historical matters in the Middle Ages, and subsequently in the modern era.

As with Rahab, Ruth was also seen as a 'type' of the Church (e.g. Isidore of Seville (*c.* AD 560–636), *On Ruth*), and the story was often read in terms of the virtues that were displayed by the various characters: 'The story of Boaz also teaches us about virtue. For he not only liberally shares his grain with Ruth but also consoles her with words. Not only does he share food with her but also was himself the minister of his kindness.'[5] The cultivation of virtue was regarded as crucial for the development of the Christian life in the early and medieval periods especially, with the development of the three 'theological virtues' of faith, hope, and love (cf. 1 Cor. 13.13) being central. In the Protestant and subsequent Evangelical traditions the language of virtue has tended to disappear, as may be seen in John Calvin's (1509–64) writings (*Inst.* 3.14.3), perhaps because of a worry that it represents 'works' rather than 'grace' or 'faith', which is a pity.

In summary, in the ancient Christian traditions stories in the Old Testament were often read either typologically or in terms of the lessons in the cultivation of virtue that may be learnt. Interpretation of the Historical Books in the early Church provided a powerful way of bringing the texts alive for Christians. Some of the books received little attention though. There is very little discussion of the books of Chronicles, for instance, in this era. However, interpretation in this period has been criticized for 'reading in' ideas to the texts that are not of concern to the story, and of focusing on isolated details while neglecting the flow of the wider story. Allegorical reading has been criticized for being wild, fanciful and without control. Can, or should, we still find these interpretations convincing? Conversely, though, can a Christian read the Old Testament without reference to Christ if one supposes that the Bible is formative for the Christian life? The challenge is perhaps to find a robustly Christological way of reading the Old Testament that does not resort to some of the extremes of allegory.

Medieval Christianity

Much of the 'spiritual reading' from the early Church was retained and developed in the medieval era, although often with some important new emphases and developments. Developed in more detail now is interpretation of Scripture in terms of 'four senses': the literal sense; the allegorical sense; the moral sense; and the anagogical sense. The foundation for interpretation was study of the literal sense, which gave rise to interpretation in terms of the other three.[6] However, there were fewer large-scale works of interpretation in this era than in the early Church. The task of Christian commentary and the Christian exposition of the Old Testament were seen as largely completed tasks. In the Western Church, excerpts from the earlier patristic commentaries were collected and compiled in the *Glossa Ordinaria* (plural *Glossae Ordinariae*). The 'glosses' on the biblical text formed notes in the margins of the Vulgate, an early Latin translation of Scripture. An influential version was compiled in the twelfth century, but various versions circulated. As well as being preached upon in sermons, the use of the Historical Books in this era was developed in large-scale theological works such as Thomas Aquinas' *Summa Theologica*.[7] This was often accomplished through discussion of earlier interpretations. The use of the Historical Books was also developed in various devotional or instructional works, such as *Speculum Humanae Salvationis*,[8] and in illustrated 'moralized bibles'. It was common to present an Old Testament 'type' juxtaposed with its Christian or contemporary fulfilment in such works, as we shall see in the excerpts below.[9]

It will be helpful to look again at the interpretation of Judges 6.19–21 in addition to some other aspects from the story of Gideon. In one *Bible Moralisée*, a lavishly illustrated work taking Old Testament stories, illustrating them, and providing contemporary application in thirteenth-century France, we read:

Bible Moralisée

(thirteenth century AD)

Here Gideon comes and takes flesh and makes an offering on an altar of stone, and an angel descends and holds a rod and strikes the flesh and fire appears which burns the flesh. [Judg. 6.19–21] That Gideon made an offering of flesh to God signifies the good man who makes an offering of his flesh to God. The angel struck the flesh with the rod and the flesh burned signifies Jesus Christ who strikes him with the Cross and with penance, and the flesh of the world burns and falls, and he tramples the world and is born again as flesh burned by fire.

...

Here Gideon comes to a beautiful field and in the middle of the field there is

---

a fleece of white wool and Gideon prays to God that he will show him through the fleece a sign of whether to go into the battle or not, and God sends a sweet dew onto the fleece and nothing around it. [Judg. 6.36–38] That Gideon came to the beautiful field and found the fleece, which was moistened by the dew from heaven and nothing around it, signifies that God scattered his grace primarily on the Jews and all other people without anything. That the dew soaked the fleece without moving a hair signifies the grace of God which conceived in the Virgin without corrupting her virginity.

Here Gideon comes and prays to God that the dew falls around it and that the fleece remains dry and God does so. [Judg. 6.39–40] That the dew fell around the fleece and not on it signifies the grace of God fell on the Christians and not on the Jews, and they remained dry like the fleece was dry.[10]

The text is still read allegorically and Christologically – that is, as referring in some way to Christ. Yet the force for the reader, and the response that is encouraged, is rather different from that of readings in the early Church. It reflects the developing theology and concerns of the Middle Ages in the West. The importance of penance for the Christian life, and the need to crucify or mortify the flesh (often literally) develops, as reflected in the excerpt here. We see too, rather sadly, a developed derogatory attitude to the Jewish people. This began much earlier, but is now developed and widespread. Moreover, we see here the development of allegorical interpretations in terms of the Virgin Mary, and, as we shall see below, the Apostles. For instance, *Speculum Humanae Salvationis* also interprets Gideon's fleece as signifying Mary, and we see such allegory again in the interpretation of the construction of Solomon's temple in 1 Kings 6—10. Here we may also see the tendency to develop allegorical interpretations of all the details of stories in the Historical Books, a tendency that would come to be seen as problematic in later eras. Every opportunity is taken to link a given Old Testament story to the Christian story, the Christian tradition, and the cultivation of the Christian life in terms of the formation of virtue:

Bible Moralisée

(thirteenth century AD)

Here Solomon comes and has built a temple at the Lord God's command, and in the middle of the temple an altar and on the altar two cherubim to guard the altar. [1 Kings 6.1, 22–23]

That Solomon had the temple built and put in the middle of the temple the altar and on the altar two cherubim signifies Jesus Christ who built the Holy

Church and put in the middle the altar which was Jesus Christ, and the two cherubim signify St Peter and St Paul who guard and govern the Holy Church.

Here Solomon comes and orders a very good craftsman named Hiram to make the temple, and he comes before him and carves pillars and borders and diverse types of capitals. [1 Kings 7.13–22]

That Solomon ordered Hiram and he carved for him pillars to hold up the temple and diverse types of capitals signifies Jesus Christ who called Jerome to Him and Jerome made for Him and carved Him pillars and capitals, which he led and brought forward by his preaching. The capitals are the Christians, the pillars are the clerics and prelates who sustain the Holy Church.

...

Here Solomon comes and has made a throne of ivory and two lions that sustain the two arms, and two lions that sustain the throne, and the throne sits on six steps. [1 Kings 10.18–20]

The throne of ivory that Solomon made signifies the throne that the Father of Heaven made on which the Son is seated, namely the Virgin. The two lions that sustained the arms signify the two volumes that Our Lady sustained. The twelve lions signify the preaching of the twelve Apostles which sustain the Virgin Mary. The six steps signify the six virtues which all live in her.[11]

We can see these themes developed also in the sermons that we have from the era, and how they are linked to important contemporary events, such as the Crusades. Let us look at a sermon on Rahab's story from this era to compare with the interpretation of her story from the early Church:

Gilbert of Tournai: *Sermon* 1.20

(thirteenth century AD)

The cross of Christ is the *scarlet string*, by which the sinners are led from their caves, meaning the hide-outs of their sins, and by which Rahab was freed, while the others perished. So while the hardened and the obstinate are killed, the faithful crusaders are drawn to Christ by this string and the promised land is given to them *by the line of distribution* [Ps. 77.54 Vg], because true crusaders, who are truely contrite, have confessed their sins and prepare for the service of God and then die, are considered true martyrs, freed from mortal and venial sins and absolved from all penance enjoined on them, the punishment for their sins in this world and the punishment of purgatory in the next, they are safe from the tortures of hell and will be invested by this sign with eternal glory.[12]

Here the traditional 'spiritual' reading of the book of Joshua is developed, but again in terms of practices of penance and an emerging idea of 'purgatory' that is important in this era. Yet what is interesting here is that although this is a sermon preached to encourage crusaders, Joshua himself is not presented as an exemplar for a crusader, and the book of Joshua does not provide a paradigm for crusading. Indeed, there is very little use of Joshua in relation to promoting the Crusades, despite the claims of a number of popular authors today. The books of the Maccabees and, perhaps surprisingly to Christian readers today, the Gospels were the texts often used to encourage participation in the crusades, as crusading was seen as a sacrificial act for the love of Christian brothers and sisters whose land had been invaded.[13]

Reformation Christianity

The Reformation marks a watershed in biblical interpretation. For some time it would seem that there was something of a desire to recover more of the 'literal sense' of the Historical Books. There was a growing tendency to wish to harmonize the biblical accounts and offer explanations of a more apologetic nature, and to explain what texts of the Historical Books meant 'on their own terms', without reference to later Christian concerns or interpretation. This trend, which becomes fully articulated in modernity, might be said to reflect an attempt of the Reformation (and post-Reformation) Christian traditions to define themselves against the Catholicism of the day. The role of individual reason in reading texts in their 'plain sense' is stressed as against the authority of a tradition that promoted allegorical excesses that were becoming increasingly detached from the biblical texts. While Joshua had been a very influential book in the early Church, its popularity gradually waned in the Middle Ages, possibly because it came to be read in more 'literal' rather than 'spiritual' terms – it is difficult to see the annihilation of whole peoples as a model for the Christian life! The Reformation emphasis on 'justification by faith' when coupled with these interpretative concerns would see the abandonment of, for example, the interpretations of the Historical Books associated with penance that we saw in the excerpts above.

John Calvin (1509–64), in his detailed commentaries, was perhaps instrumental in largely doing away with spiritual reading of the Historical Books, putting literal reading firmly in place. His style and concerns were quite different from those of earlier interpreters. He attempted to read the Historical Books very much on their own terms, and not through the New Testament or Christian theology. His commentary on Joshua is particularly interesting. There are strikingly few references to the New Testament, and his reading of the morally difficult Joshua 10 is very different from Origen's reading, which we studied above. Calvin's interpretation is, ironically perhaps, closer to the heretics' reading than established traditional Christian readings. Calvin writes on Joshua 10.18:

John Calvin: *Commentaries on the Book of Joshua*

(1563)

The enemy having been completely routed, Joshua is now free, as it were, at leisure, to inflict punishment on the kings. In considering this, the divine command must always be kept in view. But for this it would argue boundless arrogance and barbarous atrocity to trample on the necks of kings, and hang up their dead bodies on gibbets ... It would therefore have been contrary to the feelings of humanity to exult in their ignominy, had God not so ordered it. But as such was his pleasure, it behoves us to acquiesce in his decision, without presuming to inquire why he was so severe.[14]

While Origen managed to read this difficult text as a source of nourishment for the spiritual life, for Calvin this is an account of history that creates a moral difficulty requiring a theological solution – God is so far beyond us, and we are so marred by sin in our thinking, that we are unable to enquire into or rightly judge the moral issues here of the killing of kings or the annihilation of peoples. So in his interpretation of Joshua we have a reflection of Calvin's wider theology: people (and especially the Canaanites) are so depraved that condemnation may be proper. Once again, the text is interpreted in light of the prevailing concerns of the interpreter.

However, while Martin Luther (1483–1546) was also keen to develop literal readings of the Old Testament as against what he saw as uncontrolled allegorical interpretation, he would retain something of a spiritual or typological interpretation as being (prophetically perhaps) *part of* the literal sense of Old Testament texts, which spoke directly to the lives of contemporary Christians.[15] In a way, Luther collapsed the four senses of Scripture into the literal sense. Something of the sort of approach that Luther took is perhaps reflected in some of the later Puritan biblical interpreters, and would be retained in devotional reading practices into the modern and contemporary eras. Returning to the passage that we have been looking at in Judges (Judg. 6.19–21), the later non-conformist Puritan biblical interpreter Matthew Henry (1662–1714) writes:

Matthew Henry: *Commentary on the Whole Bible*

(1708)

The angel gives him [Gideon] a sign in and by that which he had kindly prepared for his entertainment. For what we offer to God for his glory, and in token of our gratitude to him, will be made by the grace of God to turn to our own comfort and satisfaction. The angel ordered him to take the flesh and bread out of the basket, and lay it upon a hard and cold rock, and to pour out the broth upon it, which, if he brought it hot, would soon be cold there; and *Gideon did so* (v. 20), believing that the angel appointed it, not in contempt of his courtesy, but with an intention to give him a sign, which he did, abundantly to his satisfaction. For,

1 He turned the *meat into an offering made by fire, of a sweet savour* unto himself, showing hereby that he was not a man who needed meat, but the Son of God who was to be served and honoured by sacrifice, and who in the fulness of time was to make himself a sacrifice.
2 He brought fire *out of the rock*, to consume this sacrifice, summoning it, not by striking the rock, as we strike fire out of a flint, but by a gentle touch given to the offering with the end of his staff, v. 21. Hereby he gave him a sign that he had *found grace in his sight*, for God testified his acceptance of sacrifices by kindling them, if public, with fire from heaven, as those of Moses and Elias, if private, as this, with fire out of the earth, which was equivalent: both were the effect of divine power; and this acceptance of his sacrifice evidenced the acceptance of his person, confirmed his commission, and perhaps was intended to signify his success in the execution of it, that he and his army should be a surprising terror and consumption to the Midianites, like this fire out of the rock.
3 He *departed out of his sight* immediately, did not walk off as a man, but vanished and disappeared as a spirit. Here was as much of a sign as he could wish.[16]

So in the Reformation and early post-Reformation readings we see a turn towards some more thorough readings and commentaries on the Historical Books as stories in their own right. There was a focus on 'literal interpretation', but different interpreters understood this in different ways. It might be fair to say that Luther's interpretation of the Old Testament stood more in continuity with earlier interpretation than Calvin's, and that Calvin's stands more in continuity with what followed in modernity in which typological or allegorical interpretations recede from view almost entirely.

Modern Christianity

Perhaps Calvin in particular initiated a trend of interpretation that led to results and conclusions that he and other reformers would not have expected.[17] Calvin stressed the importance of the original, literal meaning of the Historical Books understood in their Old Testament context. In the modern era a focus on literal reading developed which would become a focus on historical issues on the one hand, and a quest for what the author of a text had intended to say on the other.[18] When this quest for the literal meaning was coupled with the concerns regarding issues of truth and history in early modernity, a quest began to attempt to reconstruct the most original sources and history used to compose the biblical text. Early in the modern era it was assumed that there was relatively little difference between the 'real' history of Israel and that reported in the Historical Books. But with the spirit of 'criticism' in modernity things began to change, and by the end of the twentieth century there was increasing scepticism towards the historical accuracy of much of the Old Testament, even in broad terms.

Throughout much of the eighteenth to twentieth centuries, a major goal of many interpreters was to identify the original source documents or traditions behind the biblical texts, and the historical circumstances that gave rise to their production. This was modelled on the developing 'scientific method' of modernity, which was seen as the way in which certain knowledge is attained. Thus interpreters would speak confidently of the 'assured results of higher criticism' of the biblical texts in the late nineteenth century. So stories from the Historical Books have been analysed verse by verse to try to isolate the different sources or traditions used in their composition. On a larger scale, the production of whole books or sections of the Old Testament with respect to various traditions has been considered. A very popular theory can be traced back to Martin Noth's (1902–68) study of 1943 (the results of which were partially anticipated by Abraham Kuenen (1828–91) and Julius Wellhausen (1844–1918), in which he argues that Deuteronomy forms the basis and the theology for the composition of the books of Joshua, Judges and Samuel–Kings, since the language and theology of these books is very close. These books are termed the 'Deuteronomistic History' (DH), a history written using various traditions during the exile, according to Noth. Subsequent theories have multiplied regarding the origins and number of 'editions' of the DH. For example, detecting a theme of promise and a theme of judgement in the DH, in 1973 F. M. Cross proposed the existence of an original edition of the DH dating to the time of King Josiah, written to support his reforms (2 Kings 22—23), and a later edition of the DH written in the Exile in order to explain the catastrophe of that event.

The Christian reader seeking formation in the Christian life might ask if such theories of composition improve Christian understanding and use of the texts. Biblical commentaries written in the modern period, although very informative and useful for the historian, tend to prove rather inaccessible and unedifying for many Christians, with a rift developing between devotional reading and more scholarly or academic study of the Bible, even if the latter was originally pursued with the goal of serving the Church. A further rift would develop between biblical studies and theology, concerns that had gone together previously. As an example of a more readable account that is typical of later modern interpretation with its focus on 'Source Criticism', here is S. R. Driver's summary (1913) of some of the material relating to King Solomon in 1 Kings 3—11, material that overlaps with some of that treated above in the *Bible Moraliseé*:

Samuel R. Driver: *Introduction to the Literature of the Old Testament*

(1913)

The kernel of [1 Kings 11] is old; but the narrative must, in parts, have been recast, and placed in a different light ... It seems clear that the narrative itself (v.14ff) is ancient, but that the setting (vv. 9–13), which represents the events narrated as the punishment for the idolatry of vv. 1–8, was added subsequently by the compiler. In the narrative of Ahijah (vv. 29–39), vv. 32–39 must have been expanded by the compiler, as they abound with marks of his style ... 11.41–43 is the concluding formula of Solomon's reign, in the compiler's usual manner.

The work which lay at the basis of the pre-Deuteronomic account of Solomon's reign must have been one in which the arrangement of material was determined less by chronological sequence than by community of subject. In other words, it was not so much a chronicle as a series of detached notices. The description of the buildings forming the central feature in it, particulars respecting the preparations or materials required for them, and notices, or short narratives, illustrating Solomon's wisdom, or splendour, or the organization of his empire, were placed on either side of it. At the close came [1 Kings 11] (in its original form), containing some account of the political opponents who from time to time disturbed the tranquillity of his reign. Throughout, the author evinces a warm admiration for Solomon: he recounts with manifest satisfaction the evidences of his wisdom, and dwells with pride on the details of his imperial magnificence, on the wealth which streamed into Jerusalem from all quarters, on his successful alliances and commercial undertakings, and on the manner in which his fame commanded the wonder and respect of distant nations. The darker shades in the picture seem largely, though not, perhaps, entirely, to be due to the Deuteronomic compiler.[19]

In addition to the quest for identifying sources behind biblical texts the idea developed in modernity that the interpreter should be concerned with discovering what the author of a text had intended to say, this being a goal for good interpretation. So on the one hand, interpreters believed that if one could isolate the facts of the pure historical events portrayed in the Historical Books, or what the biblical author intended to say about them on the other, then one would discover God's actual revelation. Some interpreters would stress the importance of recovering the historical events themselves, while others would stress the importance of recovering what the author said about them or the traditions surrounding them. We shall return to this below when we look at von Rad, but for now we must pause to consider the role of archaeology and the attempt to discover the historical events behind the biblical texts.

A central aspect to the development of interpretation of the Historical Books in modernity was the role of archaeology, being a part of the quest for history, and thus truth as it was understood in modernity. From the nineteenth century onwards, archaeological excavations of the Near East flourished. Evidence was sought initially to confirm or illuminate the biblical history. For much of the twentieth century, following the work of William Albright (1891–1971) in particular, biblical archaeology was a flourishing discipline in which it was thought that study of the Historical Books and archaeology went hand in hand to illuminate each other. However, the excavation of Jericho was a major turning point, the results of which would gradually bring about a significant change of view during the century. Initially, the collapsed walls of Jericho were taken as dramatic confirmation of the biblical history (Josh. 6). But further analysis of the site threw this conclusion into doubt – the walls did not collapse in the era presented in the biblical account.[20] More generally, as work continued, by the end of the twentieth century a number of archaeologists and scholars were struck by the lack of archaeological evidence for a conquest, or indeed for an early United Monarchy under David or Solomon. Omri is the first king of Israel (886–74) for whom there is clear archaeological evidence. He appears to have been regarded by the Assyrians as the founder of Israel. There is a reference to Omri or an Omride king in the *Mesha Inscription*, although there is no reference to Judah. (The *Mesha Inscription* is a ninth-century BC Moabite inscription that describes how Mesha, king of Moab, captures Israelite territory.) The archaeological evidence currently available has led to a number of proposals regarding how Israel actually emerged as a nation. In the mid- to late twentieth century a number of scholars started to think that Israel emerged from indigenous tribal groups in the northern regions, perhaps only in the first millennium, rather than as the Pentateuch and Historical Books portray.[21] There is, however, a brief reference to 'Israel' in the thirteenth-century BC Egyptian *Merneptah Stele*. The stele celebrates victory in a military campaign and contains the line, 'Israel is wasted, its seed is not'. The significance of the reference is unclear, as it doesn't correspond to anything in the biblical account. Moreover, in the *Tel Dan Stele*, discovered in two parts in 1993–4, there is a reference to *bytdwd*, which might mean the 'House of David', although as in many cases this is disputed. In summary, some scholars focus on the evidence that we have to doubt the biblical history, while others point to the evidence that may yet be discovered. But the evidence that we have is partial, inconclusive, and open to different interpretations.[22]

But it is not clear that an archaeological quest, especially when pursued in apologetic terms, is helpful for Christians trying to use the Old Testament to shape their understanding of the Christian faith and live it out. If anything, although it is debatable, the available evidence would tend to point away from the historical accuracy of the Historical Books. Perhaps, to anticipate some of our discussion below, the Historical Books are best regarded as representing inspired stories that evocatively shape Christian theology, identity and worldview. They are foundational for theology and our shared identity as a distinctive community with particular values and practices. Perhaps they are more fictional (and maybe political) than was previously recognized, but this does not mean that they are untrustworthy in their theological witness, even if the Historical Books are not historical in the modern sense. Traditionalists have responded in various ways to such claims. First, even if the stories were written in the form that we now have at a very late stage, this does not mean that the stories do not reflect accurate memories passed down over the generations. Second, the archaeological evidence is debatable, and it may reasonably be claimed that archaeologists have only uncovered a small fraction of the evidence that awaits to be unearthed – 'absence of evidence is not evidence of absence'. Finally, it is claimed that an adequate theology of history will require, in broad terms at least, that the Historical Books are firmly rooted in history. But this is asserted rather than argued, and leads to theological difficulties – as Origen appreciated centuries ago. Indeed, even without recourse to archaeology, one may observe the tension in the book of Joshua between the portrayal of a complete conquest (Josh. 1—12) and partial conquest (Josh. 13—21). This casts doubt on seeking the significance of the book in historical terms. In conclusion, it is perhaps worth recalling C. S. Lewis's succinct statement, 'I think He [God] meant us to have sacred myth and sacred fiction as well as sacred history.'[23]

Another aspect to the use of archaeology and studies of the ancient Near East involves the use of texts from the ancient Near East to illuminate our understanding of the Historical Books in more literary terms, to help us to understand the customs, idioms and language of the Historical Books. Two significant texts for the Historical Books have been the *Mesha Inscription*, which has been used to try to understand the 'total annihilation' (Hebrew *herem*) in Joshua, and the records of Assyrian kings. The *Taylor Prism* is one of the most notable archaeological finds. It preserves the Assyrian text, the *Annals of King Sennacherib*, a text that is very similar to 2 Kings 18.13—19.37.[24] Yet even here caution is required in the use of such texts, as one can easily be misled by this evidence, as its relationship to the biblical text requires careful interpretation. There is no doubt, though, that the availability of a great number of texts from the ancient Near East has contributed to our understanding of the biblical materials.

Returning now to the question of the goal of good interpretation, the mid-twentieth century gave rise to renewed interest in theological issues as distinct from historical-critical issues. Interpreters often acknowledged the results of historical criticism, but regarded the task of Christian interpretation as going beyond the task of tracing sources and explicating them in terms of their original context. A particularly bold move was made by Karl Barth. While not an Old Testament specialist, Barth sparked a trend to view the task of interpretation in far more theological terms. He did not deny the validity of historical criticism, but questioned its significance for Christian interpretation of Scripture.[25] For Barth, the task of the interpreter was to elucidate the theological subject matter of the text. So, for instance, for Barth 'The Israelite monarchy ... is the prototype or copy of the kingship of Jesus Christ.'[26] A slightly more restrained way of reading the Historical Books in theological terms, and more in continuity with the modern approach and its concerns with history and authorial intention in guiding the interpretation of biblical texts, can be found in the works of Gerhard von Rad, one of the twentieth century's most influential Old Testament scholars. For von Rad, history is seen in theologically significant terms as 'salvation history', which becomes an ordering principle of the Old Testament, anticipating Christ:

Gerhard von Rad: 'The Judges', in *Old Testament Theology*

(1957)

In the Deuteronomistic historical work, the period of the Judges is set in relief against the history which precedes and follows it as an era when the emphasis is strongly on saving history. It begins with the death of Joshua in Judg. II. 6ff., and ends with Samuel's farewell address in I Sam. XII (in the same way as the Deuteronomist also solemnly rounded off the previous era by means of Joshua's speech in Josh. XXIII). This is the first place where we encounter this theology of history in all its stark individuality. To it and it alone are we indebted for the preservation of a great deal of the older traditional material belonging to this period. Of course, this school was not simply motivated by regard for old historical documents, but rather by its design to disclose that divine meaning of the events of the era which had in the interval become more clearly discernible. In so doing, it starts from the presupposition that the old narrative material already available is not in itself able to make sufficiently clear to an unaided reader what really took place between Jahweh and Israel; that is, the reader needs special theological guidance to enable him to come to an understanding of the sum total of this period in saving

---

history. How little the Deuteronomist believes in reading the old stories without commentary is shown by the weighty theological apparatus which he calls in, in order to weld the old documentary material together and interpret it. Thus the Deuteronomistic Book of Judges gives the impression of great disharmony. The old stories, taken by themselves, very directly reflect the early period, which was still largely confused: as far as culture and the things of the mind go, they take us back to a bygone world and have a freshness and originality which can only belong to traditions deriving from a nation's early days. Everything is specific and unique, and no one event is like another. In contrast, in the theological framework everything is concentrated reflexion, and reflexion which is always enquiring about what is general, typical for the time, and constantly recurring.[27]

Here we see the interweaving of a number of concerns – the acknowledgement of historical-critical study in helping us to understand the nature and formation of the text and its relation to history, but also the desire to give a theological interpretation of the text and what the authors sought to achieve through composing the text, giving a theological interpretation to history. Von Rad thus offers a synthesis of the concerns of modernity with a retrieval of theological concerns that had become eclipsed.

However, during the twentieth century the realization gradually dawned that decisions regarding the composition and history of the biblical text, and the relation of the biblical text to history, were being made on increasingly tenuous grounds. The significance and centrality of 'history' and historical concerns began to wane. A number of interpreters, especially in the light of Barth, began to question whether the results of such analysis contributed significantly to our understanding of the *message* or significance of a biblical text. The mid- to late twentieth century saw a flourishing of interest in literary and theological interpretation of the biblical texts by scholars such as R. Alter[28] and B. S. Childs. Scholars such as Childs wished to retain some of the theological and hermeneutical insights of Barth and von Rad, for example, but while being much more reserved and measured in their interpretation. For instance, Childs, discussing the interpretation of Samuel, states that von Rad's influential thesis regarding 'salvation history' is overstated.[29] Towards the end of the twentieth century Alter, and Christian interpreters who have used his work, have sought to recover the idea that the stories in the Historical Books should be read as stories rather than as sources for history, and that this is how we may understand the task of interpreting texts in their 'literal sense'. By the end of the twentieth century, unlike the beginning, scholarly commentaries could be written without lengthy discussion of the recovery of putative sources behind a given text. Rather, a commentator could take the reader through the task of reading the Historical Books as literary works.

In general terms, then, Christian commentaries on the Historical Books have, perhaps, reverted to a style somewhat closer to the Reformation commentaries by the use of literary approaches, while being informed by the results of historical criticism. Theological concerns are often in view, but are seldom Christological in focus in the style of pre-modern interpretation. In the excerpt below from Richard Nelson on 1 Kings 19 we can see how the results of historical criticism are broadly acknowledged, yet remain in the background. While there are references to 'history', there is less concern with history per se, although there are perhaps echoes of von Rad here. We can also see the influence of literary approaches to reading coupled with a desire to draw out theological implications for the contemporary Christian reader. Perhaps there are even echoes of Barth's reading alluded to above here.

Richard Nelson: *First and Second Kings*

(1987)

The context of the Old Testament as a whole points strongly to an intentional comparison between Elijah and Moses. It is possible that the Pentateuchal presentation of this aspect of the Moses tradition received its shape from this Elijah legend, although scholars have usually assumed that the direction of dependence runs the other way. Moses too grew so despondent that he wanted to die (Num. 11.15). 'Forty days and nights' sounds classically Mosaic (Exod. 24.18; 34.28). The clearest parallel is to Exodus 33.12–23; 34.33–35. Moses, disheartened about his position, asks for a special revelation of God's glory. God 'passes before' (v. 11; Exod. 33.19; 34.6) Moses, showing him divine glory, God's back but not God's face, hiding Moses in a cleft in the rock and protecting him with a hand. As a result of this experience, Moses had to hide his shining face behind a veil (a parallel to vv. 13?). Elijah falls distinctly short of Moses, however, by failing to respond to the personal revelation offered him.

In the New Testament, Jesus responds to a young man who has a request similar to Elisha's (Luke 9.61–62). This parallel is recognized by the ecumenical lectionary ... . Those committed to discipleship cannot have second thoughts. The disciple of Jesus must make the same ruthless break with the past that Elisha did in v. 21, putting forth one's hand 'against' ... the plow (to burn it?) without looking back. Thus the Elisha episode can be seen as a call to a commitment which burns all bridges to other loyalties.

This narrative also explores the mystery of God's activity in history to punish and protect the elect. Elijah's recommissioning sets a long chain of events in motion, so that he can be said to 'anoint' each of the three instruments of God's plan. In some mysterious way, God's will stands behind even such butchers as Jehu and Hazael. Somehow it is possible to equate the ministry of a prophet like Elisha with the swords of these two violent kings. On the one hand, they execute God's punishment for apostasy upon Israel. At the same time, their violence means protection for the faithful remnant of seven thousand. For the original exilic audience, who surely thought of themselves as the remnant ... this story must have been both a comfort and a warning.

This narrative explores the interplay between human despair and God's call in a way that speaks to exiles of any age. God can be counted on to provide in the wilderness (vv. 5–7). This theme is picked up in the lectionary pairing of this feeding story with the Johannine discourse on bread from heaven (John 6.41–51 ...). However, the providence of God turns out to be insufficient for the human servant, prone to despondency and depression which neither logic nor the showiest theophany can cure. But God, sovereign over both nature (vv. 11–12) and history (v. 17), refuses to accept Elijah's resignation as prophet. God induces Elijah to get back to work by giving him more to do. God shrugs off Elijah's complaints and commissions him for further tasks. There may be no theophanies in Babylonian exile (or in the modern reader's own wilderness of Damascus), but there is certainly plenty to do.[30]

It is worth observing, however, that commentaries continue today to be written in historical-critical, literary, and theological modes alongside each other. There are now several somewhat fragmented strands of biblical interpretation and scholarship. There has been a recognition that the nature of the task of interpretation is relative to the interests or concerns of the reader. The reader interested in the development of Israelite religion will have a different set of questions and a different focus from the reader coming to the text who understands it to be a resource for the Christian life, for example. Earlier in the modern era the different interpretative tasks or interests were conflated as the difference had not been recognized or articulated. The excerpt from Nelson is from a commentary series devoted to Christian teaching and preaching. A 'critical' commentary from the same era would look very different. Although written a little earlier, commentaries such as John Gray's would be typical of a more 'critical' commentary.[31]

Indeed, in the late modern or postmodern era questions of ethics, politics, power, and the influence of the context or perspective from which one reads have come to dominate much biblical interpretation. The role of the reader and their context comes to be seen as far more important than before in postmodern interpretation. Feminist interpretation is one paradigmatic expression of this trend.[32] This has often led in scholarly analysis to a questioning of the viewpoint taken in the text rather than its affirmation as authoritative and life-giving as in traditional Christian interpretation. Take R. B. Coote's reading of Joshua in 1998, for example:

Robert B. Coote: 'The Book of Joshua'

(1998)

As an expression of Josiah's reform, the story of Joshua's conquest, patterned on Josiah's reconquest, 'functions as an instrument of coercion' and intimidation, encouraging the submission of all subjects. The historian wants to terrorize the populace, particularly its recalcitrant political leaders, into submission to Josiah by showing what happens to a class of people ('Canaanites') whose interests are opposed to the interests of Josiah's monarchy and of the peasantry under him. The writer also shows that obedience to Josiah can take precedence over supposed ethnic affiliation: Canaanites can submit and be saved (Rahab, the Gibeonites), and if a Judahite belonging to the Israelite in group disobeys the Commander-in-chief, he can be repudiated and killed (Achan). 'The primary purpose of the conquest narrative is to send a message to internal rivals, potential Achans, that they can make themselves into outsiders very easily.' Josiah's historian 'uses the rhetoric of warfare and nationalism as an encouragement and a threat to its own population to submit voluntarily to the central authority of a government struggling to organize itself and to [re]create its own ideological framework of inclusion. In order to justify violent action [to that end], the dynamics of the literature of warfare usually consist of a division [often outrageously overstated] between self and other,' us and them.[33]

Here, Coote reads Joshua in political terms in the context of the assumed results of earlier historical criticism – that the book of Joshua was composed in the era of Josiah's reforms in order to support the reform. This leads to the suggestion that Joshua is a work of coercion and intimidation. But need it be a work of coercion and intimidation? Is a supposed original historical context (that might not be correct in any case) determinative for Joshua's interpretation? Could Joshua simply be encouraging the adoption of particular values and goals in a community? It is often *possible* to read a text unsympathetically, or 'against the grain', or counter to the Christian tradition. But is this a helpful or a good way of reading Scripture if one is concerned with reading it *as* Christian Scripture rather than through a political lens, as a witness to one interpretation of the political world of ancient Israel when coupled with a 'hermeneutic of suspicion'?

We see that the twentieth century gave rise to several trends in the interpretation of the Historical Books that have continued to develop alongside each other – historical-critical approaches, literary approaches, theological approaches, and various postmodern reader-centred approaches. Biblical interpreters such as Walter Moberly have sought to account for these various trends in interpretation in developing Christian theological readings of

Old Testament texts.[34] There has also been something of a rapprochement between Catholic and the various Reformation and post-Reformation traditions, with each drawing upon and valuing the insights of the other, and indeed Orthodox traditions of biblical interpretation.

Global Christianity

The interpretations above are 'global' – from Egypt, to Europe, to North America. However, these interpretations generally stem from what is known as the 'Western' tradition. In other contexts, contexts that are sometimes defined geographically – India, China, Africa, and South America, for example – the Bible may be read differently: we tend to read the Bible with our own life context, questions, and concerns in view. A church formed within an isolated tribe in South America is likely to have different questions from a church in London since the life-issues and worldviews that one is accustomed to are very different.

What makes an interpretation 'global'? Crudely speaking, perhaps there are three main types of interpretation that might be described as 'global'. First, interpretations from around the world arising immediately in the wake of (until recently, often Western) missionary activity. Second, interpretations that essentially apply political theories (often derivatives of Marxist, feminist, or post-colonial theory) to the reading of the Bible, and its interpretation by missionaries, in local contexts. Third, interpretations that seek to incorporate local culture and traditions with the Christian tradition. The first of these generally mirror the concerns of (often fairly theologically conservative) Western Christian traditions and, in a number of cases, does rather little to seek to integrate local traditions with the gospel and to value local culture. The second tends to mirror academic debates heavily influenced by contemporary political theory, and arguably represents another form of 'Western' interpretative tradition, although an essentially recent political one rather than a traditional theological one. It has, however, been able to point to the abuse of the Bible in a number of contexts, where biblical texts have been used to justify oppression. The third kind is arguably the most truly 'global', raising interesting and challenging questions regarding the relationships between culture and theology. To what extent might local culture and traditions lead to an enlarged and richer understanding of Scripture and of God, and to what extent might Scripture challenge local culture and traditions, or call for their reinterpretation? These questions are relevant to us all, as we seek to understand our own culture and context in terms of Scripture and vice versa.

First, here is an example of an African reading of Judges in which the story can be seen to resonate with the contemporary situation in the Democratic Republic of Congo in a much more powerful way than in many established Western democracies:

Fidele Ugira Kwasi: 'Judges' in *Global Bible Commentary*

(2004)

The book of Judges has much to teach to us in sub-Sahara Africa regarding how to emerge from four decades of chaotic political and economic transition, and this without paying further the high price Israel paid for having rejected YHWH. Indeed, YHWH is the only and true signpost pointing to a new social, economic, political, and cultural community order ...

Thus, this book invites us, in Africa, to look again at the long period of transition that we are in. We can recognize that, in our desperate struggle for survival we have adopted attitudes in which YHWH is not the ultimate reference point: therefore divine punishment is to be expected. It becomes apparent from what precedes that a nation is not primarily founded on a will to power, although power is a valuable tool for the service and wellbeing of others ...

In a country such as the Democratic Republic of Congo (RDC) where, according to governmental statistics, at least 80 percent of the population identify themselves as Christians ... and in a culture where the resonance between the African traditional cultures and the Hebrew Bible are numerous ... it is appropriate to emphasize that faith in YHWH is the only way to overcome our loss of community identity and of ethical grounding ...

In the present struggle of our society to survive, Congolese people need to anchor their lives in a 'law'. But rather than adopting the law of the globalization process, they should turn to Scripture and to the book of Judges. Yet, in this book, they should not expect to find ready-made models that they can passively adopt and emulate in their lives. This point is true also of the other books of Scripture, and in the case of the model judge, Jesus Christ. Rather this book and the rest of Scripture accompany us through our lives, constantly calling us to repent and to rediscover the presence of God at work among us in deliverers whom God sends to us and the empowerment we receive from God to walk together toward a time of justice and peace 'so the land [might have] rest [many] years' in Africa (3.11, 30; 5.31; 8.28).[35]

This represents a fairly traditional Christian reading in the context of the Democratic Republic of Congo, seeking to apply a traditional kind of reading of Judges to the context at hand.

Now let us look at an example of a global reading that attempts to integrate local traditions with the biblical tradition, a reading that also reflects an interest in post-colonial political concerns in which traditional Christian missionary approaches and theology are challenged:

Gerald O. West: '1 and 2 Samuel' in *Global Bible Commentary*

(2004)

Missionaries and colonial agents used the Bible to denigrate and demonize the religious and cultural practices of the Africans, insisting that their forms of Christianity were far superior. And yet, once African Christians became familiar with the Bible, they were amazed to find that their religion and culture were mirrored in texts like 1 Samuel. These similarities between the Bible and their life contexts became a resource to recover aspects of their African religion and culture that the missionaries had damaged ... Much of African biblical scholarship to date has focused on showing the similarities between precolonial African culture and religion, and the Bible, particularly the Old Testament ...

For example, the missionaries insisted that veneration of the ancestors – those 'living dead' who inhabited the spirit realm and continued to watch over and guide their people through dreams and portents – was demonic. And yet here, in 1 Samuel 28, we find Saul consulting a diviner (v. 8) who, in turn, enables Saul to consult with his ancestor, Samuel (v. 11), whom the text describes as 'a god, coming up out of the ground' (v. 13, a.t.) ... Here, we have the living dead warning Saul. And here, God as in many African traditional religions, is present but remote. It is the ancestors who are available for consultation ...

[In 1 Sam. 28] Saul asks a medium to summon Samuel. When the medium sees the spirit of Samuel, she tells Saul (literally), 'I see *Elohim* [gods or spirits] coming up from the earth' (28.13). The medium (or *sangoma*, as she would be called in Zulu) called Samuel; but what she sees are '*Elohim* [gods] coming up,' among whom is Samuel, one of the ancestors. The Israelites, like most Africans, trusted these gods because they were the gods whom their ancestors had trusted and venerated. When the living departed, they joined the living dead who watched over their people. Samuel lived on after his death, guiding those who came after him.

Texts like this, therefore, are profoundly empowering because they recover and rehabilitate damaged aspects of indigenous culture and religion.[36]

This is an interesting reading, but it has its difficulties. As with interpretation in the early Church, we might ask whether this is a *good* way to read 1 Samuel 28, and indeed what counts as a good reading. (It is interesting to note that the interpretation of 1 Samuel 28 was much debated in the early Church.) West's reading assumes that because the consultation of a 'medium' is reported in the Bible then it may be seen in positive terms. But the point of the story might be quite different. Elsewhere in the Bible consultation of mediums is seen as bad (e.g. Lev. 20.27; 2 Kings 21.6), and, in particular, the commentary on this incident in 1 Chronicles 10.13 suggests that the consultation of the medium is to be understood as a bad thing and not a good thing. West's interpretation attempts to integrate biblical tradition with local tradition. But it is not clear that it is genuinely possible if the aim of such interpretation is to remain faithful to both traditions. Sometimes the biblical tradition may affirm what is found in local tradition, and sometimes it may challenge it – the gospel message is, after all, a call to conversion.

What is, then, interesting and challenging for Christian interpreters around the globe is to see how local culture can amplify and expand our understanding of Scripture, and how Scripture might critique the local culture – be that consulting mediums in Africa or materialism in North America or Europe. But there is also a growing trend to consider how local traditions, or philosophies, might appropriately challenge biblical traditions. This is perhaps one of the main issues that the Church worldwide will grapple with in the twenty-first century. In the context of this section it is interesting to observe that in the realms of sexual ethics and marriage it is the Western traditions and associated philosophies that have become most critical of the biblical tradition, while it is the global Church that generally remains more biblically conservative, as the debates within the worldwide Anglican Communion of the early twenty-first century indicate. In terms of the Historical Books it is the interpretation of the stories of David and Jonathan, or Ruth and Naomi, that are often in question.[37] This brings us to our discussion in Part 3 on application.

Part 3: Application

There is no doubt that some of the stories and characters from the Historical Books have been widely used in the Church's ministry and mission, as we have seen. Moreover, the stories have had a pervasive influence in shaping much Western culture in particular. Here, we shall consider some further examples of the application of the Historical Books in ministry and mission. We shall consider how the books have in fact been used, before concluding with some brief remarks regarding how we might understand the task of reading and using the Historical Books well as Christian Scripture today.

Historical Books in ministry

Various stories in the Historical Books have been used as exemplars to illustrate some aspect of the Christian life. This might relate to some moral aspect of the Christian life, or offer hope and encouragement, or relate to prophecy or the demonstration of the power of God, for instance. So, for example, the story of David and Bathsheba (2 Sam. 11–12), especially when read through Psalm 51 and as reflected in Church liturgy, offers an exemplar modelling humble penitence and confession of sin following grievous moral failure. It evokes the hope of forgiveness and restoration following confession, witnessing to the gracious character of God. The story of Gideon, and in particular his use of a fleece to seek divine guidance (Judg. 6), has been taken to model one way in which God's will may be sought, figuratively speaking. Thus Christians talk about 'putting out a fleece' when seeking divine guidance. That is, 'tests' are set up, perhaps with unlikely outcomes, to discern God's will. It is not entirely clear that this reflects a good reading of the story, but it is a way in which the story is used in contemporary Christianity. To take some other contemporary examples, it has become popular to use the story of Nehemiah's rebuilding of the walls of Jerusalem as an exemplar for Christian leadership. Elijah's story is used to evoke a sensitivity to listening to God in the 'still, small voice' rather than seeking God in dramatic events (1 Kings 19.11–13), and to show that God provides for his followers (1 Kings 17.8–16). Elijah's story is also foundational for Carmelite Christian spirituality.

A number of stories have been read to indicate God's strength manifested in human weakness, or as against displays of human power and might. So, for instance, God tells Gideon to reduce the size of his army when going against the Midianites (Judg. 7), and famously the young David defeats the Philistine giant Goliath (1 Sam. 17). Stories such as these encourage and evoke the sense that the power and strength of God is with the humble follower of God even, or perhaps especially, when faced with apparently insurmountable difficulties. From the New Testament onwards, the story of Rahab (Josh. 2 and 6) has been used to demonstrate the need for faith to be accompanied by action or works. Along with various other characters from the Historical Books, she is one of the exemplars of faith in the book of Hebrews (Heb. 11.29–40). The book of Hebrews develops the idea that the crossing of the Jordan and entrance to the Promised Land in Joshua to find rest was only a temporary, earthly anticipation of the greater reality of eschatological rest in Christ. Traditionally, crossing the Jordan (Josh. 3—4) has been used to evoke Christian Baptism (e.g. Gregory of Nyssa), with life in the land evoking the Christian life and ultimately anticipating heavenly rest with God. More problematically, however, the stories of the conquest and annihilation of the Canaanites and Amalekites were used as exemplars by Puritan emigrants to North America to justify various atrocities – their treatment of the indigenous peoples and the taking of the land.[38] More generally, accounts from the Historical Books have been used in the development of 'Just War' theory, from the time of Augustine onwards. For example, Joshua 8 has been used to discuss the legitimacy of ambush in warfare, which was seen as potentially problematic as it is a form of deception.[39]

These are just some of the ways in which stories from the Historical Books have been used in Christian ministry, some of which are well established and nourishing to Christians, and some of which are problematic.

Historical Books in mission

There are various ways in which the Historical Books might be said to have been applied in mission. Some usages are explicitly evangelical, perhaps with an apologetic focus. Comparison of the Historical Books with archaeo-logical discoveries has been used to motivate the historical reliability of the Old Testament with a view to establishing its truth or trustworthiness. As we have seen, however, this is problematic. But these issues aside, stories such as Rahab's (Josh. 2 and 6), or Ruth's, have been taken to evoke conversion. Readings from the Historical Books form part of lectionary readings and the liturgy of the Church, and scenes from the books are depicted in the stained-glass windows of many churches.

More broadly, stories from the Historical Books have formed the basic repertoire for the education of many generations of children – be that in Sunday schools or Bible study classes, or religious studies classes at school. For generations children have been brought up on the stories of the tumbling walls of Jericho (Josh. 6) or the battle of David and Goliath (1 Sam. 17), for example.

Looking more broadly still, we can see the pervasive influence of the Historical Books in Western culture. This ranges from some of the everyday idioms and figures of speech that we use to fine art and music. Scenes from the Historical Books have formed the subjects of paintings from the Renais-sance to contemporary art. Depictions of David with Goliath's head are to be found in Giovanni Battista Cima de Conegliano's *David and Jonathan* (c. 1507), and Caravaggio's *David with the head of Goliath* (c. 1609). Michelangelo sculpted a statue of David that was placed in a public square outside the seat of civic government in Florence (1504). In music, stories from the Historical Books have inspired various great works. Particularly well known perhaps is Handel's 'The arrival of the Queen of Sheba' from act three of the English oratorio *Solomon* (1748), a piece often performed at weddings, and notably also at the London Olympics in 2012. The Histor-ical Books have continued to inspire artists in more contemporary styles of art – for instance, in Marc Chagall's *Joshua* (1931). In film too, the Ark of the Covenant (2 Sam. 6) inspired the 1981 Steven Spielberg movie *Raiders of the Lost Ark*. Characters from the Historical Books have influenced our language. The name 'Jezebel' has become a figure of speech or stereotype for sexually promiscuous women (introduced in 1 Kings 16.31). Abram Lyle's iconic Golden Syrup tins feature one of the UK's longest-used brand logos, introduced in 1885 and still used today. It depicts the carcass of the lion slain by Samson with a swarm of bees from Judges 14.8 and the quotation 'Out of the strong came forth sweetness' (Judg. 14.14).

Having very briefly seen something of the pervasive use and influence of the Historical Books, it is important to consider the question of what makes for a *good* interpretation or use as against a *poor* one. We have remarked on some of the difficulties associated with allegorical reading, and with historical and ethical issues. But these concerns have each in different ways been important in the interpretation of the Historical Books, representing significant theological concerns. While allegorical reading often goes too far perhaps, the New Testament's Christology implies that one ought to see Christ as fulfilling what was anticipated in the Old Testament, and that humanity and human actions are most fully interpreted with reference to Christ. As Christians confess the providential care and revelation of God, it is surely right to understand God to act in history. And as the Christian faith involves loving and living well before God and each other, it is surely right to be concerned with ethical issues too, especially in the use of scriptural narratives. But none of this is to say that one should regard Old Testament narratives as codes that need to be cracked to find Christ in allegories. Rather, we read the Historical Books in the light of Christ. Similarly, we need not understand the Historical Books as necessarily *reporting* history – rather, as stories symbolic of God's dealings with humanity, they have theologically *shaped* the histories and worldviews of people throughout the ages. If Old Testament narratives have been used badly in order to kill, steal or oppress in ethically problematic ways, this does not necessarily mean that they are reprehensible, but rather that we should recognize that they have been used badly, and that this is not Christian usage of the narratives. Indeed, if we can draw from anthropological studies regarding the kinds of story that societies use to shape their identities and worldviews, we find that such stories are often ethically problematic, being symbolic of something other than what the stories describe if read 'literally'. In other words, stories depicting violence need not be read as reporting historical fact, nor need they be read as models for ethical behaviour.[40] For example, a modern-day 'war protest movie' need not report history as such and need not commend war just because it depicts it; rather it may depict problematic aspects of warfare precisely to question them. It would seem that something like this is what we find in the book of Joshua.

'Fictional' stories may convey truth just as much as historical narratives, even if the nature and warrant for their truth-claims are different. Good fiction may be read in different ways in different contexts, requiring literary judgements as to what counts as good interpretation. It is the 'world of the text' that is the subject of interpretation.[41] For the Christian reader the Historical Books are read in a Christian theological context, and this is where they discover their meaning for Christians who will generally want to read *with* rather than *against* the grain of the texts, even though discernment is still required in forming a good interpretation of a given text. What we have been discussing is perhaps a way of appropriating Origen's insights regarding Joshua in terms that are more convincing for a contemporary reader. Many of the theological interpretations that we have considered are quite independent of their basis in history and the possible political forces that gave rise to the production of the texts. To this end it may be helpful to recall that the major Historical Books are classed in the Prophets in the Jewish Hebrew Bible. Their significance is not categorized primarily in terms of history, but in terms of a prophetic witness bringing forth the word of God. Reading the story of David and Bathsheba through Psalm 51, as evoking gracious forgiveness following humble repentance, is a good theological interpretation and use of the story quite apart from questions about the existence of a historical David and the politics of a Davidic dynasty. The story anticipates the gracious forgiveness and restoration that is most fully known and made available through Christ.[42]

Notes

1 See Young, F. M., 1997, *Biblical Exegesis and the Formation of Christian Culture*, Cambridge: Cambridge University Press, for a detailed discussion of the nature of early Christian interpretation.

2 Theodoret of Cyrus, *Questions on Joshua* Q.11, in Hill, R. C. (tr.), 2007, *Theodoret of Cyrus: The Questions on the Octateuch*, LEC, 2, Washington, DC: Catholic University of America Press, pp. 267–9.

3 Origen of Alexandria, *Homilies on Joshua*, 12.3, in Bruce, B. J. (tr.), 2002, *Origen: Homilies on Joshua*, FOTC, 105, Washington, DC: Catholic University of America Press, pp. 123–4.

4 Ambrose of Milan, *On the Holy Spirit 1, Prologue 2–3*, in Franke, J. R. and Oden, T. C. (eds), 2005, *Joshua, Judges, Ruth, 1–2 Samuel*, ACCS OT, 4, Downers Grove, IL: Inter-Varsity Press, p. 121.

5 Theodoret of Cyrus, *Questions on Ruth 2.12*, in Franke and Oden, *Joshua, Judges, Ruth, 1–2 Samuel*, p. 186.

6 For further discussion, see de Lubac, H., 1998, *Medieval Exegesis: The Four Senses of Scripture*, vol. 1, Grand Rapids, MI: Eerdmans (original 1959).

7 See Gilby, T. et al. (ed., tr.), 1964–74, *Summa Theologica: Latin Text and English Translation, Introductions, Notes, Appendices and Glossaries*, 60 vols, London: Eyre and Spottiswoode.

8 See Henry, A., 1987, *The Mirour of Mans Saluacioun: A Middle English Translation of Speculum Humanae Salvationis*, Philadelphia, PA: University of Pennsylvania Press.

9 For an overview of the development of interpretation throughout this era, see Evans, G. R., 1984–5, *The Language and Logic of the Bible*, 2 vols, Cambridge: Cambridge University Press.

10 Guest, G. B. (tr.), 1995, *Bible Moralisée Codex Vindobonensis 2554, Vienna, Österreichische Nationalbibliothek*, Manuscripts in Miniature 2, London: Harvey Miller, fol. 58vA–59rA, pp. 95–6.

11 Guest, *Bible Moralisée*, pp. 130–1.

12 Maier, C. T., 2000, *Crusade Propaganda and Ideology: Model Sermons for Preaching the Cross*, Cambridge: Cambridge University Press, p. 189.

13 See Earl, D. S., 2013, 'Joshua and the Crusades', in Thomas, H., Evans, J. and Copan, P. (eds), *Holy War in the Bible: Christian Morality and an Old Testament Problem*, Downers Grove, IL: Inter-Varsity Press, pp. 19–43.

14 Calvin, J., 1563, *Commentaries on the Book of Joshua*, 10.18, Beveridge, H. (tr.), 1854, Edinburgh: The Calvin Translation Society, reissued 1949, Grand Rapids, MI: Baker, pp. 157–8.

15 See further, Bornkamm, H., 1969, *Luther and the Old Testament*, Philadelphia, PA: Fortress Press (original 1948).

16 Henry, M., 1708, *Commentary on the Whole Bible*, vol. 2, Hendrickson Peabody (1991–4), pp. 331–2 (digital copy in Ages Digital Library, Albany, Version 1.0, 1999).

17 For an overview of some of the trends and difficulties involved in interpretation in this era from a late twentieth-century perspective, see Frei, H. W., 1974, *The Eclipse of Biblical Narrative: A Study in Eighteenth and Nineteenth Century Hermeneutics*, New Haven, CT: Yale University Press.

18 For the role of 'history' in modernity, see Stevenson, W. T., 1970, 'History as Myth: Some Implications for History and Theology', *Cross Currents*, 20/1, pp. 15–28.

19 Driver, S. R., 1913, *Introduction to the Literature of the Old Testament*, 9th edn, Edinburgh: T&T Clark, pp. 192–3.

20 For details, see Merling Sr, D., 1997, *The Book of Joshua: Its Theme and Role in Archaeological Discussions*, AUSDDS, 23, Berrien Springs, MI: Andrews University Press.

21 For an important thesis typifying this trend, see Gottwald, N. K., 1979, *The Tribes of Yahweh: A Sociology of the Religion of Liberated Israel, 1250–1050 BCE*, Maryknoll, NY: Orbis.

22 For two different interpretations of the evidence and the two sides of the debate, see Davies, P. R., 2008, *Memories of Ancient Israel: An Introduction to Biblical History – Ancient and Modern*, Louisville, KY: Westminster John Knox, and Kitchen, K. A., 2003, *On the Reliability of the Old Testament*, Grand Rapids, MI: Eerdmans.

23 C. S. Lewis, in a letter to Janet Wise, 5 October 1955, cited in Vanhoozer, K. J., 2010, 'On Scripture', in MacSwain, R. and Ward, M. (eds), *The Cambridge Companion to C. S. Lewis*, Cambridge: Cambridge University Press, pp. 75–88, at p. 87.

24 The most recent and fullest compilation of translated sources is Hallo, W. H. and Lawson Younger, K. (eds), 1997–2003, *The Context of Scripture* [COS], 3 vols, Leiden: Brill. The account of Sennacherib's siege of Jerusalem may be found in vol. 2 (2.119B), pp. 302–3.

25 See, especially, the 2nd edition of his commentary, *The Epistle to the Romans*, and the remarks in the preface. See Barth, K., 1968, *The Epistle to the Romans*, 6th edn, Oxford: Oxford University Press (original 1933).

26 Barth, K., 2004, *Church Dogmatics II.2: The Doctrine of God*, London: T&T Clark, p. 389 (original 1942).

27 Von Rad, G., 1975, *Old Testament Theology, Vol. 1: The Theology of Israel's Historical Traditions*, London: SCM Press, pp. 327–8 (original 1957).

28 Alter, R., 1981, *The Art of Biblical Narrative*, New York: Basic Books.

29 Childs, B. S., 1979, *Introduction to the Old Testament as Scripture*, Philadelphia, PA: Fortress Press, p. 279.

30 Nelson, R. D., 1987, *First and Second Kings*, Louisville, KY: Westminster John Knox, pp. 128–9.

31 Gray, J., 1964, *I & II Kings: A Commentary*, London: SCM Press.

32 See, for instance, Trible, P., 1984, *Texts of Terror: Literary-Feminist Readings of Biblical Narratives*, Philadelphia, PA: Fortress Press, and, in particular, her reading of Judges 11.29–40, at pp. 93–116.

33 Coote, R. B., 1998, 'The Book of Joshua Introduction, Commentary and Reflections', in Keck, L. (ed.), *The New Interpreter's Bible Commentary: Introduction to Narrative Literature, Joshua, Judges, Ruth, 1 & 2 Samuel, 1 & 2 Kings, 1 & 2 Chronicles*, Nashville, TN: Abingdon Press, vol. 2, p. 577.

34 Moberly, R. W. L., 2013, *Old Testament Theology: Reading the Hebrew Bible as Christian Scripture*, Grand Rapids, MI: Baker.

35 Ugira Kwasi, F., 2004, 'Judges', in Patte, D. and Croatto, J. Severino (eds), *Global Bible Commentary*, Nashville, TN: Abingdon Press, pp. 84–5.

36 West, G. O., 2004, '1 and 2 Samuel', in Patte and Croatto, *Global Bible Commentary*, pp. 94–5.

37 See, for example, Duncan, C. M., 2000, 'The Book of Ruth: On Boundaries, Love, and Truth', in Goss, R. E. and West, M. (eds), *Take Back the Word: A Queer Reading of the Bible*, Cleveland: The Pilgrim Press, pp. 92–102.

38 Warrior, R. A., 2001, 'Canaanites, Cowboys and Indians: Deliverance, Conquest, and Liberation Theology Today', in Jobling, D., Pippin, T. and Schleifer, R. (eds), 2001, *The Postmodern Bible Reader*, Oxford: Blackwell, pp. 188–94.

39 See, for example, Thomas Aquinas, *Summa Theologica*, 2a2ae, 40. Heath, T. R. (ed.), 1972, *St Thomas Aquinas Summa Theologica: Latin Text and English Translation, Introductions, Notes, Appendices and Glossaries*, London: Eyre and Spottiswoode, vol. 35, pp. 81–93.

40 See, for example, Turner, V., 1968, 'Myth and Symbol', in Sills, D. L. (ed.), *International Encyclopedia of the Social Sciences*, New York: Macmillan and The Free Press, vol. 10, pp. 576–81.

41 See Ricoeur, P., 1978, 'The Narrative Function', *Semeia*, 13, pp. 177–202.

42 For a detailed treatment of the issues discussed here, see Earl, D. S., *Reading Old Testament Narrative as Christian Scripture*, JTI Supplements; Winona Lake, IN: Eisenbrauns (forthcoming), or for the book of Joshua specifically, see Earl, D. S., 2010, *Reading Joshua as Christian Scripture*, JTI Supplements 2; Winona Lake, IN: Eisenbrauns.

4

Poetry and Wisdom

RYAN P. O'DOWD

Part 1: Introduction

Bonaventure, Columba, Thomas Aquinas, John Calvin, William Shake-speare, Mary Sidney, John Donne, Gerard Manley Hopkins, and Johann Sebastian Bach are but a few of the countless artists, mystics, and theologians who were deeply influenced by the poetry and wisdom of the Bible. The material in Job, Psalms, Proverbs, Ecclesiastes, and Song of Songs has also made its way into countless homes, worship liturgies, and the language and idioms in most of the Western world. The biblical books of poetry and wisdom are found in the third and final division of the Hebrew Bible, the 'Writings' (Hebrew *ketubim*) and in the middle section of the Christian Old Testament. Poetic writing is also found in the Pentateuch, Historical Books, and major sections of the Prophets. In fact, the total volume of poetry in the Old Testament greatly exceeds the whole New Testament, which alone should inspire us to delve into this often neglected material.

But why would God inspire so much poetry in the Bible? Perhaps because poems and poetic stories are so easily remembered, put to music, and used for teaching that they would naturally shape Israel's social and religious life. And perhaps this is because God intentionally formed us humans with a rich, poetic, and imaginative fabric that is the perfect medium to connect us with the God who made us and in whose image we are made.

As alluded to above, these books were at the heart of Israel's ancient worship. The book of Psalms not only provided prayers for the full range of experiences all humans face in daily life, but with unique emotional weight Psalms also retells and interprets Israel's history and her relationship with God and the world. It is thus natural that the Psalms, along with the other books of Old Testament poetry, stood at the centre of 'scrolls' (Hebrew *megillot*) that were read during the annual cycle of Israel's festivals (Ruth, Song of Songs, Ecclesiastes, Lamentations, Esther). In this cycle, the nation rehearsed the story from God's creation and promises to Abraham, to the laws of Moses and God's judgement of Israel for its continual decline into failure and rebellion. The fact that Psalms was so central to this cycle and to Israel's public life also helps us understand how it became the most quoted book in the New Testament, in which the early Church sought to retell

Israel's story in light of Jesus, the long-awaited Messiah. Poetry also served an important role in navigating the countless questions that arise in our day-to-day life. The poetry of the wisdom books deals uniquely with what it means to be human in this world, whether in marriage and work, parenting and politics, finance and friendship, or suffering and lament.

In all of this it cannot be overstated how powerfully the poetic and wisdom books of the Bible shape God's people through emotion, imagination, song, metre, and memory. By inspiring poetic writing, God reveals something critically important about our emotional and imaginative make-up – a fact increasingly reinforced by modern science. Old Testament poetry thus beckons us to renew the use of the arts as we relate to God, to the world, and to our neighbour.

While we will find that the books studied here provide insights for doctrines like justice, sin, salvation, and evil, they are not, as C. S. Lewis says, 'doctrinal treatises nor even sermons'. Lewis continues, '[Psalms] must be read as poems; as lyrics, with all the licences and all the formalities, the hyperboles, the emotional rather than logical connections, which are proper to lyric poetry.'[1] Each of these poetic books works in us through metre, strophe, play, and metaphor. Their sounds and images lead us not merely, or even primarily, to logical truths, but to imagining, feeling, and living obediently in the world they lay out for us. Biblical poetry also involves the full human body, from falling on our faces with Job to raising our voices with lament and our hands in praise with the psalmists. The endless web of metaphors, images of creation, and connections with our physical bodies enables poetry to become part of our daily life and transform us into ardent champions of its message. Poetry thus comes alongside the laws and narratives of the Old Testament to open up our humanity in its fullest and most wonderful potential.

Poetry and Wisdom in overview

Psalms	Praises, thanksgivings, hymns, wisdom songs, liturgies, prayers for help, laments, complaints, imprecations, and guides for spiritual discipline.
Job	A tale of divine wisdom and testing focusing on human suffering, lament, the limits of knowledge, and God's sovereign care for the world.
Proverbs	Instruction in the *ways of things* in the world: wisdom, understanding, knowledge, justice, righteousness, moral quandaries, tact, prudence, love, desire, and wonder – to name but a few.

Ecclesiastes	A candid and often jaded meditation on work, toil, meaning, the absence of meaning, pleasure, joy, loneliness, and death.
Song of Songs	A collection of songs between anonymous lovers and other voices in the community who are witnesses to their conversation.

Poetry and Wisdom in summary

Psalms

Psalms is made up of 150 prayers and is the third longest book in the Bible. Compiled sometime in the second or third century BC, the individual psalms were written over many centuries by several – and, perhaps, a dozen or more – authors. Although David's name appears in the introduction to about half of the psalms, one-third of the psalms do not have headings. Furthermore, the titles or superscriptions at the beginning of these psalms could very well identify the recipient of a psalm or the person overseeing a group of writers, rather than the author. As in most of the books of poetry, the actual authorship is uncertain. As Scripture, Psalms is God's word to us, but Psalms is also prayer – our words back to God. God's revelation of himself in the language of prayed poetry thus simultaneously gives us language necessary for navigating our way – always in search of God's presence – through the winding paths of life in this world. These sung prayers come in an almost infinite variety of forms, yet they all fit within the overarching themes of the first two psalms: Torah ('law, instruction') in Psalm 1 and kingship in Psalm 2. The opening psalm introduces us to the Psalter with a clear portrait of the ways of the righteous and of the wicked. Because the righteous delight in the Torah of God and meditate upon it day and night, God blesses them and causes all of their works to prosper. The wicked, however, perish like chaff blown away by the wind.

Significantly, like the Torah of Moses, or the Pentateuch, the Psalter has been carefully divided into five books (1—41; 42—72; 73—89; 90—106; 107—150) where each collection ends in a doxology (41.13; 72.19; 89.52; 106.48) and the book ends in five psalms of doxology (146—150). Shaped as a *prayed Torah*, Psalms carries the weight and vision of the law given on Mt Sinai. Psalm 2 continues to develop the scene in the first psalm, bidding all of the nations of the earth to bow before the kingship of the Lord and to 'kiss' his Son in worship lest they perish in the fate of the wicked. As we will demonstrate in Part 3 below, these themes of Torah and kingship appear at critical junctures in Psalms, thus reinforcing its central message: this authoritative Torah of psalms is the prayed script by which we live obediently before our God and King.

Job

'It is presumptuous to comment on the book of Job', F. I. Anderson once admitted in the first words of his commentary on the book of Job. In a story that ends with Job saying, 'I lay my hand on my mouth' (40.4), readers encounter one of the strongest lessons in the wisdom literature: there are limits to human knowledge and so also to our ability to fit language to God's ways in the world. And yet, like Anderson in his commentary, we can't help saying more about the story we find within this book of the Bible. Job is perhaps the most unusual book in the Old Testament. It is almost impossible to assign a date or author with any confidence. Its characters are not ethnically Hebrew, and its story takes place outside of Israel. The foreignness this gives to the book is likely meant to accentuate the universal nature of the message, surpassing the borders of religion and race. Similar to parts of Psalm 73 and Proverbs 30, Job portrays a 'World Upside Down' where the righteous suffer with no explanation and no apparent rescue, and God – despite having absolute and sovereign power – not only allows this suffering, but even invites it upon this man and his family. Such a captivating and tragic story forces us into direct confrontation with the problems of justice, evil, suffering, untested faith, mystery and lament in our fallen world. Job does not provide a solution to the mysteries of life; instead it offers us the words and images of the prayers of God's people in the past as they faced the same questions we face in our own lives.

Proverbs

Proverbs is the ABC of biblical wisdom. Whereas Job and Ecclesiastes take wisdom journeys through the darkness and mysterious nature of life in the world, Proverbs offers a basic guide for the order and rhythms of the well-lived life. The frequent refrain in the early chapters of Proverbs, 'Hear, my son', is by no means an indication that proverbs are only for young men. There are proverbs for children, parents, kings, farmers, shoppers, merchants, and more. The address to the son reminds us that these are the basic teachings for every human life – no one can start on the path to parenting, marriage, political rule, gardening, neighbouring, or anything in life without this guide. Because these 915 individual sayings were passed down and collected over the course of many centuries, Proverbs is impossible to tie to a particular author or date. It is likely that its final compilation was in the third or fourth century BC. Proverbs has also been constructed within a frame with two distinct kinds of sayings; each of these sections helps us understand what wisdom is. Chapters 1—9 and 30—31 are the outer frame, made up of long proverb-poems largely dominated by women: the wife, the adulteress, the 'strange' or 'foreign' women, the cosmic Woman Wisdom and Dame Folly in the first nine chapters, and the earthly woman of excellence in chapter 31 who represents expertise in human living. Both sets of female images make wisdom concrete, attractive, and memorable. The women in the first nine chapters reveal wisdom's deep rootedness in God's created order and the central role of human desire in human life. Woman Wisdom herself was the first thing created, which not only makes her an expert in God's construction of the world (Prov. 8.22–36), but also allows her to guide us back to the 'tree of life' (3.18). For the son, wisdom is a sister, wife, and lover (4.6–8; 7.4; 8.32, 36). Meanwhile, the 'valiant' woman in Proverbs 31.10–31 is a poetic vision of what would happen if the cosmic woman of creation in Proverbs 8 became a human person in Israel's ancient world. Her success in every area of life is a resounding proclamation of wisdom's applicability to *everything*. Proverbs 10—29, which reside at the centre of the book, are the more familiar form of individual wisdom sayings. Sometimes these sayings are randomly arranged – mimicking the randomness of life – but other times they are found in longer groups of sayings and proverb poems, as in Proverbs 25—27. We will say more about this arrangement under 'Modern Christianity' below.

Ecclesiastes

Proverbs offers the knowledge for living life well, and Job takes us on a wisdom journey into mystery and the problems of injustice and suffering in a world where God is good and sovereign. Ecclesiastes, meanwhile, voices the often baffling and hazy reality of trying to live such a life. The book invites us to express the sheer despair we reach when trying to be wise. Until the modern era, it was generally assumed that Solomon wrote the book; but this theory does have its problems. Most notably, Solomon is never named; we're only told that the main speaker, 'Qohelet' as he is called, was a king in Jerusalem (1.12). Recent studies of the language and content suggest a date for the book much later than Solomon, though this is not certain. The really significant issue here is that the narrator leaves us the outlines or shadow of a Solomonic persona, or guise, which subtly echoes both Solomon's great wisdom but also his utter failures as a king (1 Kings 2—11): Solomon here and not, Solomon wise and not. Would Solomon really have admitted to us that he could not find wisdom (Eccles. 7.23)? Perhaps. The very uncertainty of the main character, sitting subtly behind the scenes, adds suspense to the difficult message in the book. Could this be Solomon writing about the problem of wisdom? The author has forced us to ask, but not provided an answer.

It has been common throughout history to believe that Ecclesiastes teaches the passing futility of creation and human life, based upon the frequent refrain, 'all is vanity'. Part 2 below explores the history of interpretation in more detail. Suffice it for now to point out that many ancient and modern commentators on the book opt for a way that emphasizes the difficulty of the *search for meaning* in the book rather than the futility of the physical world around us. For one, the word translated 'vanity' is a metaphor deriving from the word 'fog' or 'mist'. Good alternatives to this frequent refrain are 'all is vapour', or 'all is obscurity', which fit well with the guise of Solomon hovering over the book. The real problems in Ecclesiastes are with our ability to *see, reason*, and find *satisfaction* in life, rather than with the stuff of the world itself. This interpretation can be seen in the fact that among Qohelet's many complaints he also affirms the goodness of the world (2.24–25; 3.12, 13, 22; 5.18–19; 8.15). Also, when we compare Ecclesiastes with the other Old Testament wisdom books, we find that they all celebrate the *goodness* of creation (Ps. 8; 19; 104; 147—148; Prov. 3.19; 8.22–31; Job 38—41) and so something deeper must be wrong with Qohelet than his view of matter. Indeed, in Proverbs, Job, and Psalms we hear often that 'the fear of the Lord' is the *beginning* or *starting point* for wisdom, but Ecclesiastes' sole reference to this theme is in the final epilogue in the words of the narrator rather than Qohelet, who says, 'The end of the matter; all has been heard. Fear God and keep his commandments' (12.13). It is highly likely that this anonymous voice at the end has clued us in to the deeper issues in Qohelet's struggle – his inability to place God at the beginning of his search for wisdom. And so the 'end of the matter' is the same as the beginning, and when wisdom comes at last through the very deep fog and friction of life, our ultimate obligation should not have changed: fear God and follow his ways.

Song of Songs

The title Song of Songs (hereafter Songs) and its other known name, Song of Solomon, come from the opening line in the book: 'The song of songs which is Solomon's' (1.1). Solomon never actually speaks in the book but makes appearances as an example or a witness of the anonymous lovers' passions. The actual author is unknown, though there are reasons to think that it might be a woman. We will say more about this below. It is also important to note that, despite an ongoing debate, most contemporary scholars do not believe that Songs is a wisdom book like Proverbs, Job, and Ecclesiastes. This is largely because of differences in the vocabulary and the subject matter. But such a view can be a little misleading, as the book is clearly about how to love well and, in that sense, a book of wisdom for romance. Further, in contrast to every other book in the Old Testament besides Ruth and Esther, the main character in this book is a woman. Yet even the stories of Ruth and Esther are relayed by a narrator and have at least some explicit theological connections, like the favour of the LORD in Ruth and the feast of Purim in Esther. Songs, however, presents the unmediated voice of a woman who speaks for the sake of expounding the beauty of love on its own merits. The reader is struck by the unashamed voice of a woman who speaks almost twice as often as her male counterpart. Many readers might think that women were expected to show greater modesty than men in the ancient world, and this is generally true. But this woman's experience of deep and passionate love has a way of refining social mores. Such passionate, even carnal, images have made Songs a controversial book in the history of the Church, particularly because the songs make no mention of Israel's God, covenants, history, or law, aside from a few references to Solomon. In Part 2 below we will discuss how this largely *secular* book was used for centuries as an allegory for the love between God and his people, and yet today is almost unanimously assumed to be a literal celebration of human sexuality. In Part 3 we will address how it is possible to receive both literal and figurative meanings.

Part 2: Interpretation

Early Christianity

Mark 15.24, 29–34

(c. AD 50–100)

And they crucified him, and divided his clothes among them, casting lots to decide what each should take ...

Those who passed by derided him, shaking their heads and saying, 'Aha! You who would destroy the temple and build it in three days, save yourself, and come down from the cross!' In the same way the chief priests, along with the scribes, were also mocking him among themselves and saying, 'He saved others; he cannot save himself. Let the Messiah, the King of Israel, come down from the cross now, so that we may see and believe.' Those who were crucified with him also taunted him. When it was noon, darkness came over the whole land until three in the afternoon. At three o'clock Jesus cried out with a loud voice, 'Eloi, Eloi, lema sabachthani?' which means, 'My God, my God, why have you forsaken me?'

As noted above, the New Testament cites the Psalms more than any other Old Testament book (approximately 360 times). Although vast in the quantity of its citations, the New Testament authors are actually very selective, choosing a handful of psalms that serve their specific theological purposes. In most of Luke and Acts, for example, Luke chooses to cite specific 'royal psalms' in order to establish Jesus' messianic kingship (e.g. Ps. 2, 16, 69, 109, 118). It should not escape our notice in the excerpt, therefore, that the crucifixion scenes in the Gospels use psalms of individual lament like 22, 31, and 69 to point to Jesus being abandoned by the Father, in Israel's stead, to fulfil his role as the redeemer. The author of Hebrews also uses Psalm 22 in teaching about the suffering Jesus endured – as God – for the world.

This is but one way the poetry is used in the early Church, for the allusive nature of poetic language and the range of content in these biblical books would inspire a diversity of interpretive methods. Psalms was the favourite biblical book of great writers like Augustine, Martin Luther, and John Donne. Writers in the first five centuries of the Church tended to read Psalms with what Susan Gillingham describes as a 'prophetic bias', seeking to show that the Jewish expectations of the Son of David in Psalm 110 and elsewhere have been fulfilled for Christians in Jesus of Nazareth.[2] This strong bias can be found in both the Eastern and Western Churches and in both literal and allegorical ways of interpretation.

The book of Job is rarely cited in the first four centuries of the Church. In those cases references are usually made to Job as a righteous man of God. Job is thus used along with Proverbs 10—29 to support preaching with didactic and moral emphases. As we will see below, however, Song of Songs, Proverbs 31, and Ecclesiastes are in a category of interpretation all their own.

Gregory Nazianzus: *Oratio* XVIII, 7–8

(fourth century AD)

I have heard Scripture saying: 'Who shall find a valiant woman?' and also that she is a gift of God … It is impossible to mention anyone who was more fortunate than my father in this respect.

While some women excel in the management of their households and others in piety – for it is difficult to achieve both – she nevertheless surpassed all in both, because she was pre-eminent in each and because she alone combined the two. She increased the resources of her household by her care and practical foresight according to the standards and norms laid down by Solomon for the valiant woman, as though she knew nothing of piety.[3]

Here Gregory gives us an example of a fourth-century literal interpretation of Proverbs 31. We know of a few other readings like this, but they are greatly outnumbered by the growing preference for allegorical interpretations. These allegorical readings dominated the Church's interpretation in AD 300–1500 and significantly coloured the popular understanding of Proverbs 31, Songs, and Ecclesiastes. These later Church Fathers who favoured the spiritual or allegorical readings of the Old Testament were heavily influenced by the rise of Greco-Roman Gnostic or Neoplatonist thought, which taught that the pursuit of spirituality and holiness meant escaping our bodily and earthly life to an existence in an immaterial state of bliss. Physical matter was believed to be inherently evil. Books and passages like Song of Songs and the valiant woman in Proverbs 31, which celebrated the bodily and material life, simply had to be understood in an allegorical way. Origen is one of the best examples of this strong resistance to literal readings of Songs: 'If these words are not to be spiritually understood, are they not mere tales? If they contain no hidden mystery, are they not unworthy of God?'[4]

The preference for allegorical readings was also helped by Jerome's interpretation of Ecclesiastes. As noted above, it was Jerome who chose to translate the oft-repeated Hebrew word *hebel* with the Latin word *vanitas*, 'vanity'.[5] Jerome was responsible for the creation of the Latin Vulgate, which became the dominant translation used by the Church for over a thousand years. Given the strong resistance to matter and sexuality, Songs was typically taken as an allegory of Jesus' love for the Church or later applied to Mary and to the individual's love for God. When the Council of Constantinople outlawed literal readings of Songs in AD 553, it secured the dominance of allegorical readings for centuries to come. Christians in the West still struggle with this embarrassment with our human sexuality.

Medieval Christianity

The Venerable Bede: *On the Song of Songs*

(pre-AD 750)

For your breasts are better than wine (S. of Sol. 1.2; Vg 1.1), as if she were to say openly: 'The reason that I long for you to come and renew your kisses is that the sweetness of your presence incomparably surpasses all those gifts that you have sent through the heralds of your coming.' For she speaks of the fermentation of knowledge of the law as 'wine,' but by 'breasts' she means the first principles of evangelical faith, concerning which Paul says: *I fed you with milk, not solid food* (1 Cor. 3.2); and again: *For I decided to know nothing among you except Jesus Christ and him crucified* (1 Cor. 2.2) ... I drink wine with my milk (S. of Sol. 5.1). In the gospel [of John] he mystically signifies how much his own wine excels the wine of the law when the old wine was running out at the wedding feast that typified the church, and from water he made new wine that was truly quite deserving of greater praise.[6]

This allegorical reading of Songs, like similar readings of Proverbs 31, became the standard throughout the Middle Ages. Both texts were used to point to the Church and its attributes, or else to the individual soul, or to Mary, the mother of Jesus. Commenting on the woman's fashioning of her own clothing in Proverbs 31.22, Bede says, 'She made for herself a *stragulatam vestem*, fine linen and purple was her clothing. A *stragulata vestis*, which is usually made very stiff by means of varied weaving, signifies the strong deeds of the church and the various ornaments of her virtues ...'

(*Proverbia Salamonis* III, xxxi, 22).[7] Bede, following what had become the authoritative allegorical interpretations of Augustine and Gregory the Great from earlier centuries, demonstrates a major link in a long history of this tradition.

Job is a different story. Although Origen, Chrysostom and Jerome commented on Job, there are few other examples prior to AD 500. Because of Job's tragic storyline and his status as a righteous man, the predominant application is moral or didactic, or for encouragement in persecution. But Job is also sometimes used as a type of the obedient Christian or a type of Christ in his sufferings. As the allegorical method prospered throughout the Middle Ages, several of the more poetic or metaphorical passages in Job attracted many spiritual readings as well.

The growing diversity of interpretation of Job in the Middle Ages is greatly exceeded by the breadth of readings that address Psalms. Medieval writers shifted their focus on Psalms from prophetic fulfilment to prayer, which in turn led to a significant rise in devotional, homiletical and liturgical writings. Psalms was a major influence on the formation of the Benedictine Rule with its daily offices, the Gregorian monastic chants, and the Roman liturgical rites that would form the basis of worship for over a millennium. Psalms also encouraged the reading method known as *lectio divina*, a divine or contemplative reading of Scripture. But Psalms was sometimes read allegorically, particularly after *c.* AD 1100, when Jews who had migrated into Christian communities began producing Jewish interpretations of the Psalter. Many Christians, intent on placing Jesus at the centre of Israel's Scriptures, responded with a full application of the fourfold sense of Psalms: a literal reading of the Davidic history; an allegorical reading of a hidden meaning pointing to Christ, the true Son of David; a tropological or moral reading; and an anagogical reading looking to the Church in eternity.

These readings become increasingly sophisticated, as can be seen in the writings of Thomas Aquinas in the thirteenth century. In the excerpt below, Aquinas comments on the Latin translation of the superscription to Psalm 8: 'unto the end; for the winepresses, A Psalm of David':

Thomas Aquinas: *Postilla Super Psalmos*

(1272/3)

Above is the Psalm in which David prayed on account of his persecution; he sets the Psalm down for the purpose of giving thanks: and, first of all, he begins the Psalm with thanks for the benefits conferred upon the entire human race ...

He says therefore for the presses, that is, the circle of the church: and he calls the church a press because, just as in a press the wine is separated from

---

the lees, so in the church the good are separated from the evil by the work of the ministers: and if not in place, at least by their state of mind ... Likewise, the presses are the martyrdoms, in which the separation of the souls from the bodies is made, for when their bodies, which are tread upon in affliction and persecution for the name of Christ, at the same time remain in the earth, their souls arise to rest in the heavens.[8]

In the way he reads Psalms as simultaneously applying to David, Israel, the Church, and Christ, Aquinas reveals the breadth of his interests in history, theology, and spirituality. Writing in the thirteenth century, he was part of two renewals: one in ancient philosophy among the scholastic thinkers, and the other in the Renaissance return to literature, language, and aesthetics. His writings in commentaries and in his *Summa Theologica* show that he is able to draw both of these movements into his own literary and theological method.

The thirteenth century, in fact, marks the beginning of a shift that would prepare the way for the Reformation. The founding of universities through-out Europe put the Bible in a realm of study that combined theology, literature, and *historia naturalis* – the history of nature. The growing academic attention to the text led to a gradual turn away from older methods of spiritual and allegorical readings. The time period also saw a renewed focus on the whole Old Testament, particularly the 'books of Solomon' – Proverbs, Ecclesiastes, and Songs – which had rarely been stud-ied in previous centuries. Albert the Great, or Albertus Magnus, inspired by the renewal of Aristotelian philosophy of his day, wrote extensively about the relationships between the divisions of the Old Testament. For him, the five books of wisdom (including Wisdom of Solomon, and Sirach, from the Apocrypha/Deutero-Canon) complement the five books of the Pentateuch. Alongside the Law, the function of the three main books of wisdom is to spell out moral goodness: Proverbs is the right middle, Ecclesiastes is the right means, and Songs is the right goal.[9] Many literal readings of Ecclesi-astes would emerge in this period, focused on the author's struggle with specific issues in his world. Still, despite these many advances, writers in this period are not prepared to do away with the older exegetical tradition or to challenge its theology.

Controversies in the Church in the next two centuries go further to pre-pare for the writers of the Reformation. As new moral readings of the Psalter emerge, the penitential psalms become a way to complain against corruption in the Church and the sale of indulgences. They are also used as cries for vindication by those who began to be persecuted for voicing their opposition.

Reformation Christianity

The long chain of allegorical readings in the Church was first seriously questioned in the Renaissance. It was then confronted directly in the Reformation era that followed. Luther, Melanchthon, Brenz, and Calvin all preached messages that reaffirmed the goodness of the created world as expressed in Genesis 1.31, which brought their theological convictions into direct conflict with the prevailing interpretations of Songs and Ecclesiastes at that time. For example, when Desiderius Erasmus produced a new translation and publication of Jerome's works in the sixteenth century, it became immediately accessible to the early Reformers, who were dismayed at Jerome's reading of Ecclesiastes, as can be seen in these excerpts:

Martin Luther: 'Notes on Ecclesiastes' (1532)	Johannes Brenz: *Der Prediger Salomo* (1528)
No less noxious for a proper understanding of this book has been the influence of many of the saintly and illustrious theologians in the church who thought that in this book Solomon was teaching what they call 'the contempt for the world' ... It was taught that to be a Christian meant to forsake the household, the political order, even the Episcopal ... office, to flee to the desert, to isolate oneself from society, to live in stillness and silence; for it was impossible to serve God in the world. The proper contempt of the world is not that of the man who lives his life in solitude away from human society, nor is the proper contempt of gold that of the man who throws it away or who abstains from money, as the Franciscans do, but that of the man who lives his life in the midst of these things and yet is not carried away by his affection for them.[10]	In short, all creatures, namely riches, honor, power, joy, pleasure, health, and other things are very good, and gifts of God. But because man is so very corrupt and ruined because of sin, they are to him a vain and empty thing, and can give him no satisfaction.[11]

According to Luther, Jerome had so strongly emphasized the helpless vanity in the world that Christians were left with no choice but to abandon it. Brenz similarly argues that Ecclesiastes was not written to condemn the physical world or even our use of it – as the creation is unquestionably good – but to emphasize the discord sin has brought on the relationship between humans and the creation. The Reformers' bold reactions to exclusive allegory and its counterpart of abandon or escape from the world are also paralleled by a growth of more literal or embodied readings throughout Europe in both Protestant and Catholic circles. The re-reading of Ecclesiastes as a more complex message about the problems of the creation – with its contradictions that both affirm and critique the physical life – goes hand in hand with new readings of the Song of Songs and Proverbs 31, taking the literal portrayals of sexuality and vocation as the central meanings:

John Donne: *Sermon* No. 9	George Herbert: 'Psalm 23' in *The Temple*
(1626)	(1633)
How plentifully, how abundantly is the word *Beatus, Blessed,* multiplied in the Booke of Psalmes? Blessed, and Blessed, in every Psalme, in every Verse; the booke seems to be made out of that word, Blessed, And the foundation raysed upon that word, Blessed, for it is the first word of the Booke.[12]	The God of love my shepherd is, And he that doth me feed: While he is mine, and I am his, What can I want or need?
	He leads me to the tender grass, Where I both feed and rest; Then to the streams that gently passe; In both I have the best ...
	Yea, in deaths shadie black abode Well may I walk, not fear: For thou art with me; and thy rod To guide, thy staff to bear.[13]

Whereas the Reformers demonstrate a strong attraction to the theological content of these books, notwithstanding an appreciation for their literary beauty, it is the poets of the seventeenth century more than anyone before them who point us to the magnificence of biblical poetry. Among these poets are John Donne, Sir Philip Sidney, Mary Sidney, George Herbert, and John Milton, all of whom leaned extensively upon Psalms for both its message and its lyrical metre. Donne tells us that Psalms was his favourite biblical book; one-fifth of his sermons come from it. The Psalms also dominate Herbert's more than 70 religious poems compiled in *The Temple*.

Donne was also fond of the books of Proverbs and Job, both of which inspired many sermons, and the latter of which inspires stanza XXIII of *A Litany*:

John Donne: *A Litany*

(1608–9)

Hear us, O hear us, Lord; to Thee
A sinner is more music, when he prays,
Than spheres' or angels' praises be,
In panegyric alleluias;
   Hear us, for till Thou hear us, Lord,
   We know not what to say;
Thine ear to our sighs, tears, thoughts, gives voice and word.
O Thou, who Satan heard'st in Job's sick day,
Hear Thyself now, for Thou in us dost pray.[14]

In the wake of the Reformation, the Bible became a book of the people. And Protestants became a people of the book – *Sola Scriptura*, 'Scripture Alone'. This new Reformation vision would clearly result in a significant increase in popular reading of the Bible. But the spirit of the Reformation also had roots in the rising secular moods of freedom, individualism, and reason that stood over against faith, tradition, and community. The Age of Reason and the Enlightenment in the next century would ride this wave to put universities in the place of churches, and scholars in the place of priests. Culture had a new emerging centre and the zenith of this new secular movement would come in nineteenth-century Germany, as we will see below.

Two other important developments occurred in the post-Reformation era that would shape wisdom and poetry studies into what they have become today. One is the sophisticated study of Hebrew poetry, fostered more than anything by Robert Lowth's *Lectures on the Sacred Poetry of the Hebrews* (1753). The second is the archaeological discovery of Egyptian and Mesopotamian wisdom and poetry in the early twentieth century. Together, these watershed events would yield fields of study that are vastly beyond all the works devoted to Hebrew poetry in the first 18 centuries of Christianity.

Modern Christianity

Inspired by developments in science and philosophy in the nineteenth century, studies in the wisdom literature, and biblical studies in general, were shaped by German scholars' search for the history and evolutionary development of Israel and its sacred texts. J. G. Eichhorn marks the end of an era. Having written the standard German *Introduction to the Old Testament* in 1803, he was sensitive to new ideas about a history behind the text, but still saw Solomon, for example, as the author of most of the wisdom literature. He also assumed that the wisdom movement was early, or dating to Solomon and earlier. The matter of Solomon's authorship is probably minor on the whole, but shortly after Eichhorn, Wilhelm Vatke (1835) would reject Solomonic authorship and begin a trend of re-dating the Old Testament that would be embodied by everyone who followed him, from the conservative scholar Franz Delitzsch to the mastermind of the Documentary Hypothesis, Julius Wellhausen. The wisdom movement was summarily re-dated as a post-exilic phenomenon, the general consensus being that wisdom was practical philosophy or humanist reflections of the Yahwist movement in late Israelite history, which, having rejected or moved away from the Law and the covenants of earlier history, sought to find new ways to live as a people dispersed and scattered throughout the Near East. The evolutionary approach to biblical studies and Israelite history became the dominant mode of research throughout universities of the West.

But the twentieth century would challenge and reframe many of these assumptions. Most notably, the discovery of ancient Mesopotamian and Egyptian artefacts (mentioned above) showed that wisdom was much older than had been assumed in recent decades and that wisdom was not a purely secular or pagan movement without theological foundations. Starting in 1970, wisdom studies expanded rapidly, particularly through comparisons with newly found ancient Near Eastern texts. The new century also brought new freedom to reading the Bible as a singular canon with a united theological message. Part of this shift was motivated by Karl Barth's commentary on Romans in 1919, which sought to recapture Christ's life, death, and resurrection as the central truth in the Old and New Testament Scriptures. Another factor that shaped the twentieth century came in the Biblical Theology Movement, which took place among academic non-conformists like Barth. The return to reading the Old Testament theologically was far from universal, but it did leave marked cultural effects. For one, the secular indifference to the Bible from the previous century was no longer the norm. Second, whereas lines between Anglican, Catholic, Lutheran, Reformed, and Jewish communities were once strong, the twentieth century saw new avenues of co-operation both in churches and among academics.

Gerhard von Rad: *Wisdom in Israel*

(1970)

… it is obvious that the fear of God is regarded as something which is given precedence over all wisdom. In its shadow, wisdom is assigned its place; it is, therefore, the prerequisite of wisdom and trains man for it … It contains in a nutshell the whole Israelite theory of knowledge. There lies behind the statement an awareness of the fact that the search for knowledge can go wrong … because of one single mistake at the beginning. To this extent, Israel attributes to the fear of God, to belief in God, a highly important function in respect of human knowledge. She was, in all seriousness, of the opinion that effective knowledge about God is the only thing that puts a man into a right relationship with the objects of his perception.

Did not Israel, in all her attempts to perceive the course of human experience, always come back to Yahweh who comprehended all things in power? … This means that Israel was obliged to remain open, in a much more intensive way, to the category of the mysterious.[15]

Von Rad writes within this new theological momentum of the twentieth century, aided by the discoveries of the ancient Near Eastern wisdom documents mentioned above. In the excerpts we can see how he highlights two unique traits in Israel's wisdom when compared with its neighbours. One is that the 'fear of the Lord' was the essential condition for Israel's view of life and knowledge. Two, and related to this, because Israel believed in a single sovereign creator rather than a competition among deities, the nation had to develop the virtue of living with mystery and wonder at the centre of the life of wisdom; if there is only one God, chaos and injustice cannot be blamed on conflicts between the gods. In many ways von Rad's work marks the point at which the modern theological study of wisdom began.

The most significant growth of renewed interfaith studies in the Church and in academic circles occurs in the 1980s, where we find renewed interest in the shape of the canon, the theological interpretation of the Bible, intertextual and modern linguistic analysis, and the study of the Bible as literature. Pre-eminent scholars like Brevard Childs, Robert Alter, Michael Fishbane, James Kugel, Meir Sternberg, Harold Fisch, and others, greatly refreshed the interest in the poetry and narrative of the Bible. Emerging scholars in these fields explored the individual and corporate voices in Lamentations and Ecclesiastes using Rhetorical Criticism, while liturgical and anthropological studies helped shed new light on rituals of lament in the book of Job. Scholars also begin to examine epistemology – what it means to know something – in books like Exodus, Ecclesiastes, and Ezekiel. And with the advent of canonical interpretation at Yale, readers began to explore the final shape of Psalms, the Minor Prophets, and the four Gospels.

Gerald H. Wilson: *The Editing of the Hebrew Psalter*

(1985)

... I am convinced by the data that there are clear indications of editorial activity throughout [the Hebrew Psalter]. These are not isolated examples of limited editorial concern, but are part of a broader editorial movement to unify the 150 psalms into a coherent whole. Further, while this movement is into a totally new rearrangement of all 150 psalms, it does move consistently and purposefully and so joins and arranges early collections, individual psalms and later groupings, that the final product speaks the message intended by the final editors(s).[16]

Riding the early wave of these expanding disciplines, Gerald Wilson sharply criticized trends within nineteenth-century Psalms studies that focused on smaller and smaller fragments of texts and supposed traditions within, or behind, the Old Testament. In his response, Wilson leveraged discoveries of ancient Near Eastern psalm collections together with advanced poetic analysis of the Psalter in order to demonstrate the strategic thinking that motivated the shaping of the 150 psalms we have in our Bibles today. His research sparked its share of controversy about the actual degree of shaping we can find in the Psalter, but he has been convincing enough to shift the lines of research significantly towards the overall unity of the Psalter when compared with the generations of scholars that preceded him. Some of the generally accepted conclusions emerging from Wilson's and others' works in this area include: (1) the Psalter was carefully divided into five books, mimicking the five books of the Pentateuch; (2) the first three books of the Psalter (1—89) are dominated by individual laments; (3) kingship and Torah stand at the introduction (1—2) and major seams between the books of the Psalter; (4) David as an author of psalms and a historical figure in the book almost entirely disappears in book III (73—89); and (5) Books IV and V (90—150) are dominated by communal praise, with significant elements of the Lord's kingship evidenced in the Enthronement Psalms (90—100), the Psalms of Ascent (120—134), and the final five doxologies (146—150).

A related path of research emerged in the study of Proverbs with an interest in the many macro- and micro-structures, poems, repeated sayings, and clusters of sayings that provide a degree of shape to the over 500 seemingly disconnected individual sayings in chapters 10—29. Scholars had already recognized that Proverbs 1—9 had been carefully shaped around poems focused on feminine metaphors and instructions from the father to his son. But now scholars came to find a conspicuous unity to the sayings in chapters 10—15 as well. In the span 10.1—15.33, 169 of the 184 sayings appear in antithetical forms, e.g. 'The prudent keep their knowledge to themselves, but a fool's heart blurts out folly' in 12.23 (NIV). Only 15 sayings appear in some other form, such as, 'Like vinegar to the teeth, and smoke to the eyes, so are the lazy to their employers' in 10.26. These six chapters also focus on two sets of opposition: the 'righteous' and 'wicked', and the 'wise' and 'foolish'. These emphases disappear sharply after 16.1. Scholars also soon recognized that chapters 25—27 showed many signs of being collected around repeated sounds, themes, and catchwords, especially chapters 25—26. The most distinct example is the sayings regarding the fool in 26.1–12.

Knut M. Heim: *Poetic Imagination in Proverbs*

(2013)

... the wisdom presented in Proverbs is not a strict system of simple rules that can be applied in all circumstances but is a more flexible understanding of the world that sheds light on the multifaceted complexities of life: many circumstances combine to form the various life situations that demand decisions informed by true wisdom. Perhaps this is reflected in the different sorts of connections that can sometimes be drawn between the various individual proverbs and their environments.

... [the] truly creative features of poetry are hard to pin down, and this is where intuition and imagination become crucial. Imaginative and skilful interpretation of poetry recognizes poetry as a normal form of human communication.

The creative repetition of repetition with variation is the very essence of poetry. What has been written with imagination, must be read with imagination.[17]

Working within these new explorations in Proverbs, Knut Heim tackles two major issues – one of identifying clusters and poems within these sayings, and the other of accounting for over 200 repeated sayings within the book. Some examples of the obvious clusters appear in the sayings regarding Yahweh and the king in 16.1–15 and the sayings about malicious and righteous characters in 16.27–33. When it comes to explaining why Proverbs repeats over 200 individual lines (almost 25 per cent of the book), Heim shows that the sayings often provide structural markers, and in most cases have been edited slightly to fit with the sounds and themes in their surrounding contexts (e.g. 10.13; 19.29; 26.3 or 11.14 and 29.18). Heim says that these new insights show us that Proverbs has been organized in a way that trains us to develop a 'more flexible understanding of the world' where our ability to find unity and affinity among various groups of sayings trains us to find order and meaning among life circumstances that otherwise appear random and senseless.

As we have moved through the early years of the twenty-first century the theological and academic consensuses of past centuries have lost the hold they had on much of biblical studies. On the one hand, the failures of strict rationalism and evolutionary social thought that fuelled two world wars, along with the critiques from postmodernism and other social studies, have together opened biblical studies into countless new and creative directions. And so we find all new areas of growing interest in the Bible and everything from philosophy, poetry, gender, and other interdisciplinary fields, to new ventures in liturgical, religious, and theological interpretation. At the same time, the uneasy sense that we have lost a grip on firm ground or boarders for the discipline has somewhat ironically re-situated historical and socio-critical studies as the default mode of interpretation in the academy. This return to nineteenth-century methodology has been largely motivated by the feeling that secular scientific readings provide a greater degree of objectivity than the many new approaches to biblical interpretation, despite what many modern philosophers would say about the illusion of objectivity within the humanities. All that said, we can fairly describe our current situation as one of fuzzy pluralism – a pluralism that sits alongside the rapidly expanding Church in Asia and the 'Global South'. As we will see below, new readings are emerging from each of these unique cultural settings where the Bible is being read.

Global Christianity

'Struggle' may be the word that best describes African and Latin American interpretation of the Bible. The struggle has two sides. The first is the *academic* and *theoretical description* of the struggle in the 'Global South'. Most of this academic writing happens to be conducted in Western universities alongside North American Black Theology and Feminist Theology. In fact, in both the West and the South, those who write academically about the struggle of the South tend to be highly educated members of privileged society, not those characterized by the struggle itself. Those masses that are the subject of their study represent the second side of struggle: the extreme poor, the oppressed, women and children of the world gathered in local churches. Largely unaware of the critical methods that universities use to describe their plight, the masses tend to read the text as a literary whole, looking for present, existential meaning – indeed, most often to cope with their own very real struggles. The pressing burden of these marginalized readers of the Bible is to identify with the physical descriptions of poverty and oppression, unlike the majority in the West who tend to give poverty and wealth purely spiritual meanings. The South also gravitates naturally to the concrete and agricultural world of the Bible as a way of understanding and living out their faith.

Dorothy B. E. A. Akoto: 'The Mother of the Ewe and Firstborn Daughter'

(2000)

1 My Mother, my shepherd,
Because of your industry as an economist, trading and toiling endlessly
I never know want; Your dependants and more are provided for.
2 You jealously guard law and order in the community as a politician,
Ensuring that they provide for the welfare of all and sundry.
3 When the community is sick and waywardness is rising,
Your instructions lead and direct toward the right ways of living,
The health of the community is restored.
4 Even when life becomes tempestuous, the future unknown and scary,
When situations are threatening and trying, there is no cause for alarm,
For your teachings, your instructions are always there to guide.
Your words of chastening are a source of purification and encouragement.
5 You jealously guard the good because you are 'nyornu' (maker of good things)
Your eyes are always fixed on the prize.
Your words of praise, comfort and encouragement make you an educator for
they nullify feelings of bitterness and hatred and restore peace and calm.
6 My Mother, my shepherd, the good and rightful paths in which you offer training,
Your tender love and care will always abide.
As long as I live, I will continue to bask in your amazing motherliness.
Surely, your guidance, your counsel, your industry will be appropriated forever and ever.[18]

In Akoto's poem quoted here we can see two sides of the struggle mentioned above: in Akoto's academic theory and in the text that speaks within the Global South. The Ewe ('Ei-way') peoples of the Volta Region of southeastern Ghana are among the struggling masses in the majority world. The Ewe are naturally drawn to the powerful liberation images in Psalm 23, Ezekiel 34, and John 10. Yet, having no shepherds in their culture, their understanding of liberation in these passages is largely abstract and distant. As a liberation scholar, Akoto frees the Ewe from the 'abstract' biblical imagery imposed on them by Western missionaries and recasts the shepherd as a woman in order to link the liberating image of the shepherd with the history of oppressed women in Ghana's history.

Akoto's creative paraphrase makes the passage immediately relevant for a people that naturally associate the woman with bringing life to a community. Yet her poetry also illumines the extraordinary range of biblical readings in African cultures and suggests why it is that many African scholars are calling for a greater understanding of their own hermeneutic, for cultural adaptation inevitably leaves gaps in meaning. For example, in the ancient Israelite Hebrew world the shepherd is also a symbol of kingship and rule echoing back to humans exercising care for the animals in Genesis 1. But these connections cannot be reproduced in Akoto's poem. That does not diminish her efforts, but it does raise questions about the methods and aims of translation, exposition, and preaching. Just what are the benefits and dangers of paraphrases and cultural adaption? These are questions that many African scholars seek to address today.

When Liberation Theology first emerged in Latin America 50 years ago, it was characterized by what Néstor Míguez has called the 'fundamentalism of the left', which read the Bible to make explicit connections with the conditions of the poor and oppressed.[19] This movement was reinforced by the success of the Cuban revolution, which led to Latin American resistance and revolt. Two major factors then continued to shape the new fundamentalism from the left. The first was the exposure to European and North American writings that gradually broadened theological reading of the Bible. At the same time, the hopes of liberation in the middle of the twentieth century were crushed as dictators and oppressive governments rose to power. Latin America now exists under a new age of exploitation and repression, where the Bible continues to be a message of hope for liberation, but even more as a source of comfort in continued suffering.

Elsa Tamez: *When the Horizons Close: Rereading Ecclesiastes*

(2000)

God made human beings straightforward, 'but they have devised many schemes' (7.29). For Qohelet, then, the world as *hebel*, is not the work of a star-crossed, tragic destiny; rather it is human beings themselves who turned it upside down. An inverted reality complicates the possibility of finding new horizons under the sun ...

Justice for the poor and oppressed is an implicit desire behind Qohelet's rejection of the present. That is obvious; the key points of his discourse reveal it. Society is inverted, with wickedness in the place of justice (3.16); power is in the hands of the oppressors; the poor are violently oppressed, and there is no one to comfort their tears (4.1). The state does not fulfill its task of administering justice and social welfare (5.8), and the tyranny of the king is unbearable; no one can reproach him, for he does whatever he pleases as if he were God (8.3–4), and his spies are all around (10.20).[20]

Tamez's feminist reading of the Bible cited here represents a large and growing trend in Latin America. Scholars like Tamez are not in the least unaware of the fact that children and men also suffer under the same economic and cultural conditions, as can be seen in Tamez's application of the message in Ecclesiastes to modern Latin America. But women occupy a unique place. The suffering of the men in Latin America has indeed been humiliating and dehumanizing, but has also fuelled a masochistic response in which men cope by turning to alcohol, sexual licentiousness, and oppression of their own women. The situation is complex, with one set of injustices leading to another. The woman stands in a symbolic place, able to give new life to the people of Latin America and be an example of endurance and courage when there is often little sign of hope.

Africa and Latin America have both attracted a breadth of non-governmental organizations who work against oppression in labour, treatment of children, and care for the land. Not only are these groups more academically aware, they are prone to read the Bible through the framework of their political or social interests. As we see in the excerpt below from Mark Fang, the same is true in Asia:

Mark Fang: 'Translating and Chanting the Psalms'

(2008)

The psalms that Jiang Wenye had set to music [1946] played a significant part in the vigorous development of the Taiwanese Catholic Church at this key time in the 1960s and 1970s. The success of the Jesuit Guangqi Press at Taizhong, for example, is generally recognized as resting on two books: ... the *Complete New Testament* ... and the collected assortment of ritual songs, *Collected Sacred Songs*. This was the first such scale edition of collected religious songs published by Taiwanese Catholics, and included a dozen of Jiang Wenye's compositions. The second hymn collection, which followed on from this was the truly epoch-making: *Shengjing Yuezhang*, the Chinese edition of *Biblical Hymns and Psalms* ... This volume was published in September 1970 by the Guangqi Press in a run of 5,000, which rapidly sold out, with a revised reprint of 3,000 coming out in November. This collection of songs clearly met the needs of the post-Vatican II era.[21]

The prolific growth of Christianity in Asia testifies to Scripture's power to communicate across cultural lines. Although the first modern missionary effort reached China in the nineteenth century, it was not until after the Second World War that the most significant growth began. Fang chronicles the Taiwanese Catholic use of Psalms as a part of a larger discussion on use of the Psalter throughout Asia's post-war era. The renowned Chinese musician Jiang Wenye, cited above, is said to have devoured the Psalter on his first reading, feeling compelled to vow to God to set the whole collection to music, which he did. The Chinese appreciation for poetry and music led to a natural attraction to the Psalms and to their rapid assimilation into Chinese Christians' life and worship.

But Bible interpretation in Asia, and especially in China, is still in its infancy and has to be understood in the context of these cultural traditions and history, particularly the cultural power of authoritative Chinese writings like Confucius. On the one hand, this has made the Bible easy to receive as a book of powerful moral instruction. On the other hand, it tends to inhibit the full reception of the whole of the Christian message. For example, Chinese tradition is sometimes used to critique Scripture as a source of roughly equal authority and, though Jesus has been culturally understood as a wise moral teacher, the importance of the Old Testament is often lost.

Above all, the language gap in Asia and the difficulty in translating the Bible into so many dialects are the greatest concerns. For one, most of Asia faces a clash with the West in its encounter with modernization and education, leading to the need to differentiate Western culture from Western Christianity, and both of these from biblical Christianity. An even deeper issue in translation arises out of the way the first Western missionaries taught and selectively reproduced texts and expositions of the Bible for rather narrow purposes (usually to plant more churches), a selectivity that colours most reception of the Bible in Asia. With its enormous population and growth, the Church in China in particular is in need of consistent theological education and training in reading the Bible.

Part 3: Application

Poetry and Wisdom in ministry

The advent of the twentieth century marks a break with 2,000 years of tradition in which the Psalms were read or sung in almost every church in weekly worship. Aside from the random church here and there, the wisdom literature has not been a major focus in the last century either. While poetry does not feature centrally in our lives, it did in Israel's and does in much of the non-Western world today. This lack of interest in the developed world is partly due to overstimulation. Poetry demands focused attention for it to work in us through its pictures, emotions, places, and memories. Biblical poetry is also laden with images and metaphors from the natural world, and the fact that most of us live increasingly urbanized lives sheltered from stars, wildlife, forests, and natural sources of water increases the distance we feel from these books. The ancient appreciation for the grandeur and necessity of biblical poetry needs to be renewed today.

In this light, while it is well recognized that the basic shape of the Bible is narrative, poetry is the flare that brings the story to life in manifold ways.

It comes from within the story and goes beyond it to achieve something narrative cannot on its own. In his recent work on cultural practices, James K. Smith alerts us to how poetry and liturgies, or practices, are interwoven with our affections and emotions.[22] In the West, our poetry and practices are more or less dominated by television, the internet, shopping malls, video games, college dormitories, advertising, and sport stadiums, whose catchy music and addictive rituals capture our affections and loyalties. Ancient Israel lived with similar temptations and alternative rituals that came from neighbouring cultures. But Israel also had deeply traditioned ways of turning to poetry in the home, in the festival seasons, and at the temple and synagogue. These poetic readings inspired Israel in embodied and creative ways to remember and return to worship Yahweh and follow his revelation. The Church needs to discover that these biblical prayers, poems, and narratives have immense power to recapture our affections for God and his Kingdom.

Another important reason to attend to poetry is the way it works to heal and shape us spiritually and psychologically. The medical and psychiatric professions today attest overwhelmingly to the way poetry, music, and art bring integration and wholeness out of anxiety, loneliness and depression. The psychiatrist Curt Thompson explains that, 'Reading poetry has the effect of catching us off guard. Our imaginations are invigorated when our usual linear expectations of prose … don't apply. This can stimulate buried emotional states and buried memories.'[23] As we move between processing in the left brain (analytical) and right brain (emotive and imaginative), new neural pathways form that allow understanding, integration, stability, and resolution. How significant then that the Bible gives us so much poetry. Rather than telling us to pray, praise, or be wise, it repeatedly *involves* us in confessing, lamenting, proclaiming, and imagining: 'the earth is the Lord's'; 'he founded it upon the waters'; 'save those who pursue me … lest he rend me to pieces like a lion'; 'he makes wars to cease to the ends of the earth'; 'he stores up wisdom for the upright; he is a shield to those who walk in integrity'; and '[wisdom] is a tree of life to those who grasp her'.

Such insights into poetry open new windows into the interpretation of the book of Songs. While it is true that the early ascetic theologians were embarrassed by its literal descriptions of sexuality, and thus refused to read it as such, it does not follow that their allegorical readings are without merit. Songs has ways of resisting a narrow or singularly literal interpretation of marital love. Notice that the nuptial imagery in the book was already one of the most familiar images used by the prophets to symbolize the relationship between God and Israel. It is likely that the author(s) of Songs adopts these familiar prophetic images of women and marriage for a new purpose, yet without excluding the symbolic meaning from which they came. Notice also how we can see the nuanced meaning of Songs in the way it was placed in the Hebrew and Christian canons, respectively. In the Jewish canon, Songs was placed among the wisdom Writings, after Proverbs and Ruth, and before Ecclesiastes. Brevard Childs observes that in this place Songs was naturally read within the emphasis of the wisdom literature: the pursuit of life in the world and 'the mystery of love within the created order'.[24] When the Christians reordered these books, they placed Ecclesiastes and Song of Songs between Proverbs and Isaiah. In this place, says Childs, 'the book is made to symbolize the prophetic themes of God's love for his people, of the new exodus, etc. ... themes which are missing in the wisdom corpus'.[25] Childs thus shows that Songs was naturally written in a way that could serve multiple meanings.

Paul Ricoeur explains how this double meaning works at a literary level, noting that Songs is both 'over-' and 'underdetermined'. By this he means that the specific identity of the lover in the book (a Shulamite), her friends and parents, and the references to places and meetings, give us a sense of over-determination that wants us to imagine a literal couple. But then the book withholds many expected things, such as names or any connection to God, Israel, the Law or the covenants. This under-determination works against the literal sense in favour of a more symbolic meaning. While this may not warrant an allegorical reading of Proverbs 31 – which does not have the same sense of a particular person in the past nor the absence of clear references to God – it does suggest that the poetic texts of the Bible, as C. S. Lewis says, are naturally given to second meanings, which keep the interpreter from closing them down with analytical certainty. And as recent science of the mind reveals, this kind of imaginative activity is essential to our spiritual and psychological health.

The wisdom books also provide endless resources for ministry. Africa and China share traditions of wisdom, proverbs, and folk sayings that have allowed for a greater appreciation of wisdom than in the West. But the fragmented nature of life in the West, accentuated by the cultural power of technology, is urgently in need of the concrete guidance that wisdom gives for daily life. Grounded in the creation, wisdom ties even the smallest things we do to the grand cosmic order of God's universe. Wisdom thus gives back the sense of an integrated whole that the Western world does so much to destroy.

Wisdom and poetry also foster spirituality and a life of prayer. Whether through Job's candid prayers to God, the massive collection of sung prayers in Psalms, or the 14 refrains in Proverbs that proclaim the 'fear of the Lord is the beginning of wisdom', wisdom and poetry lead us to worship the one true God and to live our lives in constant conversation with him. Consider further how individual proverbs invite careful meditation to search through their many sayings for the guidance to navigate through the grey and uncertain circumstances of daily life. The 'fear of the Lord' imagines the prayerful way this is to be done. It is perhaps well known in New Testament studies that Paul's prayers in Ephesians, Philippians, Colossians, and Philemon all ask for *wisdom*, *understanding*, and *insight*. In the larger context of these prayers, Paul wants people to connect the radical fact of Jesus' resurrection to its power to make all the people and the things of the world new again.

Paul's model for getting such wisdom is prayer – a spiritual discipline of coming into the presence of God to have him put the pieces in place for us so that we may see our place in God's reconciling all things to himself.

Poetic and wisdom literature are also helpful in times of anguish, confusion, and suffering. The book of Ecclesiastes, often preached or read in small parts, tends to be overlooked as one person's vexing journey to find wisdom and meaning in life. Qohelet's encounters with obscurity and despair, sitting alongside his hope and faith, assure readers that confusion is endemic to the human condition. But Ecclesiastes also encourages us to wrestle prayerfully through our experience with faith in God. Job's message, meanwhile, takes us on a journey through the terror of suffering and injustice in the world. Characteristic of wisdom literature, it connects Job's suffering to God's cosmic designs for the universe. And there are times when that must suffice for an answer. To be sure, God does not seek to justify himself against the claim that the existence of evil taints his character. Thus a large part of wisdom is developing habits of affirming the goodness of God in the face of mystery – but not without prayer and complaint. The dozens of lament psalms reinforce, along with Job, God's invitation to us to pray honestly and often in our journey through the dark night.

Poetry and Wisdom in mission

According to Christopher Wright, mission is God's work to make himself known to every person in every nation, deal with the offences of sin, defeat evil, destroy death, remove enmity between Jews and Gentiles (and all nations), and heal the whole creation.[26] The gospel invites us to believe in the victorious work of Jesus the Messiah and become participants in this work. Wisdom and poetry are essential companions for the journey before us, for, like wisdom and poetry, the eyes of mission are on the creator and his work to bring the world to its final, ordered, and glorious end.

From start to finish, the Psalter looks through Israel to its role in being a blessing to the nations. Psalm 2 calls for the kings of the earth to bow before the Lord's anointed, and this anticipates Psalm 72, the last psalm in book III as it envisages all rulers and nations bowing before Israel's king because he has modelled the worship of Yahweh and manifested his just and righteous government among all people. The string of Enthronement Psalms from 96 to 99 all hope for the conversion and praise of the nations, ending with Psalm 100, which calls for all the earth to praise him. The same climactic note ends the Psalter: 'let everything that breathes praise the LORD' (150.6). The image of a reconciled humanity is unmistakable: the divisions between Jew and Gentile, slave and free, North and South, will be broken in the gathering before the Lord at his throne.

Old Testament wisdom and poetry also ground *worship* in a missional, world-gathering vision. In the West, worship has been formed primarily around abstract theological ideas that make it uninviting to outsiders, especially those in severe physical or emotional suffering, children, the mentally handicapped, and those from foreign cultures or non-Christian backgrounds. Worship that is more intentionally grounded in aesthetics, ritual, and participation – poetry, colour, music, physical movement, creative lighting, and liturgical seasons – crosses these barriers and provides a context in which people can enter into God's presence in mutual participation: mind and body, together. After all, the dual focus of word and sacrament – proclamation and enactment – in the historic Christian Church takes its roots from ancient Jewish liturgy, which seamlessly blends festival, song, story, law, and ritual.

The wisdom literature spends a considerable amount of space helping us to understand and respond to the wounds within individual humans and society as a whole. Job's non-Jewish identity is a reminder to the reader that the suffering of humanity crosses all boundaries and that we all need comfort and wisdom as we make our way through life. A major portion of the book of Proverbs is devoted to the issues of wealth and poverty, both to the fact of their inevitability and to the reality that they represent the broader areas of injustice and suffering in all their manifestations. Wisdom takes a stand against oppression, calling for just weights and measures (Prov. 20.10, 23), honest handling of private affairs (3.27–30) and justice and righteousness in all our ways (1.3; 2.8–9; 8.20; 21.3). Proverbs also ends with strong images of just and righteous behaviour. When King Lemuel recounts his mother's instructions, justice, mercy, and care for the poor appear centrally: 'Open your mouth for those who are mute, for the cause of all those who are passing away. Open your mouth, judge righteously; plead the cause of the poor and oppressed' (31.8–9). Proverbs fittingly ends with a celebration of the valiant woman of wisdom. Not only does she excel at everything she does, from marriage and parenting to industry, teaching and crafts, but she also cares for her servant girls (31.15), and 'opens her hands to the poor and stretches out her hands to the needy' (31.20). Wisdom thus leads us to gaze on the order and wholeness in God's own creative work and then seek to restore whatever we find in our world that is broken and out of place.

The books of poetry and wisdom are also distinctly rooted in the celebration of the goodness of God's creation. In Job, the theme of creation offers a testimony of God's power and wisdom that go beyond the limits of our reason. Psalms and Proverbs call for celebration of the exquisite order in creation: 'O Lord, how wonderful are your works; in wisdom you have made them all' (Ps. 104.24). This echoes the experience of the Woman Wisdom in Proverbs 8, who, in witnessing the creation of the world, exclaims, 'I was dancing for his world, his earth, and delighting in the sons of men' (8.31). Song of Songs meanwhile celebrates the goodness of sexuality in the context of love. Given these many positive views of the world we are able to paraphrase Paul's statement in Romans 8.22 and say: the whole creation groans with longing for redemption from prostitution, human trafficking, global warming, soil erosion, pollution, and the destruction of habitats that lead to extinction of species. Paul's personification of a groaning creation reinforces the goodness of creation in the Old Testament, emphatically echoed throughout literature of wisdom and poetry.

The poetry and wisdom of the Bible has enormous potential for the life of a culturally and globally diverse Church today. Accompanying the narrative that runs from creation, promise, law, and covenants to gospel and mission, poetry constantly reorientates us to our embodied humanity and our place in the world as creatures of dust, image, rhythm, feeling, and hope for a new creation.

Notes

1 Lewis, C. S. 1958, *Reflections on the Psalms*, New York: Harcourt, Brace and Company, pp. 2–3.

2 Gillingham, S., 2008, *Psalms through the Centuries*, Oxford: Blackwell, vol. 1, pp. 24–46.

3 McCauley, L. P. (tr.), 1953, *Funeral Orations by Saint Gregory Nazianzen and Saint Ambrose*, FOTC, 22, Washington, DC: Catholic University of America Press, pp. 124–5.

4 Lawson, R. P. (tr.), 1957, *Origen: The Song of Songs: Commentary and Homilies*, Westminster, MD: Newman Press, p. 270.

5 Kallas, E., 1979, 'Ecclesiastes: Traditum et Fides Evangelica', PhD dissertation, Graduate Theological Union, Berkeley, CA, 1979, pp. 58–88.

6 Holder, A. (ed.), 2011, *The Venerable Bede: On the Song of Songs and Selected Writings*, New York: Paulist Press, pp. 38–9.

7 Wolters, A., 2001, *The Song of the Valiant Woman: Studies in the Interpretation of Proverbs 31:10–31*, Carlisle: Paternoster, p. 84 (his translation).

8 Gillingham, *Psalms through the Centuries*, p. 92.

9 Froehlich, K., 1996, 'Christian Interpretation of the Old Testament in the High Middle Ages', in Saebo, M. (ed.), *Hebrew Bible/Old Testament: The History of its Interpretation*, I/2: *The Middle Ages*, Göttingen: Vandenhoeck & Ruprecht, pp. 535–6.

10 Luther, M. 'Notes on Ecclesiastes', in Pelikan, J. (ed., tr.), 1972, *Luther's Works*, St Louis, MO: Concordia Publishing, vol. 15, pp. 4, 9.

11 Brenz, J., 1970, 'Der Prediger Salomo. Faksimile-Neudruck der ersten Ausgabe Hagenau 1528. Mit einer Einleitung von Martin Brecht: Glaube und Skepsis. Die erste evangelische Auslegung des Predigers Salomos von Johannes Brentz', Stuttgart-Bad Cannstatt: Frommann, pp. 6–7, in Wolters, A., 2013, 'Ecclesiastes and the Reformers', in Boda, M. J., Longman, T. and Rata, C. (eds) *The Words of the Wise are like Goads: Engaging Qohelet in the 21st Century*, Winona Lake, IN: Eisenbrauns, pp. 55–68, at p. 65.

12 Simpson, E. M. and Potter, G. R. (eds), 1954, *The Sermons of John Donne, Edited with Introductions and Critical Apparatus: In Ten Volumes*, Berkeley, CA: University of California Press, vol. 7, p. 243.

13 Gillingham, *Psalms through the Centuries*, p. 177.

14 Carey, J. (ed.), 1990, *John Donne The Major Works*, OWC, Oxford: Oxford University Press, p. 167.

15 Von Rad, G., 1972, *Wisdom in Israel*, London: SCM Press, p. 67 (original 1970).

16 Wilson, G. H., 1985, *The Editing of the Hebrew Psalter*, SBLDS, 76, Chico, CA: Scholars Press, p. 11.

17 Heim, K. M., 2013, *Poetic Imagination in Proverbs: Variant Repetitions and the Nature of Poetry*, BBRS, 4, Winona Lake, IN: Eisenbrauns, pp. 459, 644, 645.

18 Akoto, D. B. E. A., 2000, 'The Mother of the Ewe and Firstborn Daughter', in West, G. O. and Dube, M. W. (eds), *The Bible in Africa: Transactions, Trajectories, and Trends*, Leiden: Brill, pp. 266–7.

19 Míguez, N., 2006, 'Latin American Reading of the Bible: Experiences, Challenges and its Practice', *The Expository Times*, 118/3, pp. 120–9.

20 Tamez, E., 2000, *When the Horizons Close: Rereading Ecclesiastes*, Maryknoll, NY: Orbis, pp. 10, 20.

21 Fang, M., 2008, 'Translating and Chanting the Psalms: A Retrospective on the Use of the Bible in the Chinese Catholic Church in the Second Half of the Twentieth Century', in Starr, C. (ed.), *Reading the Christian Scriptures in China*, London and New York: T&T Clark, pp. 184–5.

22 Smith, J. K., 2009, *Desiring the Kingdom: Worship, Worldview, and Culture Formation*, Grand Rapids, MI: Baker, pp. 17–73.

23 Thompson, C., 2010, *Anatomy of the Soul: Surprising Connections between Neuroscience and Spiritual Practices that Can Transform Your Life and Relationships*, Carrollton, TX: Tyndale House Publishers, p. 150.

24 Childs, B. S., 1979, *Introduction to the Old Testament as Scripture*, Philadelphia, PA: Fortress Press, p. 576.

25 Childs, *Introduction to the Old Testament*, p. 575.

26 Wright, C. J. H., 2006, *The Mission of God*, Downers Grove, IL: Inter-Varsity Press, pp. 67–8.

5

Prophetic Books

LENA-SOFIA TIEMEYER

Part 1: Introduction

The Prophets is the name of the second canonical section in the Hebrew Bible. It consists of two subsections: the Former Prophets and the Latter Prophets. The Former Prophets (whose books are among the Historical Books in the Christian Bible) feature prophetic activity (e.g. Elijah, Nathan), whereas the Latter Prophets contains three long books (Isaiah, Jeremiah, and Ezekiel) and the so-called Book of the Twelve (Hosea, Joel, Amos, Obadiah, Jonah, Micah, Nahum, Habakkuk, Zephaniah, Haggai, Zechariah, and Malachi). The prophetic books share certain theological viewpoints, yet each book also has its own characteristics. They call the people of Israel to repentance, threaten that Israel will be punished for their sins unless they repent, and promise salvation if they do. The prophetic books also speak of the nations around Israel and assure them that God will punish them for their acts of violence against Israel.

The books in the Latter Prophets were composed over an extended period of time, ranging from the eighth to the fifth centuries BC, possibly even the fourth century, and address different historical and geographical situations. It is likely that a prophetic book originated around a specific prophet's teaching. The disciples of that prophet subsequently added to the growing corpus of texts as they applied the prophet's teaching to new historical circumstances.

Some texts in the Old Testament testify to the actual composition of prophetic texts. Most of our information comes from the book of Jeremiah. Jeremiah 36.1–8, for example, tells us how God commanded Jeremiah to take a scroll and to write down all the words that God spoke to him. Jeremiah accordingly employed Baruch, son of Neriah, as his secretary and dictated to him the words that God had spoken to him. Moreover, Baruch accompanied the prophet and read out aloud the prophet's words. Later on in the same passage, we are told that King Jehoiakim burned this scroll as he did not approve of its content when it was being read to him (Jer. 36.9–26). This, in turn, forced Jeremiah and Baruch to create a new version of the scroll (Jer. 36.27–32).

During the third to the first centuries BC, the books of the Old Testament were translated into Greek. In the second century AD, the translated books were gathered together into books (codices). The compilers placed the books of the Old Testament in a new order. Most modern Christian Bibles follow that new order. First, because Daniel shared many features with the prophetic books, it was placed after Ezekiel. Second, because of a deeply rooted tradition that Jeremiah had written Lamentations, it was placed after Jeremiah. Third, all the prophetic books were moved to the end of the Old Testament, and are known in Christianity as the Major Prophets and the Minor Prophets because their books are longer and shorter respectively.

Prophetic Books in overview

The prophetic literature does not portray a chronological sequence of events. Instead, the various books primarily address theological topics: they depict God's glory and majesty, they highlight the correlation between sin and punishment, and they speak about God's salvation of Israel and of all of humanity. In addition, they also touch upon a wide range of military, political, and sociological matters. What is the role of a good king? How shall we relate to the poor in our society? And what is the right way of treating not only our friends and relatives but also the strangers in our midst? It is not possible to do justice to the width and variation of all those topics that are covered by the individual prophetic books. The following overview therefore merely singles out a few of their key themes:

Isaiah	God's majestic glory and holiness; God's love for his city Jerusalem; the present and future role of the Davidic kings; the return of the exiles to Judah; the restoration of the people in Judah.
Jeremiah	God's use of Babylon in order to punish his people; insights into God's character; criticism of Judah's leaders; Jeremiah's lament over God's destruction of Judah and Jerusalem; promises of God's restoration of his people.
	Lamentations, traditionally understood to have been written by Jeremiah, laments the fall of Jerusalem in 586 BC.
Ezekiel	God's awe-inspiring glory, which demands the people's obedience and their punishment when they disobey; the exile of the people to Babylon; a vision of the future temple.
Daniel	Six stories about Daniel, a faithful Jewish man living in Babylon; a sequence of visions that speak mainly about the persecution of the people in Jerusalem during the second century BC.

The Book of the Twelve Prophets (Hosea–Malachi)

The Book of the Twelve Prophets is a diverse corpus of texts that traditionally are understood to form a textual unit. In Jewish tradition, these twelve books were written on a single scroll. Likewise, in Christian tradition, the same twelve books (sometimes called the Minor Prophets) were often considered to be a single book that should be read sequentially. Despite their diversity, at least four themes appear in many of the books in the Twelve: the Day of the Lord, fertility in the land, the fate of Israel, the problem of theodicy.[1]

Hosea	God's heartfelt sorrow at Israel's sins and his deep love for his people; Hosea's marriage to a faithless woman (named Gomer), their marriage forming a picture of God's relationship with his people; critique of Israel's royal politics.
Joel	A call to lament the devastation caused by a locust plague (or by human enemies described as locusts); a promise that God will pour out his Spirit upon everyone.
Amos	A call to oppose social injustice; the condemnation of much of the cult of God as it was performed during Amos's time.
Obadiah	A vision of the fall of Edom (the territory to the east and south of the Dead Sea).
Jonah	The story of Jonah's refusal to preach repentance to Nineveh (the Neo-Assyrian capital); Jonah's subsequent time inside the fish; Nineveh's repentance; God's compassion.
Micah	Critique of Israel's idolatry; critique of injustice and of any cultic performance that is unaccompanied by love of God and by respect for one's fellow human beings.
Nahum	A poem about the fall of Nineveh.
Habakkuk	A plea to God to end violence and injustice; a vow against Babylon.
Zephaniah	God's punishment of his people and of the surrounding Gentile nations at the coming terrible 'Day of the Lord'; God's victorious reign over a redeemed remnant.
Haggai	A call to rebuild the temple in Jerusalem that the Babylonian armies had destroyed more than half a century earlier.
Zechariah	A sequence of visions and accompanying oracles that speak about the new political and religious situation in Judah in the sixth century BC; a sequence of oracles that foresee a new king and a new, reunited kingdom.
Malachi	Critique of, and an attempt to reform, the cult in the newly rebuilt temple in Jerusalem.

Prophetic Books in summary

The prophetic individuals and the prophetic roles

Many of the books in the Latter Prophets feature a prophetic individual who functions as an intermediary between God and Israel. God called a prophet to convey his words to the people of Israel. The prophetic literature contains many 'call narratives' that tell us how God called an individual to prophethood. For example, Isaiah 6 and Jeremiah 1 give us glimpses as to how God would call a prophet. God conveys his message to the prophet through speech (oracles) or visual impressions (visions). The prophets can also communicate with God. In particular, they can pray to God for mercy on behalf of Israel (e.g. Jeremiah, Amos; cf. Jer. 27.18). At times, the prophets are filled with or moved by God's spirit (e.g. Isa. 61.1; Ezek. 3.14–15).

Some books tell us a lot about the prophets who have given them their name (e.g. Jeremiah, Ezekiel, Hosea) while others (e.g. Obadiah, Haggai) tell us nothing. Prophetic individuals appear outside of the Latter Prophets. Judges, 1 and 2 Samuel and 1 and 2 Kings contain narratives about prophets (i.e. Deborah, Samuel, Nathan, Elijah, Elisha, Huldah). Material in the Pentateuch calls Abraham (Gen. 20.7), Aaron (Ex. 7.1), and Miriam (Ex. 15.20) 'prophets', and portrays Moses as a prophetic figure (e.g. Num. 12.6–8; Deut. 34.10–12).

Prophets could work full time as prophets (e.g. Elijah, Elisha) but most appear to have had another job as well. For example, Amos took care of cattle and cultivated vine (Amos 1.1; 7.14), Nathan, Gad, and Isaiah held advisory positions at the royal court (2 Sam. 7; 12; 22; 24; Isa. 36—39), and Jeremiah might have been a priest (Jer. 1.1). It is further possible that prophets could serve for a limited time in order to preach a specific message. Haggai's prophecies, for example, all stem from the years 522–521 BC, and concern the rebuilding of the temple in Jerusalem.

Sin, punishment, and redemption

The Prophetic Books contain primarily oracles – that is, God's speech, via the prophet, to Israel and Judah. Oracles often begin with the statement 'thus says the Lord' and frequently contain the phrase 'oracle of the Lord'. The oracles from the time period leading up to the destruction of Jerusalem in 586 BC are chiefly oracles of judgement (e.g. Ezek. 1—24; Jer. 2—25). They accuse the people of Israel for having failed in their covenant duties towards God by doing such things as worshipping foreign gods. Unless they repent (e.g. Jer. 18.5–11), or unless the prophet intercedes on their behalf (e.g. Amos 7.1–6), God will punish them.

The prophetic literature also contains oracles of salvation. After the destruction of Jerusalem, God promises to return to his people (e.g. Isa. 40.1–11; 52.7–10; 59.20–21; 60—62; Zech. 1.16–17) and to build up the ruins of Jerusalem (e.g. Isa. 54.11–14). Other oracles from the same time accuse the leaders in Judah for failing in their duties towards the people and God (e.g. Isa. 56.9–12; Hag. 2.10–14; Mal. 1.6–14). Yet others criticize the people for not making God a priority in their lives (e.g. Hag. 1.4) and for participating in unorthodox worship (e.g. Isa. 57.3–13).

Oracles against the nations

God, as the sovereign ruler of the whole world, relates to nations other than his covenant partner Israel. Many of the prophetic books (e.g. Isaiah, Jeremiah, Ezekiel, Amos, Obadiah, and Nahum) contain so-called 'oracles concerning the nations', which predict the nations' future punishment. The nations will be punished because they act with violence against Israel and against each other (Amos 1.3—2.3), or because they are inherently wicked (Jer. 25.31), proud (Jer. 50.31–32), and trust in their own gods (Jer. 50.38; 51.47, 52). These thoughts form part of ancient Near Eastern ethics that proscribe the destruction of 'the other' who deviates from one's own social and religious order.

Social critique

The prophetic literature voices sharp critique against Israel's leaders. Isaiah 58.1–14, for example, criticizes employers for not caring for their workers. Isaiah 56.9–12 admonishes Judah's leaders for failing to lead the people. Micah 3.5, 9–12 exclaim that the ruler of Israel and Judah accept bribes, priests will teach only if they get paid for it, and prophets will prophesy in exchange for money and their teaching will cause the people to err. Other texts condemn the lack of social justice in general. Amos 5.12b criticizes the people for taking bribes and for denying justice to the poor, and Ezekiel 22.29 states that the people oppress the poor, take plunder, and use violence against strangers. Yet other texts reprimand the rich for not sharing their riches with the poor (e.g. Amos 4.1; 5.10–11; 6.1, 4–6).

Future restoration

Many prophecies portray a future existence where things will be fundamentally different from, and better than, what they are in the present. In this eschatological future, God will transform the land of Israel. God will also live in Jerusalem permanently, his glory will be manifest in the temple (e.g. Isa. 60.1–2; Ezek. 43.7–9; 48.35), and people from all over the world will come to Jerusalem and worship God (e.g. Isa. 27.13; 66.18–21; Mic. 4.1–4).

God will change nature. God's creation will cease to hurt itself (Isa. 11.6–9), there shall be no more weeping, and illness and premature death will disappear (Isa. 65.18–25). In a similar way, God will change humanity. He will give the people of Israel a new heart and a new spirit, which will help them act in accordance with his will (Jer. 24.7; 32.39; Ezek. 18.31; 36.24–32; 37.23). God will also restore communication between God and Israel. All men and women in Israel will have direct access to God (Joel 2.28–29, cf. Ezek. 39.28–29).

God will gather together his people from all corners of the earth and punish those nations who have caused suffering to the people of Israel (e.g. Isa. 11.11–16). In parallel with this, people from all over the world will come to Jerusalem and worship the God of Israel (Isa. 27.13; Zech. 14).

Part 2: Interpretation

Early Christianity

The writings of the early Church form a disparate body of literature, yet they are unified by its ongoing struggle with the Old Testament: what is its meaning and its significance in the new era after Jesus' death and resurrection? On the one hand, the Old Testament was Sacred Scripture for the first Christians, who firmly believed that Jesus was the fulfilment of its many prophecies. On the other hand, much of the content of these same prophecies did not appear to be directly relevant to the newly founded Christian community, due to their focus on the land of Israel and its history. In short, the early Christian authors battled with the question of how the Church could make Israel's Scriptures its own, in light of the radical newness and transformative power of the gospel.[2]

Revelation 6.1–8

(first century AD)

[1]I watched as the Lamb opened the first of the seven seals. Then I heard one of the four living creatures say in a voice like thunder, 'Come!' [2]I looked, and there before me was a white horse! Its rider held a bow, and he was given a crown, and he rode out as a conqueror bent on conquest. [3]When the Lamb opened the second seal, I heard the second living creature say, 'Come!' [4]Then another horse came out, a fiery red one. Its rider was given power to take peace from the earth and to make people kill each other. To him was given a large sword. [5]When the Lamb opened the third seal, I heard the third living creature say, 'Come!' I looked, and there before me was a black horse! Its rider was holding a pair of scales in his hand. [6]Then I heard what sounded like a voice among the four living creatures, saying, 'A kilogram of wheat for a day's wages, and three kilograms of barley for a day's wages, and do not damage the oil and the wine!' [7]When the Lamb opened the fourth seal, I heard the voice of the fourth

---

living creature say, 'Come!' [8]I looked, and there before me was a pale horse! Its rider was named Death, and Hades was following close behind him. They were given power over a quarter of the earth to kill by sword, famine and plague, and by the wild beasts of the earth. (NIVUK)

Revelation reports John's visions. The book can be categorized as an apocalypse, which means that it seeks to 'unveil' or 'reveal' hidden events. As such, much of its message deals with eschatology – that is, the study of the end times. It speaks of the end of life on earth as we know it, and the beginning of the Kingdom of God. The apocalyptic genre is characterized by specific literary features, themes, and concepts. It has been defined as 'revelatory literature with a narrative framework, in which a revelation is mediated by an otherworldly being to a human recipient, disclosing a transcendent reality which is both temporal, insofar as it envisages eschatological salvation, and spatial insofar as it involves another, supernatural world'.[3] Revelation has a very clear Christian content. In the quoted passage, the 'lamb' is Jesus and he is responsible for 'opening the seals' – that is, revealing the future to come. 'Apocalypse' is not an exclusively Christian genre, though, even if many people recognize its significance in Christian writings. In the Old Testament, the second half of the book of Daniel (chs 7—12) is often considered to be apocalyptic literature. There are also several examples of early Jewish apocalypses, among them 3 Baruch and the book of Enoch.

Revelation contains close to 400 allusions to the Old Testament. It picks up and transforms motifs and images from Ezekiel's, Daniel's, and Zechariah's vision reports. The careful reader of the excerpt of Revelation 6.2–6 will be able to detect allusions to Zechariah 1.8–11, 6.1–8, Ezekiel 1 and 10. Revelation 6.2–5 also reuses Ezekiel's description of a creature in the likeness of four living creatures (Ezek. 1.5) that carry God's throne (1.26–28). Ezekiel had earlier identified the same creature(s) with cherubim (Ezek. 10.22) who removed God's glory from Jerusalem (11.22–23).

Revelation often uses images from the Old Testament as literary prototypes. Revelation 6.2–8 draws on Zechariah's motifs of horses with distinct colours. In Zechariah, the horses symbolize God's omniscience as they patrol the earth in search of information (Zech. 1.8–11). They also represent God's military and executive power as they, attached to chariots, set out to act according to God's command (Zech. 6.1–8). In their new context in Revelation 6.2–8, the coloured horses keep the notion of God's military might over the nations (6.2).

Revelation uses the Old Testament texts to help readers understand the theological impact of later events. Revelation 6.4 alludes to the statement in Zechariah 1.11 that the earth is resting peacefully. Both texts view the state of peace as a sign of God's inaction, and both employ horses as the means by which God brings about havoc to the earth. In this manner, Revelation portrays events in the end times as already foreseen by the Old Testament prophets.[4]

Jerome: *Commentary on Jonah*

(end of fourth century AD)

1.3a. *But Jonah rose up to flee unto Tarshish from the presence of the LORD.* The Septuagint here is similar. The prophet knows by an inspiration of the Holy Spirit, that the repentance of the people is the destruction of the Jews ...

4.1. *But it displeased Jonah exceedingly and he was very angry.* Seeing the crowd of Gentiles enter (Rom. 11.25), and that fulfils what is written in Deuteronomy: 'they annoyed me with these gods who are not gods, so I will annoy them with a people that is not one; I shall anger them like a foolish nation' (Deut. 32.21). He despairs of Israel's safety and is hit by a great suffering which breaks out in words. He shows the signs of his suffering and more or less says this: 'I have been the only one of the prophets chosen to announce my people's ruin to them through the safety of others'. Thus he is not sad that the crowd of Gentiles should be saved, as some people believe, but it is the destruction of Israel. Moreover our Lord wept for Jerusalem and refused to take bread away from the children to give to the dogs (Matt. 15.26; Mark 7.27). And the apostles preach first to Israel, and Paul wishes to be anathema for his brothers who are Israelites (Acts 13.46) and have adoption, glory, alliance, promises and law, and from whom the patriarchs come, and from them to according to the flesh came Christ (Rom. 9.3–5).[5]

Jerome (AD 347–420) was born in the village of Stridon in what is nowadays Croatia. At this time the Roman Empire had been Christian for decades. Jerome was sent to Rome for his advanced education, where he became familiar with the rules of grammar and encountered the classical Latin literature. He also learnt rhetoric, a talent that is evidenced in his writings. Jerome left Rome in AD 368 and settled first in Trier, and later in Antioch. It was during this period that he decided to devote his life to the study of the Bible. He also became attracted to an ascetic lifestyle and, at times, withdrew to the desert to study and write. He learnt Hebrew and corresponded with a group of Jewish Christians.

Later in life, Jerome returned to Rome and began what came to be his most lasting legacy, namely, the translation of the Bible into Latin. This translation is known as the Vulgate. Until then, Christians had read the Old Testament in Greek, using the translation called the Septuagint (LXX), or they had access to the so-called 'Old Latin' (*Vetus Latina*), a collection of translations based on the Septuagint. At first, Jerome followed the practices of the day and used the Septuagint as the basis for his new translations.

Gradually, however, he came to work from the original Hebrew text. His Vulgate became the official Bible of the Western Church.

Jerome left Rome in AD 385 and returned to Antioch. From there, he continued on to the Holy Land where he stayed, often in a hermit's cell near Bethlehem, but also in more urban lodgings in Jerusalem, until his death. During these years, he translated the Old Testament from the original Hebrew into Latin, and he wrote most of his commentaries to the individual biblical books.[6]

In his commentary to Jonah quoted above, Jerome bases his interpretations on the original Hebrew text, which he further tries to render as faithfully as he can into Latin. In parallel, he also refers to the Greek translation in the Septuagint. Jerome's penchant for the Hebrew text was still a novel concept at this time, when most Christians read the Greek text and in some cases also actively argued against using the Hebrew text, which was the text preferred by the Jewish community. Jerome's commentaries show knowledge of and dialogue with prevalent Jewish interpretations of the same text.

In the excerpt, Jerome is confronted by the difficult task, on the one hand, of staying true to the meaning and message of the book of Jonah and, on the other hand, of seeking to explain – and to a certain extent also to exonerate – Jonah's behaviour. Why did he flee from God, and why did he initially refuse to preach repentance to the people of Nineveh (the Neo-Assyrian capital)? Jerome, like many Jewish commentators before and after him, realized that the willingness of the people of Nineveh to repent reflected badly on the Israelites who had failed to turn to God despite the many prophets that God had sent to them. Many Jewish exegetes explain Jonah's reluctance to go to Nineveh as a heroic attempt to prevent Israel's destruction. First, if Nineveh did not repent, then God would destroy them, which in turn would mean that Assyrians would not sack the Northern Kingdom of Israel in 721 BC. Second, if Nineveh did not repent, then the Israelites' lack of repentance would not be compared unfavourably with the Gentiles' turn to God.[7] In contrast, Jerome regards Israel's destruction as necessary, yet he acknowledges the grief that this event caused not only Jonah but also God himself.

Theodore of Mopsuestia: *Commentary on the Twelve Prophets: Hosea*

(fourth century AD)

The fact that God had the prophets do a number of things that to the general run of people seemed unseemly, like ordering Isaiah to appear naked and barefoot in the midst of everyone [Isa. 20.2–6], clearly has the following explanation. Since we general run of people normally listen to words idly, but are startled at the novelty of what happens and comes to our attention, especially if it is a variance with the normal behaviour of the one doing it, it made sense for God with the Jews' disobedience in mind to have the prophets frequently perform such things so that the people might in some fashion be converted by the novelty of what happened, and come to learn the reason and be instructed in their duty. Accordingly, he bade the prophet marry a prostitute: it would have been unusual for the prophet to choose such a woman to take into the marriage relationship – which is exactly what God ordered him to do ... the novelty of the event provided the prophet with the occasion of ... demonstrating the greater marvel of God's condescending to choose such ungrateful men for special attention by the powerful example – namely, the remarkable prophet's doing his duty by entering into association with a prostitute.[8]

At Antioch a theological school existed that explored the ways in which the Church could and should interpret the Old Testament. This particular school insisted on the literal and historical senses of the text, as opposed to the allegorical approach advocated by the school of Alexandria. Influenced by the teaching of Aristarchus, the exegetes in Antioch interpreted the prophetic literature within the Old Testament context. Theodore (c. AD 350–428) was born in Antioch, and later became bishop of Mopsuestia in Cilicia from 392 to 428. He wrote a commentary on the Book of the Twelve. This commentary, written in Greek, depends on the Greek text known as the Septuagint (LXX), rather than the Hebrew text. In general, Theodore set out to identify the historical situation of the different prophets. In this, he challenges the tendency, common among the Church Fathers, to read the Old Testament Christologically – that is, as speaking about Jesus.

Although Theodore did not exclude Christological interpretations, he argued that the Old Testament spoke primarily about events contemporary with the authors. He therefore assumed that every character that the prophetic literature mentions was a historical person and every event that it refers to happened. For example, considering the excerpt, it probably struck Theodore as odd that God commanded the prophet Hosea to marry a prostitute, yet, as it was by no means beyond belief, he proceeded to justify God's and the prophet's behaviour and to claim that this marriage really took place. This approach sometimes causes problems for Theodore. For example, in the case of the book of Jonah, Theodore has to justify Jonah's behaviour, lacking, as he does, the possibility of treating the portrayal of the prophet as a satire of a particular brand of exclusive and self-obsessed 'prophetism' in Israel – which was probably the original author's actual intention.

Medieval Christianity

By the time of the Middle Ages the Church had spread beyond the Mediterranean world. There were five ancient centres – Rome, Constantinople, Jerusalem, Antioch, and Alexandria – but Christianity had grown and also become the religion of places farther afield such as northern France, Germany, the Netherlands, the British Isles, Scandinavia, and Eastern Europe. Christianity also began to diversify. It was split mainly between the Western Catholic Church and the Eastern Orthodox Church and there was a growing tension between these two branches. Medieval Europe also saw the rise of monasticism. Some key monastic orders were the Benedictine order, the Cistercian order, as well as the Franciscan and the Dominican orders. The nuns and monks in the latter two orders were often called 'friars' and emphasized a simple life of poverty, missionary activity, and education.

The Venerable Bede: *On the Canticle of Habakkuk* 3.6

(sixth to seventh centuries AD)

The mountains were violently shattered. He gives the name mountains to the proud and those giving themselves airs because of the power, wisdom or wealth of this world. These, when the Lord turned his gaze on them, were not just shattered but violently shattered; whereas when he showed compassion, some of these people not only renounced their vain and proud haughtiness but even impugned it by their lifestyle as well as by their preaching. Finally Saul and Matthew were mountains, the former raised up from the wisdom of the human word, the latter from the mammon of iniquity; but when each of them had been converted to the tutorship of humility, and became a disciple of Christ, the mountains were indeed violently shattered.[9]

Bede (AD 672/3–735) grew up and was educated in the twin monasteries of St Peter and St Paul at Wearmouth and Jarrow, a major centre of learning and knowledge in Anglo-Saxon north east England. He was later ordained a deacon and priest of the same monastery. The twin monastery had a library of about 300 volumes, mostly copies of the Latin (Vulgate) translation of the Old and the New Testament. For Bede, the study of the Bible was 'the bread of life' – that is, an integral part of life. Although he did not read Hebrew, he was aware of the importance of the Hebrew text underlying the Latin translation to which he had access. In his commentaries, Bede drew upon the Latin Church Fathers (e.g. Jerome, Augustine, Gregory, and Ambrose). Bede's interpretations focused on the spiritual and devotional aspects of the text. Influenced by the daily recitation of the Bible in the liturgy in the monasteries, Bede saw the biblical texts as the means through which we can communicate with God.

Bede saw the Old Testament characters as prototypes for Jesus and he sought to show that the Old Testament foreshadows Jesus' life and death. He adhered to a variant of the typical medieval fourfold method of Old Testament interpretation: a given passage has a historical meaning (pertaining to the history of Israel), an allegorical meaning (events in the Old Testament that signify events or concepts in the New Testament), a tropological meaning (specific statements in the Old Testament provide general moral instruction), and an anagogical meaning (that interprets plain statements as referring to the future life in heaven). That Old Testament prophecy could be freely applied to the lives of later Christians is evident in the excerpt.

Habakkuk 3.2–19 was used in the monastic liturgy every Friday as part of the proclamation of the mysteries surrounding Jesus' death and resurrection. Bede's commentary is a detailed and beautiful analysis of the inner meaning of the words of Habakkuk 3.2–19. He sought to draw out the spiritual and mystical meaning embedded in the text and how it points towards Jesus. As can be seen from the opening line of his commentary, his word is dedicated to 'my dearest sister' (on Hab. 3.1) – Bede composed his commentary for a woman, presumably the abbess of one of the convents in the north of England. Bede intended his commentaries to be used by the clerical elite. They served to enhance private devotional study and the public reading of the Bible in church and monastic service, as well as to train English clergy to improve their missionary activities.

Nicholas of Lyra: *Commentary on Daniel* 4.29–37

(1322–7)

... first it is not likely that the King would have been allowed to run in the fields with the beasts; but rather he would have been chained and imprisoned. Likewise, he would not be able to live for such a long time nude and in the open. Third, it seems impossible that he could survive on such food as it says: 'You will eat grass like a cow'. Fourth, the beast would devour him over such a long time, as it seems. Fifth, it is not likely that the entire kingdom would be without a king for seven years. Moreover, there is no record that another king took the throne and if he were enthroned, he would not likely yield to Nebuchadnezzar after his madness. Thus they say that Daniel speaks here *ad litteram* about the Devil, and *sub metaphora* of Nebuchadnezzar.

... On the other hand, it can be said that his son Evilmoreodach ruled at that time. How did he yield to his father afterwards? He was forced by the princes who hated his evil ways.[10]

The Franciscan exegete Nicholas (1270–1349) was born in the town of Lyre in Normandy, France. He possibly learnt Hebrew with Jewish teachers in the nearby centre of Jewish learning in Evreux. It is, however, unlikely that he himself stemmed from a Jewish family or had any other ties to the Jewish community. In 1300, at the age of 30, Nicholas entered the Franciscan convent in Verneuil, near Lyre. The brothers discovered his talents and sent him to study in Paris. He later became a doctor at the Sorbonne (1309) and eventually came to be the head of all Franciscan monks in France.[11]

Nicholas was a prolific exegete. He first authored the so-called *Literal Postill to the whole Bible* (1323–31). It demonstrates an extensive knowledge of Hebrew and draws on Rashi's (Rabbi Solomon ben Isaac) commentaries on the Old Testament, written in Hebrew. Nicholas's interpretations favour the literal sense of the text, in contrast to the prevalent custom of allegorizing the Bible. Nicholas is also one of the earliest critical scholars insofar as he argues that the obscurity of many Old Testament passages is the result of copyists' carelessness or translators' mistakes. The task of the exegete is thus to reconstruct the original Hebrew text.

Later in life, Nicholas wrote the *Moral Postill to the whole Bible* (1333–9), a brief typological and allegorical series of notes on those passages in the Bible that Nicholas thought should be given 'moral' interpretations. Nicholas comments on issues pertaining to ecclesiology, the life of the faithful soul, and the world to come. Nicholas intended it to be an economical and practical handbook for preachers.

These two postills were printed together as *Postillae perpetuae in universam S. Scripturam*, the first printed commentary on the Bible (1471). Nicholas's commentary and hermeneutical principles later influenced Luther. In this manner, it was through Nicholas of Lyra that Rashi's earlier commentaries became widely known to the Christian Protestant world. Nicholas's interpretation of Daniel 4, in the excerpt, displays many of the characteristics of his commentary. He keeps the discussion close to the biblical text, interacts with previous scholarship, and challenges those who deny the literal and historical sense of the text.

Reformation Christianity

The sixteenth century saw a great upheaval in the Christian world. The Reformation began properly in Germany with Martin Luther and was soon taken up by John Calvin, Huldrych Zwingli, and others. These men sought to 'reform' the Catholic Church by bringing its beliefs and practices in line with the teaching of the Bible. The Reformation soon split into two chief branches, with the Lutheran Church following the teaching of Luther, and the Reformed Church following the teaching of Calvin.

Martin Luther: *Commentary on Isaiah* 60.3

(1527)

And nations shall come to your light. He simply cannot get away from the light. He is clearly repealing all of Moses and enlarging the church beyond the limit of the synagogue and extending it to the Gentiles, since the light and the glory will be spread and poured out. There will be no law to oppress the people.

And kings to the brightness of your rising. That light and glory is multiplied for the nations, that is, the gospel will be a proclamation to illuminate the whole world. This text does not persuade us that we have this light, since it says *the nations shall come*, although it is a light not of the Gentiles but of the Jews.

And kings to the brightness of your rising, that is, all walk in the very brightness of the Gospel. Light, brightness, rays, these are the greatest names of the Gospel. The first designation of dignity is light.[12]

Martin Luther (1483–1546) was born in Eisleben in Germany. His schooling when a boy was in Latin, and later on he entered the University of Erfurt where he received his Master's degree in 1505. Shortly afterwards, he decided to become a monk and entered the Augustinian monastery in Erfurt. He also studied theology. He was ordained as priest in 1507 and began learning and teaching at the University of Wittenberg, where he received his Doctor of Theology degree in 1512. Luther completed his translation of the New Testament in 1522, and of the Old Testament in 1534. His translations are not always word-for-word translations. Instead, he argued that the task of the translator was to render the same *meaning* as clearly and faithfully as possible in the receptor language. In a sense, Luther's translation of the Bible is its interpretation.

Luther saw Jesus as the centre of both the Old and the New Testament. He states that 'every prophecy and every prophet must be understood as referring to Christ the Lord, except where it is clear from the plain words that someone else is spoken of'.[13] The primary purpose of the whole Bible is to preach Jesus, and the goal of studying the Bible is to gain knowledge of him. Luther held on to the unity of the two Testaments and saw Jesus as the unifying factor. He also rejected any dichotomy between the two Testaments. The same merciful God reveals his grace in *every* book in the entire Bible. At the same time, Luther endeavoured to understand the Old Testament in the context of its own history.

In his commentary on Isaiah, Luther divides the book into three interlocking parts. First, many texts threaten sinful and idolatrous Israel with divine punishment, and it foretells God's Kingdom and Jesus' coming (e.g. Isa. 7.14; 53). Second, other texts deal with Assyria and its ruler Sennacherib (e.g. Isa. 36—99). Third, yet other texts deal with the Babylonian captivity and predict the exiles' return to Jerusalem during Cyrus' reign (539–530 BC). Luther argued that Jesus is the main point of all the parts of the text. In the case of Isaiah 60.3, in the excerpt, Luther interprets the prophecy as speaking about the coming of Jesus, and he takes the notion of 'light' as a symbol of the gospel.[14]

John Calvin: *Commentary on Malachi 2.4*

(1558)

Here he addresses in particular the priests; for though the whole people with great haughtiness resisted God, yet the priests surpassed them. And we know how ready men are to turn to evil whatever benefits God may bestow on them … This evil however has ever prevailed among men – that they have defrauded God of his glory, and have turned to an occasion of pride the favours received from him. But it is an evil which is very commonly seen in all governors; for they who are raised to a high dignity, think no more that they are men, but take to themselves very great liberty when they find themselves so much exalted above others … For when God favoured the priests with the highest honour, they became blinded, that they thought themselves to be as it were semi-gods; and the same thing has taken place in the kingdom of Christ. For how have arisen so great impieties under the Papacy, except that pastors have exercised tyranny and not just government?[15]

Calvin (1509–64) was born in Noyon in France. At a young age he learnt Latin and philosophy, and also served as a bishop's clerk. He later studied law at the University of Orléans. In 1533, Calvin had a religious experience that in all likelihood coincided with his break with the Catholic Church. He published his major theological work in 1536 which, among other things, represented a statement of faith for Reformed Christianity. In 1538–41, Calvin moved to Strasbourg where he worked and preached in several churches and also continued to write on Reformation matters. In 1541, Calvin travelled to Geneva where he went to live and preach, until his death in 1564.

Calvin's commentary on the twelve Minor Prophets, finished in 1558, is not a commentary in the modern sense of the word. Instead, it is a compilation of material that Calvin's friends gathered together from his lectures in the Academy of Geneva (1556–8). Calvin himself lectured directly from the biblical text without written lecture notes. The original audience consisted of adult male students, many of whom later became Church leaders in the French Reformed Church, seeking to evangelize their home country. The depth of Calvin's knowledge of Hebrew is debated, yet he clearly strove to interact with the original Hebrew text, and he offers his own translation of the text under discussion. We also do not know to what extent Calvin was familiar first-hand with the writings and interpretations of the Church Fathers and the Rabbis. He refers to them, yet seldom by name or in any great detail.

Calvin sought to establish the plain sense of the text. He maintained that prophecy had three interpretative layers. First, any given prophecy refers to events that are in the near future from the perspective of the prophetic author. Second, it speaks of Jesus and his life and teaching, as well as of the apostolic era. Third, it applies to the whole course of history up until the end times. The excerpt from Calvin's commentary on Malachi 2.4 illustrates his approach. He comments operate on more than one level. First, he interprets the text in its historical context and speaks about those priests contemporary with Malachi. He then uses the text to make statements about humankind in general, and people's tendency to think more of themselves than is appropriate and to place themselves above God's laws. Finally, he applies the passage to his own times and likens the behaviour of the priests that Malachi criticized with the contemporary priests within the Catholic Church.[16]

Modern Christianity

Biblical studies changed irrevocably with the rise of critical biblical scholarship at the end of the nineteenth century. Influenced in part by the new archaeological discoveries from the ancient Near East, scholars started to explore the world of the Bible and began to ask new questions of the biblical texts. For example, it was no longer enough to say that Isaiah wrote the book of Isaiah. Rather, scholars wanted to find out what it meant that Isaiah was a 'prophet' and which particular historical circumstance each text in the book addressed. The focus of biblical research further shifted from 'What can the Bible tell us about our faith?' to 'What can the Bible tell us about the faith of the ancient Israelites?'. By the end of the twentieth century, however, the pendulum swung back and many scholars saw the need to revisit the first question and to explore yet again how the Israelite prophetic texts can be, and indeed should be, relevant for the Church today.

Herbert B. Huffmon: 'A company of prophets: Mari, Assyria, Israel'

(2000)

In the royal archives of Mari, the Neo-Assyrian texts, and the Hebrew Bible, together with related texts, we find a commonality in distinctive settings and with differing manifestations. The commonality is that prophets (1) present communications from the divine world, normally for a third party, and serve

---

as mediators who may or may not identify with the deity; (2) draw upon inspiration through ecstasy, dreams, or what may be called 'inner illuminations'; (3) offer messages, often unsolicited, that are immediately understandable by the audience addressed; and (4) not only offer assurance but frequently admonish or exhort the addressee. This prophetic activity, however, takes place within different contexts and develops in different ways. Within each community the prophets are perceived in different ways by different people, reflecting the particular settings and perspectives of those involved.[17]

Until the twentieth century most readers of the Bible considered the Israelite prophets and the prophetic literature in the Old Testament to be unique and distinctly different from prophetic phenomena in other cultures. The discoveries from Mesopotamia have changed that situation. We now have access to non-biblical texts that speak about prophets and that contain prophetic sayings. There are two main types of prophetic texts, found at different places and stemming from different time periods: the royal archives of Mari and the Neo-Assyrian prophetic texts.

The archives of Mari (c. 1800–1750 BC) contain prophetic texts, primarily addressed to the king, that assure him of success or warn him of possible dangers. They also express concern with cultic issues – for example, that sacrifices to a particular deity have been neglected. The prophets at Mari could be either male or female and they received the divine communication primarily through dreams. On occasion, some prophets were ecstatic or in a special state of consciousness when receiving the deity's message. The king took these messages seriously but often demanded that they were verified by another form of divine communication – for example, by divination. From the later period, the Neo-Assyrian prophetic texts contain primarily material from the reigns of Esarhaddon (681–669 BC) and Assurbanipal (668–627 BC). The prophets were predominantly female, and many of them were associated with the cult of Ishtar, the Mesopotamian goddess of love and war. The prophets had access to the royal court and their messages, mainly words of reassurance, were taken seriously by the kings.

These Mesopotamian texts can, together with the biblical material, shed light upon the lives, activities, and social roles of the prophets in the ancient Near East. The Mesopotamian texts suggest that the Israelite prophets were part of a wider social phenomenon, as Huffmon itemizes in the excerpt. Male and female prophets functioned as intermediaries – that is, persons who enabled communication between a deity and his/her worshippers. Yet these comparisons also emphasize the differences between prophets in different cultures, in particular the uniqueness of the extended literary compositions found in the Old Testament of which there is no counterpart in Mesopotamia.

Julia M. O'Brien: *Nahum*

(2009)

The book of Nahum both attracts and repels me ethically. On the one hand, I find much of it disturbing. The violence of the book feels all too familiar in a world of the Holocaust and Palestinian refugee camps; of Armenian, Cambodian, Rwandan, and Albanian genocides; of skinheads; of students who gun down their classmates and their teachers – a world that I want to change. I tend towards pacifism, and Nahum celebrates war.

Even more disturbing to me is the relish with which the destruction of enemies is described, the joy that it takes in envisioning, in painstaking detail, the humiliation and death of others. Nahum tries to keep the enemies generic, so that I need never look into their eyes. But my own commitments conjure the faces of Nahum's enemies. As a woman, I see myself and women like me as the Nineveh who is stripped and raped, and I am horrified that someone would gloat over 'our' degradation. As a mother, I want Nahum to express regret that the innocent suffer for the crimes of the guilty, and I cringe when, in an offhand remark, it mentions the death of children (Nah. 3.10).[18]

O'Brien, alongside many other contemporary exegetes, encounters problems when they look to the Bible for guidelines for contemporary Christian living. Nahum brings many issues to the forefront, as seen in the excerpt. How can we approach Nahum's violence and sexually charged rhetoric that modern society no longer finds acceptable, yet stay faithful to our Christian faith? It is tempting to explain the violence in Nahum historically in the light of the Neo-Assyrian oppression of Israel and Judah. God's destruction of Nineveh, the capital of Israel's brutal enemy, appears justified. This reading carries its own problems, however. Even though we may be able to trace Nahum's message back to the time of the destruction of Nineveh, we still have to explain the fact that it was preserved and accepted into the biblical canon. Its message must have been deemed relevant even *after* the fall of the Neo-Assyrian Empire.

It might well be attractive to consider the claim that Nahum is less about Nineveh and more about God. After all, God's justice compels him to destroy evil in order to establish his just and sovereign rule. His anger thus reveals his love and care. Yet this particular reading is also problematic: it forces the reader to accept the validity of God's estimation of Nineveh as totally corrupt, and it disregards the realities that the destruction of any city brings to its inhabitants. It also ignores the issue of Nahum's *pleasure* in the downfall of Nineveh, as evidenced by the detailed descriptions of its destruction (e.g. Nah. 3.5–7).

Nahum is a literary presentation and its rhetoric portrays Nineveh as the faceless and anonymous enemy rather than a nation filled with suffering human beings who were created by God. At the same time, Nahum is a vivid reminder of what it feels to be the victims of the horrors of war who long for revenge and imagine the destruction of their oppressors at the hands of their God. Nahum gives a voice to the underdog that we, from our often privileged Western situation, cannot easily dismiss. O'Brien looks for readings that deal with Nahum's disturbing message and resist its tendencies to reduce Nineveh to a faceless 'other'. We must recognize the difficulties inherent in the book and give Nineveh a face in order to recognize that Israel and the enemy are victims alike, locked in a conflict of war.

Christopher R. Seitz: *Prophecy and Hermeneutics*

(2007)

The canonical form of the twelve Minor Prophets is concerned both to protect the original witness and to comprehend how that witness is meant to speak meaningfully across the ages, through time. The mature provision of a form that teaches us this is to be respected. In this way, the prophets' association with one another is clarified and their common legacy is confirmed without loss of their individual features and historical productivity. By this I mean the capacity to generate fresh reflection on the abiding features of God's word as spoken in times past, yet always straining for a new hearing and application. The association of the prophets, through a canonical form, is intended to enable us to see how time and history work and what they mean. The stability of the form also allows us to comprehend the dynamic dimension of the terms of its mature presentation and also better to appreciate the way the New Testament asserts its accordance with this.[19]

The study of biblical prophecy has shifted in the last 25 years, from a focus on the individual prophets, understood to have been the authors of at least parts of the books bearing their names, to the prophetic literature – that is, the books containing material that can be associated with prophets and their prophecies. Roughly along similar lines, many scholars have ceased trying to isolate the original and authentic prophetic word (*ipsissima verba*, 'the very words') and to set it apart from later editorial comments (and dating each textual strand to its own historical context), and have instead begun to investigate the thematic continuity or discontinuity of larger sections of texts, books, and sequences of books.

This new approach highlights a number of issues. For instance, what does it mean that two texts appear in the same biblical book, even if it is reasonably clear that they were penned by two different authors? Redaction Criticism – that is, the study of the work of the later editors responsible for the putting together of the prophetic texts as we have them today –

explores the shape and message of the final form of a given text. Why did the redactors structure the text in the way that they did, and what is the message of this final form? To give an example, what is the message of the (entire) book of Isaiah? Although the individual texts in the book most likely were written at different times and address diverse matters, the Isaiah scroll forms a single textual unit. Someone thus decided that these texts should be incorporated into a single book. The question is: Why?

Turning from redactor to reader, questions arise as to what happens in the reader's mind when texts are being read together. What is, for instance, the significance of the fact that the Book of the Twelve (known also as the Minor Prophets) was traditionally written on one scroll? Furthermore, how does the order of the books, with Hosea first and Malachi last, influence the reader's perception of the overarching message of the Twelve?

This renewed interest in the prophetic *books* also raises important questions with regard to the understanding of the canon of the Old and the New Testament. How can texts that are more than 2,500 years old still communicate with us? More specifically, what happens when Christians read the prophetic texts of the Old Testament? Does a prophecy in the Old Testament change *meaning* when it is juxtaposed with the New Testament (it used to mean X but now, applied to Jesus, it means Y), or does it rather change *significance* (it means X but it can now also, in tandem, mean Y)? Furthermore, is a prophecy in the Old Testament a witness to God in its own right, shared by both Christians and Jews, or does it have a different meaning for the Church that is distinct from its meaning when being read in the Synagogue and also different from the meaning that it had for its original ancient Israelite audience? Also, should Christians read the entire Old Testament or should they rather read only those passages that are highlighted by the New Testament and understood by it to point towards Jesus (*Vetus Testamentum in Novo receptum*)? These are no easy questions and scholars continue to debate them.[20]

Global Christianity

Christianity began as a small Jewish movement in an obscure part of the Roman Empire. It soon spread across the Mediterranean world and, 300 years later, had become the state religion of the same Empire. In the subsequent millennium, Christianity spread across Europe and for much of its history it has been considered a European religion. This, however, is no longer the case. In fact, some people would claim that the centre of Christianity has shifted during the twentieth and the beginning of the twenty-first century in a monumental way; that it has by now become primarily an African and an Asian movement. While this specific claim may be contested, it is nevertheless true that people across the world confess that Jesus is Lord, and many Christians read the Bible from a global perspective.

Renita J. Weems: *Battering Love*

(1995)

The *dramatis persona* in Ezekiel is Jerusalem. The capital city is the promiscuous wife. The prophet details the city's rape, violation, and humiliation. Like Jeremiah, Ezekiel overwhelms his audience with one image after another, offending every sense of decency and propriety his audience must have held, exploiting each element of the metaphor for its ability to represent adultery, harlotry, and humiliation. The prophet goes to great lengths to detail the extent and nature of Jerusalem's punishment. Whereas rape was mostly only alluded to by the other two prophets, it and other sexual activities become decidedly explicit in Ezekiel. In fact, so extensive is the prophet's commentary on the woman/Jerusalem's ruin that many of the prophet's descriptions fall into the category of what some today might classify as pornographic ... The woman's punishment in Ezekiel is so savage and outrageous that it is difficult to imagine anyone hearing of her plight and not feeling empathy for her and disgust at the way she is treated. It is almost impossible to believe that anyone could conclude that this woman, or anyone else for that matter, deserved to be treated as cruelly as she is in the Ezekiel narrative.[21]

Modern biblical scholars investigate the metaphorical language in the Old Testament and highlight the ways in which metaphors shape and influence our reality and ways of looking at contemporary issues. In particular, scholars focus on the sexual and marital metaphors that appear throughout the prophetic literature (e.g. Hos. 1—3; Jer. 2—3; Ezek. 16; 23). In these texts, the nation of Israel/Judah, or the city of Jerusalem, is personified as a woman who has been unfaithful to her husband. Her adultery justifies her husband's punishment of her. By analogy, God is justified in punishing his people because they have been unfaithful to him as they have worshipped other gods. In these texts, the wife's punishment is described in forceful and explicit sexual terms, as the excerpt highlights.

Feminist and womanist biblical scholars around the world resist these metaphors in two ways. First, they seek to uncover the patriarchal assumptions that are embedded in the text. Second, they strive to read the texts from the perspective of the women within the text. Many feminist and womanist readers refuse to side with God, the male protagonist in the text, and instead choose to side with the woman whom they see as a victim rather than a perpetrator. They resist readings that accept terms such as 'whore' at face value and they reject the view that rape and other forms of sexual violence are justifiable acts of punishment of adultery.

Renita Weems examines this issue from an African-American womanist perspective. 'Womanist Theology' (see, further, the writings of Jacquelyn

Grant) stems from the realization that the oppression of black women is different from the oppression of black men, and it proposes that Jesus suffered in his time in the same manner as black women suffer today. Weems acknowledges that her own interest in this type of language has to do with her own identity as a black African-American woman, and that she wishes to challenge biblical language that condones violence against socially marginalized women.

In her reading of Hosea 1—3, Jeremiah 2—3, and Ezekiel 16 and 23, Weems discusses the sexist language and highlights its dangers to modern readers. In our own society, as long as women continue to be victims of sexual and other types of violence, the metaphor of the battered wife is dangerous. Moreover, if we accept the prophets' portrayal of God as a husband who allows his jealousy to sanction acts of violence towards his wife, how does this type of metaphoric language influence our image of God? These are undoubtedly important questions to ask.

Weems also, however, lifts up the positive aspects of the marital metaphoric language such as the promise of love and healing after a period of violence and estrangement (e.g. Jer. 2.14–23). Even though the idea of a husband and wife reuniting after domestic violence is unsatisfactory for many modern readers, the prophetic image of reconciliation between God and his people may nevertheless provide a way forward. We need to reflect on the fact we, women and men alike, have wounded one another and that the only way forward may be the hope of forgiveness and grace.

Rachel Bundang: 'Home as Memory, Metaphor, and Promise in Asian/Pacific American Religious Experience'

(2002)

If Jeremiah were writing to the exiles today, what would he say? What would become of his directives and promises, his prophecies and calls to remembrance? The sadness, nostalgia, and sense of elusive, ever-fading memory would outweigh the anger, I suspect. I chose to focus here on Jeremiah's letter to the exiles (Jer. 29.4–23) not because it has any special significance to Asian American Christian communities ... but rather because in those lines I sense historical, emotional, and spiritual resonance with Asian Pacific American experiences of uprooting and building new homes both physical and spiritual as depicted in our histories, arts, and literature ... The task of rebuilding, however temporary or permanent, is informed by memories of homes we left behind, dreams of homes we have only heard about in ancestors' and travelers' stories, and experience of homemaking and settlement in an often indefinite present.[22]

Bundang looks at Jeremiah's letters to the exiles in Babylon (Jer. 29.4-23) from an Asian-American perspective and offers an ethical and moral theological reading. She writes from an American Roman Catholic perspective, yet she is also influenced by the traditions and practices of her native Philippines. As the excerpt indicates, Bundang highlights the sense of displacement that the Jewish exiles in Babylon must have felt after the fall of Jerusalem. Without the city and the temple to bind them together, how could they find God and how could God find them? The exilic community felt the need to replace the pre-exilic importance of the temple and the nation with other matters such as the keeping of the Sabbath in order to understand and re-define themselves as a distinct people. In this sense, the Exile gave birth to Jewish religious life in the Diaspora.

Bundang compares the experiences of the exiles from Judah in Babylon with the experiences of the Asian and Pacific Island communities in North America. Regardless of the reasons for the displacement of the individual members, they all consider themselves as living in 'exile' (the first generation) or the diaspora (subsequent generations). As the experience of the homeland fades, the displaced communities cling to memories, real and imagined, about their distant 'homeland', and yet, at the same time, they also create a new culture that is distinct from that of the 'homeland'. In some cases, the diaspora community will hold on to a practice more tightly than those in the homeland will because it serves as an identity marker. The meaning of the practice will, however, change in order to meet the new demands of the diaspora setting.

In his letter to the exilic community in Babylon, the prophet Jeremiah encourages the exiles to settle down (Jer. 29.4-7). Seen through the lens of the experiences of the Asian Diaspora in North America, we can interpret Jeremiah's words as an invitation to rediscovery. By settling down and living out the memories of home and by adhering to the practices of home, rather than waiting passively for redemption, the exiles can *rediscover* their religious beliefs and practices. By planting and growing – that is, every-day acts of care for home and family – they recommit themselves to the covenant. In this manner, rather than giving up, they preserve their identity, their independence, and their way of life.

This rediscovery should not, however, be done without critical reflection. On the contrary, Bundang argues, the exiles, both in Babylon and in North America, need to re-examine their cultural heritage and decide ways of reconciling new values with their old ones. Not everything from the old culture can, or even should, be translated into the new exilic or diaspora setting. In this matter, Jeremiah teaches both communities that 'prudent discernment with God at the forefront of the concern is vital in determining what course of action would be most sustaining and life-giving for them in relation to God, each other, and the world beyond themselves'.[23]

Makhosazana K. Nzimande: 'Isaiah'

(2010)

Under neo-colonialism and globalization, black South Africans are the 'Suffering Servants' who constantly seek to remove the Babylonian hegemonic yoke while others benefit tremendously from it. This is mostly manifested in increased class stratification of postapartheid South Africa and the concomitant class consciousness. ... Therefore, black South Africans identify with the 'Oppressed Servant' of Deutero-Isaiah ... Black South Africans eagerly await a 'Cyrus of Persia' figure to rescue them from the stranglehold of globalization and neo-colonialism (Isa. 48.14). Hopefully, in God's appointed time, Babylon will be toppled over and justice shall prevail! But while 'Cyrus' rescues us from Babylon, the peculiar South African situation demands a concomitant rescue from dehumanizing black-on-black class exploitation, especially if it takes place between women.[24]

Post-colonialist interpretations of the Bible are readings that consist of reactions to, and analysis of, the cultural legacy of colonialism. During colonial times, it was common for the colonizers to read themselves into the biblical narrative. For example, the colonizers of Africa saw themselves as re-enacting the Exodus and entering into the Promised Land, while they saw the indigenous population as 'Canaanites'. There is also a sharp division between the colonizers who are articulate and civilized and the colonized who are lazy, exotic, disorganized, and helpless.

After independence, many of the African nations sought to free themselves from these kinds of worldviews, and to find new ways of reading the Bible that integrate their own cultural and religious experiences. They seek to uncover interpretations and ways of interpreting the Bible that are biased in favour of the Western world. Post-colonialist approaches offer ways to read the Bible in one's own cultural terms, and challenge those who insist that Western modes of interpretation are the only acceptable ones. For example, they argue that Historical Criticism emerged within a Western context and, as such, prioritizes Western ways of thinking about the Bible.

Post-colonial scholarship points out that much of the Old Testament emerged within the context of colonialism and reflects a colonial perspective. Israel and Judah were for many years living under the indirect or direct influence of colonial powers (Assyria, Babylon, Persia, Greece, and Rome), and many texts criticize the colonial powers. For example, select parts of the book of Isaiah speak up against the oppression of Assyria and Babylon, subvert both the imperial powers and the imperial sympathizers among his own people, and envisage God's wrath upon its oppressors (e.g. Isa. 14; 36—37).

Nzimande reads Isaiah from a South African post-colonial perspective (*Imbokodo*, a term that refers to the hard grinding stones used for food preparation, is often used to denote the resilience of African women).[25] She notes that post-apartheid South Africa seeks to rediscover its history that imperialism suppressed, and to create a counter-memory – that is, a new, positive, black historical collective memory that can serve as the counterpart to the history of apartheid and white supremacy. Nzimande acknowledges that this is to a large extent a patriarchal endeavour in which women are historically silenced, misrepresented, and sometimes negatively depicted.

In her essay, Nzimande addresses this imbalance and seeks to portray black African women as active participants in history. She first notes that a black woman reader faces difficulties when seeking to identify women's socio-economic struggles in the text. The biblical book focuses on injustice affecting males in high positions of power within an imperial setting. Women can therefore only identify with the general national struggles in the book. Despite these difficulties, Nzimande suggests that poor South African women can identify themselves with the so-called Suffering Servant in Isaiah 52.12—53.13. Most Christian interpretations identify the servant figure with Jesus, either as a direct prophecy concerning Jesus' death and resurrection or, more indirectly, as a model that prefigures Jesus' own life.

While not negating these interpretations, Nzimande argues that the servant figure can *also* be a model for the kind of suffering that many black women in South Africa endure under the yoke of globalization and socio-economic exploitation. She highlights that the recent increase in upper-class women working outside their homes have increased the demand of lower-class black women to work as maids. In this manner, poor women are now working as domestics in black households, just as they did in white ones. While benefiting economically from such arrangements, poor black women are being typically reduced again to positions of inferiority. Black South African women can nevertheless, alongside the servant, wait for the day when Babylon – that is, the current oppressive situation – will be finally destroyed.

Part 3: Application

Prophetic Books in ministry

The prophetic literature offers us glimpses as to who God is. Words can never fully describe or define God, and they cannot give us a complete picture of God's nature. The prophetic literature conveys, through the use of images, metaphors, and similes, the prophet's understanding of his character and his actions. More than any other part of the Bible, the prophetic literature reveals to us God's grandeur. The vision report in Ezekiel 1, envisaging God enthroned in splendour upon a flying chariot carried by otherworldly creatures, paints a mind-blowing picture of God's awesome majesty and incomprehensibility. Likewise, Isaiah's vision of God, seated upon his throne in the temple and surrounded by heavenly creatures (Isa. 6), reveals God's absolute magnificence. As evidenced by 2,000 years of Jewish and Christian Reception History, these images have informed our view of God. Among the earliest examples of this reception is the account of John's visionary experience of 'the Son of Man' in Revelation 1.12–20 and in Revelation 4.

The prophetic literature also gives us images that help us to understand God's acts towards his people and his relationship with them. God has made a covenant with Israel and they now share a bond of mutual obligations as well as feelings for one another. According to the prophetic literature, God is in dialogue with Israel and he adapts his actions to Israel's actions (Amos 7.1–6; Jer. 18.7–10; 26.3; cf. Jon. 3.9–10). Many texts describe God in terms of his strength: he is a mighty warrior (Isa. 42.13; 63.1–6) and a rock (Isa. 26.4; Hab. 1.14). Other passages emphasize God's loving care for us as they liken him to a parent: God behaves as a mother who cries out in childbirth (Isa. 42.14), a mother who carries Israel as a baby (Isa. 46.3–4), and who nurtures (Isa. 49.15) and comforts (Isa. 66.13). Alternatively, God is portrayed as a loving father who teaches Israel to take his first steps (Hos. 11.1) and who gives good gifts to his children (Jer. 3.19). Yet other texts, wishing to express God's ardent love for Israel, as well as his jealous and proprietorial feelings towards *his* people, liken God to a spouse. They describe God as a wronged husband who seeks his wife's (i.e. his people's) repentance and reconciliation (Jer. 3.6–11; 31.31–32), or, alternatively, as a violent, cuckolded husband who seeks vengeance (Ezek. 16), or, yet again, as a loving husband who longs for his wife to come back to him (Isa. 54.4–6). A few texts also portray God as overcome with emotions for Israel that his whole inner being is in torment (Hos. 11.8).

The prophets, as God's spokespersons, strove to give the people of Israel ethical guidelines according to which they could model their lives. The prophets proclaimed that God looks for people with integrity, equipped with a strong social conscience and filled with burning compassion. His people should do what is morally right, and they should care for the poor, the marginalized, and the downtrodden in society: often epitomized by 'orphans' and 'widows'. In the case of an individual's own life, Isaiah proclaims the desired state forcefully: 'Wash, clean yourself, remove evil from your actions from before my eyes, cease to do evil, learn to do good, seek justice, straighten what is oppressed, defend the orphan, advocate for the widow' (1.16–17). In other words, do what is right, and bring about social justice. According to Amos (4.1; 5.1–11; 6.1, 4–6), the people of Israel should share with their poorer brothers and sisters instead of hording riches for themselves. In the same vein, Isaiah speaks of the Israelites' social duties (58.6–7, 10). God wishes each and every one of them to 'open evil bonds, to unbind bonds of oppression, to let those crushed go free, and to break every yoke of oppression'. They should share their food with the hungry, provide a home for the homeless, dress the naked, and show solidarity with their relatives. If they do that, then God promises to be near them and to hear their prayers. On a national level, the prophetic literature criticizes Israel's leaders for their failure to lead and care for the people (e.g. Ezek. 34.1–6). A good leader should be like God who satisfies his people's needs in terms of food, rest, and security. A good leader seeks those who are lost, heals those who are broken, and strengthens those who are ill (Ezek. 34.11–16).

The Church will never *replace* Israel as God's chosen people. Rather, we are grafted into Israel through God's grace and by Jesus' death on the cross (Rom. 11). As such, the Church can partake of many of the promises to Israel. When the Bible describes God as caring for Israel as a parent, then the Church can translate this promise into our own context and we, as Christians, can share Israel's place and relate to God as our heavenly father and mother. Likewise, when the Bible describes God as chastening Israel for failing to put him first in their lives and for giving their devotion to other matters, then the Church, alongside the synagogue, should also stand corrected. It is also important that the Church incorporates the whole range of divine imagery into its image of God as it teaches and preaches God's words. God, according to the prophetic literature, is not a passive God who created the world and then left it to its own devices. Rather, God is compassionately involved in the affairs of his creation; he rejoices when Israel or the Church rejoices and he grieves when they go against his will and when they act without compassion and mercy towards one another.

Most of us today would agree wholeheartedly with the aforementioned ethical guidelines. There is, however, much in the prophetic literature that is foreign to our modern sensibilities and ethics (as pointed out above by O'Brien and Weems). The rhetoric of violence in warfare in the book of Nahum is a case in point. Likewise, passages such as Isaiah 34.5–7, which glorifies God's bloodshed as he destroys Edom, and the similarly gory portrayal of God's destruction of his enemies in Jeremiah 46.10, should cause modern readers to pause. In a similar manner, most readers, male and female alike, are shocked by the rhetoric of sexual violence in the book of Ezekiel (Ezek. 16 and 23).

When dealing with this issue, we need to be aware that the prophetic literature is a time-bound collection of documents that reflects the knowledge and values of 3,000 to 2,000 years ago. At that time, the earth was considered to be flat and at the centre of the universe, slavery was accepted, and women and foreigners were second-rate human beings. The ancient Israelite prophets were children of their time and, as such, restricted in its understandings. In the same way as the biblical material cannot contribute to the modern study of astronomy, so we cannot take for granted that we can adopt all prophetic values without serious reflection. For instance, more than one prophetic text in the Old Testament (e.g. Isa. 10; 17; Nah. 2—3) prescribes that the correct way of dealing with political enemies is their total annihilation. The Church today cannot allow this commandment to form the basis of modern Christian ethics.

It is important for contemporary readers to confront such passages and not explain them away as something that happened in the past and thus of no concern for us. We should also take care not to omit them from our reading or seek to redeem them by claiming that they are not as bad as they look. Instead, we must read them at face value and battle with them. Although we may never really find the optimum way of relating to the difficult texts in the prophetic literature, we must continue to *engage* with them so that we do not become complacent about human suffering.

Prophetic Books in mission

As Israel's prophets were in the past, so Christians today are sent by God to preach God's words, to encourage one another, to act justly and mercifully, and to intercede before God on behalf of sinners. Just as God commissioned Isaiah as his mouthpiece, and just as Isaiah responded with the words 'Here I am; send me' (Isa. 6.8b), so we are invited to be carriers of God's words. Indeed, the so-called prophetic 'call narratives' have been particularly important in helping to articulate the discernment of Christian vocations to ministry and mission. For example, in the Church of England's service of ordination to the deaconate, prior to the priesthood, the narrative of Jeremiah's prophetic calling (from Jer. 1) is read publicly.

From a Christian perspective, the reality of Jesus links both Testaments. The New Testament confesses the continuity, yet also the radical newness of the gospel. Within this perspective, the prophetic literature contains texts that speak about Jesus. In other words, the prophetic books 'foretell' Jesus' future acts of salvation. Accordingly, the majority of Christian exegetes throughout the last two millennia, including not only the Church Fathers but also the exegetes of the Reformation, have searched the prophetic literature for predictions about Jesus, his nature, life, work, death, resurrection, and glorification. For instance, most Christians today would agree that Isaiah 9.2–7 foreshadows Jesus' birth, and that Isaiah 52.12—53.13 refers to Jesus' death on the cross. In other cases, the suggested link between the Old and the New Testament is weaker. The prophet Jonah, his three-day stay in the belly of the fish, and his preaching to the people of Nineveh have commonly been understood as a precursor to Jesus' death, resurrection, and the offer of salvation to the Gentiles (Matt. 12.38–40; Luke 11.29–30; cf. Theodore of Mopsuestia's *Commentary on Jonah*, Introduction). The parallels between Jonah and Jesus can be challenged on several levels: most obviously, there are not three days between Good Friday and Easter Sunday, and Jonah had no desire to preach to the Gentiles.

More recently, Brevard S. Childs, followed by other scholars, advocated a modern variety of this kind of approach. Even though Childs differentiates between theological and historical readings of the Old Testament, and stresses the importance of reading a text in the Old Testament in its literary and historical context, he nevertheless maintains that that text receives a new *significance* when read canonically – that is, within the context of both the Old and the New Testament. A canonical approach, although not in itself incorrect, nevertheless faces several problems. First, the discovered parallels between the prophetic literature in the Old Testament and Jesus' life and death are often not self-evident, as in the case of Jonah (above). Second, a canonical approach runs the danger of creating a Christian 'canon within a canon' where the Church only reads those passages that can be understood as predictions about Jesus. This, in turn, leads to the neglect of approximately 90 per cent of the prophetic literature.

And third, it is unlikely that the ancient Israelite prophets *intended* their prophecies to be mainly about Jesus and the future. Thomas of Aquinas argues that although the human prophets intended the 'plain sense' of the text, God, as the ultimate author and the one who comprehends everything, embedded a multiplicity of meaning, including allegorical and typological interpretations, into the text.[26] This is a possible approach, yet its inevitable side effect is that it silences the plain sense of the Old Testament. It also fails to take into account the fact that the Old Testament passages, in their own context, do not always speak about the future but rather address the prophet's contemporary audience. In other words, the prophetic books also 'forthtell', in the sense that they speak out publicly against sin and injustice. In addition, the neglect of this impedes fruitful dialogues between Christians and Jews about the content and meaning of the Old Testament.

As a Church, it is important that we read *all* of the prophetic books in the canon in their original context and listen attentively to the plain sense of the *whole* text. We must first ascertain that we understand a text in its original context before we seek to read it canonically as prefiguring Jesus. Only when we understand the text in its own right can we begin to look at how the Church has understood it traditionally, and how we can understand it for today. At that point, we have a choice of whether to hold on to the plain sense, to adhere to a traditional Christian interpretation, or somehow to straddle both meanings. Yet the canonical sense should never erase the plain historical meaning of the text.

The prophetic literature has served as the inspiration for many great works of art, music, and literature. To begin with the obvious examples, few people are unfamiliar with Handel's *Messiah* (1741). The oratorio, written by Charles Jennens, reflects on Jesus' role as the Messiah. Its opening words are taken directly from Isaiah 40.1–3, which proclaim 'comfort, comfort my people'. The ensuing scenes 1–5 proceed with other parts of Isaiah 40.1–9, as well as with Isaiah 7.14, 9.2–6, 35.5–6, 60.1–3, Haggai 2.6–7, Zechariah 9.9–10, and Malachi 3.1–3, which together announce the splendour of the temple in Jerusalem, the coming of the messenger (identified with John the

Baptist) who will purify the people and prepare the way for the Messiah, and the Virgin Birth.

The text of Zephaniah 1.14–18, often called the *Dies irae* (from the Latin Vulgate translation, meaning 'Day of Wrath', Zeph. 1.15) takes another prominent position in music. It is an integral part of many requiems through the ages. The requiems by Mozart, Verdi, Berlioz, Vaughan Williams, and Britten, to name but a few, all employ this text. The same passage also appears frequently in literature. Harriet Beecher Stowe, for example, refers to this text in chapter 19 of *Uncle Tom's Cabin* (1852).[27]

The prophets themselves, as well as many images from the prophetic literature, have been commemorated in art. Michelangelo's depiction of the prophets and sibyls in the Sistine Chapel (1508–12), for instance, features seven Israelite prophets (Jonah, Jeremiah, Ezekiel, Joel, Zechariah, Isaiah, Daniel) who all foretold the coming of Jesus the Messiah. These characters are the largest figures in the Vault of the Chapel and thus command the viewer's attention.

Jonah and Daniel are by far the most commonly depicted prophets, probably due to the narrative quality of the books bearing their names. There are many famous depictions of the character of Jonah. The so-called *Jonah Sarcophagus* (c. AD 300), presently in the Vatican, portrays key passages of the Jonah narrative: Jonah paying the fare to the sailors, Jonah being thrown into the sea, the fish vomiting him out, Jonah warning the Ninevites, and Jonah sleeping in the shade of a plant.[28] Many years later, Jan Brueghel the Elder painted his famous painting *Jonah Leaving the Whale* (1600), on display in the Alte Pinakothek in Munich.[29]

Among the most famous paintings of prophetic themes is Rembrandt's *Belshazzar's Feast* (1636–8), inspired by the narrative in Daniel 5 and presently in the National Gallery in London. It depicts how the hand of God appeared to Belshazzar, the Neo-Babylonian ruler, and wrote the cryptic words *mene, tekel, upharsin*, which are given their explanation in verse 25.[30] Another renowned painting by Rembrandt is his *Jeremiah Lamenting the Destruction of Jerusalem* (1630), on display in Rijksmuseum in Amsterdam, which depicts the prophet Jeremiah leaning his tired head on his hand as he mourns the destruction of Jerusalem.[31]

Turning to literature, novels and poems have picked up many of the key topics of the prophetic literature. The fall of Nineveh as depicted in the book of Nahum, for example, has often exemplified 'how the mighty have fallen'. In his poem 'The Fall of Nineveh' (1847), the poet Edwin Atherstone depicts a city filled with splendour. Fifty years later, the author Rudyard Kipling compared the British Empire with Nineveh in his poem 'Recessional' (1897).[32]

The vivid and frequently bizarre images in the book of Ezekiel have often been alluded to in literature. Let us end with the words of John Milton, who employed Ezekiel's depiction of the heavenly chariots (Ezek. 1) in his *Paradise Lost* (1667) to portray God's glory and majesty:

Flashing thick flames, Wheele within Wheele, undrawn,
It self instinct with Spirit, but convoyd
By four Cherubic shapes, four Faces each
Had wondrous, as with Starrs thir bodies all
And Wings were set with Eyes, with Eyes the wheels
Of Beril, and careering Fires between;
Over thir heads a chrystal Firmament,
Whereon a Saphir Throne, inlaid with pure
Amber, and colours of the showrie Arch.[33]

Notes

1 See further, Nogalski, J. D., 2011, *The Book of the Twelve*, 2 vols, Macon, GA: Smyth & Helwys Bible Commentary, vol. 1, pp. 1–17.

2 For an easily accessible introduction to the relationship between the Old Testament and the early Church, see Heine, R. E., 2007, *Reading the Old Testament with the Ancient Church: Exploring the Formation of Early Christian Thought*, Evangelical Ressourcement: Ancient Sources for the Church's Future, Grand Rapids, MI: Baker.

3 This definition is taken from 'Apocalypse Group' of the Society of Biblical Literature (SBL), published in Collins, J. J., 1979, 'Introduction: Towards the Morphology of a Genre', in *The Morphology of a Genre*, Semeia 14, Chico, CA: Scholars Press, pp. 1–20, at p. 9.

4 For further discussion of the use of the Old Testament in Revelation, see Beale, G. K., 1998, *John's Use of the Old Testament in Revelation*, JSNTS, 166, Sheffield: Sheffield Academic Press.

5 MacGregor, R. (tr.), 2014, *Ancient Bible Commentaries in English: Commentary on Jonah by St. Jerome*, Ashland, KY: Litteral's Christian Library Publications, pp. 8, 39.

6 For a good discussion of Jerome, his life, and his background, see Williams, M. H., 2006, *The Monk and the Book: Jerome and the Making of Christian Scholarship*, Chicago, IL; London: University of Chicago Press, pp. 1–23. For a discussion of the relevance of Jerome's thoughts for today's Christians, see Hall, C. A., 1998, *Reading Scripture with the Church Fathers*, Downers Grove, IL: Inter-Varsity Press, pp. 108–16.

7 For a discussion of rabbinic exegesis of this notion, see the 'Overview' by Rabbi Nossom Scherman in Zlotowitz, M. (tr.), 1980, *The Twelve Prophets: Yonah*, The Artscroll Tanach Series, New York: Mesorah Publications, pp. ccviii–ccxxix.

8 Hill, R. C. (tr.), 2004, *Commentary on the Twelve Prophets*, FOTC, 108, Washington, DC: Catholic University of America Press, pp. 37–102, at p. 41. For a general introduction to his life and work and approach to the Old Testament, see the same volume, pp. 1–34; Hill, R. C., 2005, *Reading the Old Testament in Antioch*, BAC, 5, Leiden: Brill; and Hall, C. A., 1998, *Reading Scripture with the Church Fathers*, Downers Grove, IL: Inter-Varsity Press, pp. 163–9.

9 Connolly, S., 1997, *Bede: On Tobit and On the Canticle of Habakkuk*, Dublin: Four Courts Press, p. 75. For a discussion of his methods of interpretation, see further, Ward, B. (Sister), 1998, *The Venerable Bede*, London: Geoffrey Chapman, p. 74.

10 Zier, M., 2000, 'Nicholas of Lyra on the Book of Daniel', in Krey, P. D. W. and Smith, L. (eds), *Nicholas of Lyra: The Senses of Scripture*, SHCT, 90, Leiden: Brill, pp. 173–93, at p. 179.

11 For more detailed discussion of Nicholas of Lyra, see Skevington Wood, A., 1961, 'Nicolas of Lyra', *The Evangelical Quarterly*, 33/4, pp. 196–206.

12 Oswald, H. C. (ed.) and Bouman, H. J. A. (tr.), 1972, 'Lectures on Isaiah', *Luther's Works*, St Louis, MO: Concordia Publishing, vol. 17, p. 313.

13 Oswald, H. C. (ed.) and Bouman, H. J. A. (tr.), 1974, 'First Lectures on the Psalms', *Luther's Works*, St Louis, MO: Concordia Publishing, vol. 10, p. 7.

14 For Luther's exegetical methods, see, further, Thompson, M. D., 2009, 'Biblical Interpretation in the Works of Martin Luther', in Hauser, A. J. and Watson, D. F. A. (eds), *A History of Biblical Interpretation. Vol 2: The Medieval through the Reformation Periods*, Grand Rapids, MI: Eerdmans, pp. 299–318.

15 Owen, J. (tr.), 1986, *Zechariah and Malachi*, GSC, The Minor Prophets 5, Edinburgh: Banner of Truth Trust, pp. 518–19.

16 See further discussion of Calvin's way of interpreting the Old Testament in Wilcox, P., 2006, 'Calvin as Commentator on the Prophets', in McKim, D. K. (ed.), *Calvin and the Bible*, Cambridge: Cambridge University Press, pp. 107–30.

17 Huffmon, H. B., 2000, 'A Company of Prophets: Mari, Assyria, Israel', in Nissinen, M. (ed.) *Prophecy in its Ancient Near Eastern Context: Mesopotamian, Biblical, and Arabian Perspective*, SBLSS 13, Atlanta, GA: SBL, p. 47.

18 O'Brien, J. M., 2009, *Nahum*, 2nd edn, Readings: A New Bible Commentary, Sheffield: Sheffield Phoenix Press, p. 18.

19 Seitz, C. R., 2007, *Prophecy and Hermeneutics: Towards a New Introduction to the Prophets*, STI, Grand Rapids, MI: Baker, pp. 150–1.

20 For a recent and well-informed discussion, see Poulsen, F., 2014, *God, His Servant, and the Nations in Isaiah 42:1-9: Biblical Theological Reflections after Brevard S. Childs and Hans Hübner*, FAT, 2/73, Tübingen: Mohr Siebeck.

21 Weems, R. J., 1995, *Battering Love: Marriage, Sex, and Violence in the Hebrew Prophets*, OBT, Minneapolis, MN: Fortress Press, pp. 59–60, 96.

22 Bundang, R. A. R., 2002, 'Home as Memory, Metaphor, and Promise in Asian/Pacific American Religious Experience', *Semeia*, 90/91 (The Bible in Asian America), pp. 87–104, at p. 88.

23 Bundang, 'Home as Memory', pp. 99–102.

24 Nzimande, M. K., 2010, 'Isaiah', in Page, H. R. (ed.), *The Africana Bible: Reading Israel's Scriptures from Africa and the African Diaspora*, Minneapolis, MN: Fortress Press, pp. 136–46, at pp. 143–4.

25 See further, www.elcsadurban.co.za/Home/Leagues_-_iMbokodo.html.

26 Thomas Aquinas, *Summa Theologica*, 1a1, 10; Gilby, T. (ed.), 1963, *St Thomas Aquinas Summa Theologica: Latin Text and English Translation, Introductions, Notes, Appendices and Glossaries*, London: Eyre and Spottiswoode, vol. 1, pp. 37–41.

27 For these and other references in music and literature to the *Dies irae*, see Han, J. H., 2011, 'Nahum, Habakkuk, and Zephaniah', in Coggins, R. and Han, J. H. (eds), *Six Minor Prophets Through the Centuries*, BBC, Chichester: Wiley-Blackwell, pp. 96–9.

28 See further, www.livius.org/jo-jz/jonah/jonah-sarcophagus.html.

29 See further, www.artbible.info/art/large/330.html.

30 See further, www.nationalgallery.org.uk/paintings/rembrandt-belshazzars-feast.

31 See further, www.rijksmuseum.nl/en/collection/SK-A-3276.

32 See further, Han, 'Nahum, Habakkuk, and Zephaniah', pp. 9–11.

33 Milton, J., 1667, *Paradise Lost*, 6.751-9. See further discussion in Lieb, M., 1998, *Children of Ezekiel: Aliens, UFOs, the Crisis of Race, and the Advent of End Time*, Durham, NC: Duke University Press, pp. 21–41.

6

Apocrypha/Deutero-Canon

HYWEL CLIFFORD

Part 1: Introduction

The collection of ancient texts that is printed under the title 'Apocrypha' in many English editions of the Bible comprises texts that have acquired variable status in the different traditions of Christianity. They are therefore encountered in different ways. In Roman Catholic Bibles, they are integrated as canonical texts among the books of the Old Testament (e.g. 1 and 2 Maccabees with the Historical Books, Sirach in Poetry and Wisdom); whereas in Protestant Bibles they are either placed in a separate appendix to the Old Testament (before the New Testament) or they are omitted from Bibles altogether. The adjective 'apocryphal' can refer to one of these texts. But due to the legacy of the dispute over their status since the Protestant Reformation, it frequently refers to a story of doubtful authenticity, if not false or misleading content – as in popular parlance. For this reason, in Roman Catholic and Orthodox Christianity, at least, the alternative term 'Deutero-canonical' is generally preferred, as it indicates not only that these texts are canonical but also that they are secondary ('Deutero'), in terms of both their later periods of composition and later formal recognition as authoritative texts. The more ancient 'proto-canonical' texts of the Old Testament are common to all Christian traditions.[1]

To begin to make sense of these less well-known texts, it is helpful to approach them with the more ancient, canonical Old Testament texts in view. To give some examples: the Wisdom of Solomon uses the voice of ancient Israel's famously wise king; Psalm 151 is a short poem just like many of the 150 canonical psalms; and the Additions to Esther are about the very same Jewish heroine exiled in Persia. Indeed, all of them have a close relationship to the more ancient biblical texts, as is evident from their genres, which may be similarly classified: history, poetry, story, wisdom, and apocalyptic (the order followed below under 'Apocrypha/Deutero-Canon in Summary'). Some are directly dependent for their content and literary form on the older canonical texts, as 'Rewritten Bible' (e.g. 1 Esdras), 'Additions' (i.e. to Daniel, Esther), and imitations (e.g. Baruch). Others, which still depend in various ways on the older texts, are best seen as independent compositions: history (e.g. 1 and 2 Maccabees), story (e.g. Tobit, Judith), and wisdom (e.g. Sirach, Wisdom of Solomon). Taken together, they are about one-fifth of the length of the canonical Old Testament.

As individual texts they are diverse. Sirach is the longest at 51 chapters, whereas Psalm 151 has just seven verses. While some are about the biblical era (e.g. an exiled Daniel) or might have had early post-exilic origins (e.g. Tobit), they were largely composed later: between the third century BC and the first century AD. Some were composed in Hebrew or Aramaic and then translated into Greek (as were the biblical texts in the translation known as the Septuagint). Others were originally composed in Greek. Who wrote them? They were written by various religious, literary Jews living under Persian, Greek (Hellenistic), and Roman rule, whether at home in Palestine or abroad in the Jewish diaspora (the Christian additions in Latin to 2 Esdras are the obvious exception). But they are largely pseudonymous – written in the name of another ancient figure; there are hardly any indications within them about their authorship (e.g. Sir. Prologue; 50.27; 2 Macc. 2.23; 2 Esd. 14). Nevertheless, they provide a valuable and unique window on aspects of the early Judaism of those periods. They did not form a distinct or coherent collection from the start (as if there was an 'Apocrypha' in Jewish antiquity) and they have never been treated as canonical texts by most religious Jews.

Apocrypha/Deutero-Canon in overview

Books and Additions that are in the Roman Catholic, Greek, and Slavonic Bibles: Tobit, Judith, The Additions to the book of Esther, Wisdom of Solomon, Sirach (= the Wisdom of Jesus son of Sirach, or Ecclesiasticus), Baruch, The Letter of Jeremiah (= Baruch 6), The Additions to the book of Daniel (The Prayer of Azariah and the Song of the Three Jews, Susanna, Bel and the Dragon), 1 Maccabees, 2 Maccabees.

Books in the Greek and Slavonic Bibles; not in the Roman Catholic Canon: 1 Esdras (= 2 Esdras in Slavonic = 3 Esdras in an Appendix to the Vulgate), Prayer of Manasseh (in an Appendix to the Vulgate), Psalm 151, 3 Maccabees.

In the Slavonic Bible and Appendix to the Latin Vulgate: 2 Esdras (= 3 Esdras in Slavonic = 4 Esdras in the Vulgate) (Note: in the Vulgate, Ezra-Nehemiah = 1 and 2 Esdras).

In an Appendix to the Greek Bible: 4 Maccabees.

Apocrypha/Deutero-Canon in summary

1 Esdras

Covering a long time-span (*c.* 622–*c.* 428 BC), the continuity of Israelite religion is the underlying theme of this book, and its central concern is the restoration of temple worship in Jerusalem in the Persian period. It is a shorter parallel history to Chronicles, Ezra, and Nehemiah, based specifically on 2 Chronicles 35—36 (Josiah and the last kings of Judah), mostly Ezra, and Nehemiah 7—8. It also contains new text that recalls more ancient court tales (e.g. Joseph, Daniel, Esther). Three bodyguards compete for high position, with each arguing for that which has the strongest influence: wine, kingship, or women, and then truth. The latter, deemed the winner, is argued for by Zerubbabel, the protagonist and governor in Yehud (= Judah) after the Exile. Various compositional matters are debated: its date (perhaps the second century BC), its original language (Hebrew, Aramaic, or Greek), and its relationship to the canonical texts (whether it is part of a larger work, or complete in itself).

1 Maccabees

This book tells how Jewish leaders of the Hasmonean dynasty defended Judea in the second century (175–135 BC). Following Alexander the Great's conquests, the Seleucid king Antiochus IV (Epiphanes), a descendant of Alexander's generals, invaded Jerusalem. He desecrated its temple and banned the practice of Judaism. Mattathias of Modein led a successful revolt, and nearing death announced his sons as his successors. The book's 16 chapters are dominated by the famous exploits of Judas Maccabaeus (Maccabee means 'hammer') who won a series of battles in a struggle for Jewish independence (3.1—9.22). This included purging the Jewish community of its traitors, rededicating the temple in 164, conquering surrounding peoples, and making a treaty with Rome. Judas was succeeded by Jonathan Maccabaeus (Apphus) in 160. There followed internal Seleucid power struggles (between Demetrius I and Alexander Balas, who both courted Jonathan's allegiance) and also externally with the Ptolemaic rulers of Egypt. Jonathan was made High Priest and governor by Alexander, and he renewed the Jews' friendship with Rome. Jonathan was killed in 143 by Antioch's governor Trypho, and was succeeded by Simon, who engaged in hostilities with Trypho but was honoured as High Priest by Rome and Sparta. Simon was killed in 134, and was succeeded by John (Hyrcanus). This book, based on second-century events, and probably written in Hebrew *c.* 100 BC, was translated into Greek (and versions dependent on the Greek). It is in the style of older Historical Books, with its heroes modelled on biblical figures (e.g. Joshua). It contrasts Jews and Gentiles sharply, but its Hasmonean protagonists, dedicated to their ancestral religion and its laws (which helps justify their questionable roles as High Priests), are portrayed as being pragmatic about political relations for the defence of the nation.

2 Maccabees

This book is not simply a continuation of 1 Maccabees. It is comprised of two letters and an 'epitome', a summary of a historical work, by Jason of Cyrene (2.23), that overlaps with 1 Maccabees. The first letter (1.1–10a), from Jerusalem, exhorts Egyptian Jews to celebrate the festival of Hanukkah (the rededication of the temple in Jerusalem). The second letter (1.10b—2.18) is similar, but includes an account of the death of Antiochus IV, and emphasizes the traditional importance of temple worship. The core, the epitome (3.1—15.37), is about the Maccabean revolt (187–161 BC), but it differs from, and does not always agree with, 1 Maccabees. Much more attention is given to the attacks of Antiochus IV, and also to the defeat of Nicanor (for which 'Nicanor's Day' was celebrated until AD 70). Also, in 2 Maccabees there is more divine involvement: Judas and his men often pray before battle, they are helped by angelic epiphanies, and the Jewish martyrs hope for resurrection. A major theme is the struggle of the Jews and 'Judaism' (first used here in Jewish literature in Greek, 2.21) against the brutal political imposition of 'Hellenism' (4.13), its religion and culture (e.g. sacrifices to Zeus, to Dionysus, the forced eating of pork, naked athletics). Jewish leaders seek good relations with the Greeks but, while some are compromised by this, others such as Judas are bound to their God, the nation, and its laws – such as not fighting on the Sabbath. They will die for them too, whether in battle or through torture (i.e. Eleazar, the seven brothers, and their mother). Based on second-century events (after 163) and probably compiled in the first century, it was written in Greek. It follows some conventions of Hellenistic history-writing – such as how a god defends a temple – as well as echoing earlier Historical Books (e.g. 2 Kings).

3 Maccabees

This book portrays an attempt by Ptolemy IV Philopator to destroy the diaspora Jews in Egypt (217–216 BC). The book's title misleads: it is not about the Maccabees, even if some of its themes echo their later period (e.g. the holiness of the Jerusalem temple, loyalty to the covenant laws, divine providence). After defeating Antiochus III at Raphia, and touring his conquered territories and their temples, Ptolemy was invited to Jerusalem. But he wished to enter the Holy of Holies, which only the High Priest was permitted to do once each year, so the Jews, supported by Simon the High Priest, lamented and prayed for divine intervention. God answered the prayer by paralysing Ptolemy temporarily. He was offended and returned to Egypt, determined to wreak vengeance on the Jews: he removed their rights as citizens, unless they apostatized, and commanded that they be registered for execution in a hippodrome. These, and other attempts to kill them (e.g. their trampling by 500 drugged elephants), failed in farce and comedy, as God repeatedly intervened in response to the Jews' prayers. The unstable king, now forced to acknowledge God, decreed a celebratory Jewish festival of deliverance, and the Jews returned to their Egyptian homes. The few who had apostatized were violently purged by the Jewish community, whereas the majority celebrated their new-found security. The book's central theme is divine providence: God intervenes in response to prayer from those loyal to the covenant and its laws. There is no individual human hero: Simon the High Priest in Jerusalem, and a priest Eleazar in Alexandria, support the Jews who act together as a people. It was originally composed in Greek, probably in the first century BC, and was translated into various languages (Syriac, Armenian, Old Slavonic). Its style and content recalls Hellenistic romance literature: a historical framework, whether or not based on actual events (cf. Josephus C. *Ap.* 2.5), is expanded with the motifs of divine rescue and human folly. It recalls other diaspora Jewish novels (e.g. Esther, Judith).

Prayer of Manasseh

Whether originally a Jewish or Christian composition (its earliest form is found in the *Didaskalia Apostolorum,* an early Christian text concerning Church order during the second or third centuries AD), this Greek text is presented as Manasseh's penitential prayer (see 2 Chron. 33.18-19). Its portrayal of Manasseh depends on 2 Kings in which he is blamed for the Babylonian Exile, and 2 Chronicles in which he repents and is restored. The first half (vv. 1–7) is a hymn of praise to the covenantal God of Israel's ancestors, who is the creator and is merciful. After lamenting his sins, Manasseh appeals sincerely to God for mercy and restoration (vv. 8–15).

Psalm 151

This is placed at the end of the Psalms in ancient Greek Bibles (and dependent versions in Latin, Syriac, Ethiopic). While it is described as 'outside the number' in Greek Bibles, it is canonical in the Greek and Russian Orthodox Churches. In verses 1–5 (based on 1 Sam. 16) David recounts his calling by a messenger (or angel) while still a young shepherd and musician, and his anointing to be king rather than any of his seemingly more impressive brothers. In verses 6–7 (based on 2 Sam. 17) his killing of Goliath for cursing him and disgracing Israel is recited. The Dead Sea Scrolls include a Hebrew version in two fragmentary parts.

Tobit

Set in the eighth-century-BC exiled community in Nineveh, Assyria, Tobit was an official of King Sennacherib. It was written in Hebrew or Aramaic (second-century BC fragments in both languages were discovered at Qumran), and translated into Greek (short and long forms) and Latin. In the first part (chs 1—3) Tobit is presented as a model of Jewish piety, unlike his fellow exiles, seen in his faithfulness to ancestral Jewish customs (e.g. sacrifice, tithing, burial, marriage, almsgiving). While relaxing outside, after burying a fellow Jew killed in Nineveh, Tobit is blinded by sparrow droppings. He unjustly accuses his wife Anna of stealing her employer's goat, which Anna laments. Meanwhile, in Ecbatana (Media), Sarah the daughter of Raguel, Tobit's cousin, laments the successive killing of seven husbands by a demon. The angel Raphael is sent to answer both Tobit's and Sarah's prayers.

In the second part (chs 4—6) Tobit, thinking of death, exhorts his son Tobias to be pious, and to retrieve money held in trust in Media. Raphael (whose angelic identity is not known to Tobias) is sent by God to accompany Tobias on his travels. By the River Tigris, a fish grabs Tobias' foot, but Raphael says it will be useful medicinally. Approaching Ecbatana, Raphael and Tobias discuss Sarah's marital eligibility as a kinswoman. In the third part (chs 7—10) they are welcomed by Raguel and Edna, Sarah's parents, and Tobias marries her. The fish's liver and heart are burned on the embers of incense to repel the demon – and they all give thanks to God that Tobias did not die on their wedding night. Raphael collects the money from Gabael in the town of Rages. Tobias insists that they must return to Nineveh. In the fourth part (chs 11—14) there is resolution. With the fish's gall bladder, Tobit heals his father's blindness. Raphael reveals his angelic identity, commends piety, and tells Tobias to write down his experiences. Tobit praises God, and calls the exiles to praise and confession. Tobit instructs Tobias to leave Nineveh, whose downfall has been prophesied (it happens within Tobias' lifetime); the Babylonian attack on Jerusalem is also anticipated. The families live out their days in prosperity, and are buried with honour.

Judith

This book is about a pious Jewess who assassinates an Assyrian general through her beauty and cunning, saving Israel from almost certain defeat. Its mixture of Assyrian, Babylonian, Persian, and Hellenistic details, and errors (e.g. Nebuchadnezzar was not the king of Assyria but of Babylon), shows that it is a work of historical fiction (cf. 3 Maccabees). It was written originally in Aramaic or Greek, in the second or first centuries BC (as implied by its Maccabean allusions). The first part (chs 1—7) begins with Nebuchadnezzar making war against Arphaxad of Media. He calls on western states to assist, but they refuse, which prompts his revenge, led by general Holofernes. After a destructive western campaign, Holofernes ends up in Galilee, near to Judea. Fearful for the temple's destruction once again, the High Priest in Jerusalem leads the preparations for war. Achior the Ammonite warns Holofernes that an Israel obedient to their God will be defended – but this advice is arrogantly rejected. Achior is expelled and handed over to the Israelites in the city of Bethulia. The Assyrians, Ammonites, and Edomites surround the Israelites, who debate whether to surrender, but the elder Uzziah asks the people to hold out for five days.

Judith is then introduced at the start of the second part (chs 8—16). After criticizing Uzziah's outlook, she determines to act secretly. Judith intercedes in prayer for Israel, beautifies herself, and then leaves Bethulia with her maid. They approach and enter the Assyrian camp. Claiming to be fleeing Israel's imminent judgement for having eaten the consecrated first fruits of the harvest, Judith offers military intelligence to Holofernes. Admiring her beauty, he and his servants believe her. Judith comes and goes regularly from the camp for prayer and purification. She is then invited to a private banquet, where Holofernes becomes very drunk – but Judith observes Jewish dietary regulations (*kashrut*). Left alone in his bedchamber and invoking God's help, Judith beheads Holofernes, and leaves the camp with her maid. Judith parades Holofernes' head back in Israel, amazing all of the people. Also amazed, Achior the Ammonite joins the Israelite community and is circumcised. Discovering Holofernes' headless body, the Assyrians flee, and Israel plunders their camp. Judith sings a song of victory – the enemy was undone by a woman – and offers her own shares of war as a votive offering in Jerusalem. Judith lives out her days in honour.

Additions to Esther

The Greek version of Esther contains the same story and characters as the Hebrew version: the Jews in the Persian Empire faced genocidal destruction by King Artaxerxes (= Ahasuerus), but through Esther's efforts they enjoyed deliverance and vengeance, which they celebrated in the festival of Purim. Like other biblical figures and post-exilic texts (e.g. Joseph, Daniel, Judith, 3 Maccabees), it is a story of the reversal of fortunes. But the six additions (A to F) render the original (which does not mention God) a more religious account with many references to God (some of which were also added to the canonical text) and various theological aspects (e.g. deliverance, providence, fasting, prayer). They also expand on the inner personal struggles of its characters and the story's drama (e.g. Esther's prayer, and her approach to Ahasuerus). The additions were composed later than the original Hebrew story (and placed after it by Jerome), even though some of them (A, C, D, F) were most likely translated into Greek from Hebrew or Aramaic originals. According to its colophon (the scribal notes about its publication), Esther's Letter about Purim was translated into Greek by Lysimachus, a resident of Jerusalem, during the reign of Ptolemy and Cleopatra (11.1; cf. 9.29). This suggests the late second or early first century BC as the period of composition, although the identification of Ptolemy is uncertain since several rulers had this name and wives named Cleopatra. There is yet another Greek version, the 'Alpha Text', but this was based on a different Hebrew text.

Additions to Daniel

Like the stories in Daniel 1—6, these additions are about the deliverance of righteous Jews in Babylon in which Daniel is the most prominent figure. Sometimes placed between Daniel 3.23 and 3.24 (about Daniel's three friends in the fiery furnace), the 'Prayer of Azariah and the Song of the Three Jews' emphasize the martyrs' piety. 'Susanna' (Greek Bible ch. 13) is about how a young Daniel defends this Jewess against contradictory sexual accusations by two wicked judges and the threat of the death penalty; and he becomes famous following her exoneration. 'Bel and the Dragon' (Greek Bible ch. 14) are two stories about how Daniel exposes to King Cyrus the foolishness of idolatry. These three additions are part of a book with complex origins and growth: in different languages (Hebrew and Aramaic) and genres (stories and visions). Alternative versions of its stories circulated in antiquity (e.g. the madness of King Nebuchadnezzar, in Daniel 4, is attributed to the earlier King Nabonidus in some Dead Sea Scrolls fragments). It is likely that the three additions were originally composed in Hebrew or Aramaic, perhaps circulating as stories from the third century onwards, and translated into Greek by c. 100 BC. The Greek translations survived in two main versions: an initial 'Old Greek' translation, and the second-century AD translation by Theodotion, which differ from one another in places (e.g. in the Septuagint version, the cross-examination of the men takes place in a synagogue, not Susanna's husband's house).

Wisdom of Solomon

This book was most likely composed in Greek, in first-century BC or AD Alexandria. It is a fine illustration of Hellenistic Judaism: literary evidence for the influence of Hellenism on Judaism (e.g. non-biblical Greek, didactic and poetic genres, Platonist and Stoic ideas). But its biblical-style wisdom and other Jewish traditions remain core and paramount in its outlook. Perhaps intended for apologetic use within the Jewish community, its explicit addressees, 'rulers' (chs 1 and 6), are called to live by wisdom, an idea that has rich meaning and application throughout (e.g. morality, virtue, knowledge, revelation, desire, love, spirituality, cosmology, afterlife, justice). The first part (chs 1—6) is about the incompatibility of wisdom and wickedness, and the final rewards of the righteous (immortality) and the wicked who persecute them (punishment). Marked by a zeal for righteousness and virtue, this part ends with an exhortation to seek wisdom. The second part (chs 7—10) describes and praises wisdom, which is personified as a desirable, virtuous and cosmically powerful woman. It includes a mystical prayer and quest, in King Solomon's voice, for the gift of divine wisdom to be given him to enable his just rule, and to bring him immortality. The third part (chs 10—19) is an interpretation of the history of Israel, from Adam to the Exodus (although after chapter 10 the keyword *sophia* 'wisdom' occurs only at 14.2, 5; this could imply chs 11—19 were written by a different author). Its recurrent themes are divine providence for the people of God during the Exodus, and a defence of God's justice by means of naturally opposed outcomes (11.5): salvation or destruction, respectively. For instance, the plague of darkness overcame the Egyptians, but light guided the holy ones 'through whom the imperishable light of the law was given to the world' (18.4). The Law that was given to the world. The book includes a polemic against idolatry, especially among the Egyptians, by identifying its foolishness, origins, and damaging moral effects.

Sirach

Sirach (Ben Sira in Hebrew, Ecclesiasticus in Latin) was originally written in Hebrew while or after 'Simon son of Onias' (50.1, either Simon II or Simon the Just) was High Priest in Jerusalem (219-196 BC). It was translated into Greek in the second century BC, according to its Prologue, by the author's grandson (after 132 BC when he arrived in Egypt). Fragments in Hebrew (e.g. Dead Sea Scrolls, Masada, Cairo Geniza), and versions in Greek, Latin, and Syriac, have survived from antiquity and the medieval period. Probably written by a scribe or teacher (51.23 mentions 'the house of instruction'), he names himself 'Jesus son of Eleazar son of Sirach of Jerusalem' (50.27; incidentally, Jesus, the Greek form of Joshua, was a widespread name). This long book, in two parts (chs 1—24 and 25—51), contains discussions of standard wisdom topics (e.g. creation, death, honour, shame, money, women, justice). Its outlook is socially conservative and patriarchal but not without nuance (e.g. 26.1–18; 42.9–14). While it strongly resembles earlier biblical wisdom in its literary forms, content, and religious emphases (e.g. the fear of the Lord, the praise of wisdom, theodicy), it also contains ideas and sections untypical of earlier wisdom (e.g. the law as wisdom, prayers and hymns, and the history of famous Jewish ancestors). The book's poetry begins in praise of the wisdom that comes from God (1.1-10), and it ends with three additional poems – the last of which is an acrostic on the search for wisdom (51.13-28).

Baruch

This book addresses challenges to the faith of the Jews in exile and in Jerusalem. Attributed to Jeremiah's scribe, Baruch, living in Babylon (although according to the book of Jeremiah he went with the prophet to Egypt), it is a collection of narratives and poems. Begun in the second century BC, the book quotes extensively from earlier biblical texts. Ancient translators depended on a Greek version, even if the first part might have been originally composed in Hebrew. In the first part, in prose (1.1—3.8), Baruch reads to the exiles who, in humble confession, send money and return to Jerusalem the temple vessels that had been looted by the Babylonians. It advocates prayers for rulers, especially Nebuchadnezzar, and appeals to them to protect those in exile. Its theology, like Jeremiah, is that of the forced exile of the Jews from their homeland as punishment for rejecting the laws of God, but it includes appeals to God for mercy and restoration. The second part, in poetry (3.9—4.4), calls on the exiles to learn wisdom, which is identified with the Law that was given to Israel alone (as in Sir. 24). The third part, in poetry (4.5—5.9), addresses the Jews in exile and Jerusalem, much like Isaiah 40—66, with both challenge and encouragement about future restoration.

Letter of Jeremiah

While said to be a letter by Jeremiah to the exiles in Babylon (recalling Jer. 29), this is a second-century BC Jewish warning against apostasy. It is a satire on Babylonian idolatry that includes quotations from earlier biblical books on the same theme (e.g. Jer. 10; Isa. 44; Ps. 115). Its refrain is 'they [idols] are not gods' (6.16, 23, 29, etc.). It might have originally been composed in Hebrew, although it only survived in Greek and other versions (e.g. Syriac, Latin, Sahidic). In the Septuagint, Lamentations is placed between this letter and Baruch; whereas in the Vulgate this letter is known as Baruch 6, due to the association of all these texts with Jeremiah and his scribe of that name.

4 Maccabees

This first-century BC or AD Jewish work begins: 'The subject that I am about to discuss is most philosophical, that is, whether devout reason is sovereign over the emotions' (1.1). This is illustrated by the virtue and courage of the Jewish martyrs of the Maccabean period – Eleazar, and the seven brothers, and their mother – who were faithful to the observance of the Jewish laws. The core section (3.20—17.1) develops 2 Maccabees (especially chs 3, 6—7) with speeches and didactic insertions. The death of Eleazar also draws from Plato's *Gorgias*, on the death of Socrates: both were old, revered teachers, and faced death faithfully because of their prior allegiances. It contains a eulogy on the brothers' mother, explains the significance of the martyrdoms (17.2–22), and closes by contrasting the final destinies of the brothers with that of the tyrant Antiochus IV, who nevertheless commended their endurance to his own soldiers (17.23—18.23). Its main theological ideas are election, obedience, atonement (especially the Jews' propitiation for Gentile wickedness, and the martyrs' vicarious expiation and ransom for the Jews), salvation, and eschatology (in particular, everlasting life at peace versus the torment of the wicked). Written in Greek, whether in Alexandria, Antioch, or elsewhere, its philosophical content, especially the Stoic term for reason (*logismos*), and the four cardinal virtues of Plato ('rational judgement, justice, courage, self-control', 1.6, 18), place it within the sphere of Hellenistic Jewish philosophical writing (cf. Wisdom of Solomon; and, above all, Philo of Alexandria). The book also echoes earlier biblical figures (e.g. Abraham, Isaac, Jacob, Moses, David, Daniel). The closing section implies that there was an ancient festival in memory of the martyrs.

2 Esdras

The core of 2 Esdras, chapters 3—14 (= 4 Ezra), is a first-century AD Jewish apocalypse (with some Christian insertions: e.g. 7.28). Written in the name of the post-exilic Ezra, it contains seven visions that move from lament to consolation over the destruction of Jerusalem by Rome in AD 70. It recalls Jewish and Christian apocalypses such as Daniel, Enoch, and Revelation, in its literary forms (e.g. visions and angelic interpretations), its concerns (lament over Israel's unjust tribulations, the questioned fairness of God in judging sinful humanity), and its outlooks (i.e. the limitation of human wisdom; divine wisdom and justice; cosmic battle and Messianic victory; the resurrection to paradise of the elect and hell for rebellious sinners). Noteworthy features are an apocalyptic timetable and cosmography, an allegory about Jerusalem and Rome, and a description of its composition. Chapters 1—2 (= 5 Ezra) are a Christian addition in Latin that laments Israel's history of rebellion and foresees apocalyptic blessings for a new people of God (the Church). Chapters 15—16 (= 6 Ezra) are also a Christian addition in Latin that envisages upheavals and disasters, judgement against those who persecute the elect, and exhortations for the elect (of the Church) to be faithful because God will guide and purify them. Originally written in Greek, 2 Esdras was transmitted in the Latin Vulgate as a unified work, but parts translated from Greek have survived in other languages (e.g. Syriac, Ethiopic).

Part 2: Interpretation

Early Christianity

The New Testament texts provide some reflection of the diverse matrix of Jewish groups that existed in antiquity (e.g. Pharisees, Sadducees, Jewish-Christians). This is also borne out by some of the texts of the Apocrypha, and other writings (e.g. the Dead Sea Scrolls, Pseudepigrapha, Philo, Josephus). These texts were largely written in the later part of the broad period that is conventionally called Second Temple Judaism (c. 515 BC–AD 70). They show not only that there were many religious texts in circulation, but also that the categories of the Jewish canon had already begun to be established (e.g. 1 Macc. 9.27; 2 Macc. 2.13-14; 15.9; 2 Esd. 14.44-46; Josephus C. Ap. 1.37-43; Luke 24.44; Acts 28.23) – with the Torah as the undisputed foundation of all the 'Judaisms'. But while the texts and ideas of the Apocrypha were read and known in various Jewish communities (e.g. at Qumran: Sirach, Tobit; by Josephus: 1 Esdras, 1 Maccabees; among the Rabbis: 1 and 2 Maccabees, Sirach), they had less prominence than the more ancient canonical texts.

This was also the case for the New Testament writers. The more ancient canonical texts were primary for them. It is true that they do not quote formally from every Old Testament text (e.g. Joshua, Song of Songs, Zephaniah), and that they sometimes alluded to or quoted from others, both Jewish and non-Jewish (e.g. the Jewish 1 Enoch 1.9 in Jude 14—15; the Greek didactic poet Aratus in Acts 17). Still, it remains the case that, unlike the vast majority of the more ancient canonical texts, no text from the Apocrypha is quoted with a standard formula (e.g. 'it is written') by the New Testament writers. The near-contemporary Jewish philosopher Philo of Alexandria did not quote from them either. Nevertheless, the texts of the Apocrypha are important for making sense of parts of the New Testament texts within that ancient Jewish matrix.

Many Jewish-Christian concerns, well known from the New Testament, are also mentioned in the texts of the Apocrypha: the importance of the Law, the hope of a Messiah, and God's sovereignty over earthly nations and rulers. More than this, certain New Testament texts and ideas are helpfully explained by some of the texts in the Apocrypha. One clear example is 'the Feast of Dedication', or Hanukkah, referred to in the Gospel of John (10.22–23), for the celebration of the rededication of the Jerusalem temple since the Maccabean period. Other details might suggest direct influence from them on the New Testament writers. The sayings of Jesus are similar to the wisdom sayings of Sirach (e.g. Matt. 7.16–20 and Sir. 27.6; Matt. 6.12 and Sir. 28.2–4). The Letter to the Hebrews evokes the exalted figure of wisdom (Heb. 1.1–4; Wisd. 7.25–26; cf. Col. 1.15) and also the Maccabean martyrs (Heb. 11.35–36; 2 Macc. 6—7). Revelation 12.9 identifies the devil with the serpent of Genesis, as had Wisdom of Solomon 2.23–24. Paul's Letter to the Romans, in particular, echoes Wisdom, as the following excerpts indicate:

Wisdom 12–14 (selections)	Romans 1.20–32
(first century BC)	(late 50s AD)
13.5 For from the greatness and beauty of created things comes a corresponding perception of their Creator. Yet these people are little to be blamed, for perhaps they go astray while seeking God and desiring to find him. For while they	Ever since the creation of the world his eternal power and divine nature, invisible though they are, have been understood and seen through the things he has made. So they are without excuse; for though they knew God, they did not honour him

live among his works, they keep searching, and they trust in what they see, because the things that are seen are beautiful. Yet again, not even they are to be excused; for if they had the power to know so much that they could investigate the world, how did they fail to find sooner the Lord of these things?

13.1 For all people who were ignorant of God were foolish by nature; and they were unable from the good things that are seen to know the one who exists, nor did they recognize the artisan while paying heed to his works;

12.24 For they went far astray on the paths of error, accepting as gods those animals that even their enemies despised; they were deceived like foolish infants.

14.24 they no longer keep either their lives or their marriages pure, but they either treacherously kill one another, or grieve one another by adultery, and all is a raging riot of blood and murder, theft and deceit, corruption, faithlessness, tumult, perjury, confusion over what is good, forgetfulness of favours, defiling of souls, sexual perversion, disorder in marriages, adultery, and debauchery. For the worship of idols not to be named is the beginning and cause and end of every evil.

as God or give thanks to him, but they became futile in their thinking, and their senseless minds were darkened. Claiming to be wise, they became fools; and they exchanged the glory of the immortal God for images resembling a mortal human being or birds or four-footed animals or reptiles. Therefore God gave them up in the lusts of their hearts to impurity, to the degrading of their bodies among themselves, because they exchanged the truth about God for a lie and worshipped and served the creature rather than the Creator, who is blessed for ever! Amen.

For this reason God gave them up to degrading passions. Their women exchanged natural intercourse for unnatural, and in the same way also the men, giving up natural intercourse with women, were consumed with passion for one another. Men committed shameless acts with men and received in their own persons the due penalty for their error. And since they did not see fit to acknowledge God, God gave them up to a debased mind and to things that should not be done. They were filled with every kind of wickedness, evil, covetousness, malice. Full of envy, murder, strife, deceit, craftiness, they are gossips, slanderers, God-haters, insolent, haughty, boastful, inventors of evil, rebellious towards parents, foolish, faithless, heartless, ruthless. They know God's decree, that those who practise such things deserve to die — yet they not only do them but even applaud others who practise them.

There is a similar Jewish thought-pattern about Gentiles in evidence here: creation points to its creator God, but the foolish and inexcusable rejection of this leads to idolatry, and then to a catalogue of sins. But their overall message is different: the distinction between the wicked Gentile and the righteous Jew recurs in Wisdom, whereas Paul argues that both are guilty before God and both need the redemption of Jesus Christ.[2] Thus, although influence from the texts of the Apocrypha on the New Testament writers may be detected, here and elsewhere, they did not simply 'copy and paste' but interpreted that Jewish heritage in new ways, guided by the example and teaching of Jesus Christ. Attitudes to dietary laws (e.g. 4 Macc. 5; Matt. 23.23; Acts 10.9–16), help for the outsider (e.g. Sir. 12.7; Luke 10.29–37), and the role of religious violence (e.g. 1 and 2 Macc.; John 18.36) are other examples.

This development continued in the early Church, as it emerged out of its Jewish setting. The following excerpt from an ancient Christian commentary on Susanna, one of the three Additions to Daniel, by the theologian Hippolytus of Rome (AD 170–235), illustrates this well. Hippolytus read this text not only literally but also figuratively (i.e. by typology and allegory) in terms of Christ and the Church, and in so doing articulated beliefs and practices in ways that distinguished Christians from Jews, and also non-Christian Gentiles.

Hippolytus of Rome: 'On Susannah'

(second century AD)

What is narrated here, happened at a later time, although it is placed before the first book (at the beginning of the book). For it was a custom with the writers to narrate many things in an inverted order in their writings. For we find also in the prophets some visions recorded among the first and fulfilled among the last; and again, on the other hand, some recorded among the last and fulfilled first. And this was done by the disposition of the Spirit, that the devil might not understand the things spoken in parables by the prophets, and might not a second time lay his snares and ruin man.

7. 'And at noon Susannah went into (her husband's garden).' Susannah prefigured the Church; and Joakim, her husband, Christ; and the garden, the calling of the saints, who are planted like fruitful trees in the Church. And Babylon is the world; and the two elders are set forth as a figure of the two peoples that plot against the Church – the one, namely, of the circumcision, and the other of the Gentiles. For the words, 'were appointed rulers of the people and judges', (mean) that in this world they exercise authority and rule, judging the righteous unrighteously. 8. 'And the two elders saw her.' These things the

---

rulers of the Jews wish now to expunge from the book, and assert that these things did not happen in Babylon, because they are ashamed of what was done then by the elders.

52. 'O thou that art waxen old in wickedness.' Now, since at the outset, in the introduction, we explained that the two elders are to be taken as a type of the two peoples, that of the circumcision and that of the Gentiles, which are always enemies of the Church; let us mark the words of Daniel. And learn that the Scripture deals falsely with us in nothing. For, addressing the first elder, he censures him as one instructed in the law; while he addresses the other as a Gentile, calling him 'the seed of Canaan', although he was then among the circumcision.

55. 'For even now the angel of God.' He shows also, that when Susannah prayed to God, and was heard, the angel was sent then to help her, just as was the case in the instance of Tobias and Sara. For when they prayed, the supplication of both of them was heard in the same day and the same hour, and the angel Raphael was sent to heal them both.

61. 'And they arose against the two elders;' that the saying might be fulfilled, 'Whoever digs a pit will fall into it.' To all these things, therefore, we ought to give heed, beloved, fearing lest anyone be overtaken in any transgression, and risk the loss of his soul, knowing as we do that God is the Judge of all; and the Word Himself is the Eye which nothing that is done in the world escapes. Therefore, always watchful in heart and pure in life, let us imitate Susannah.[3]

Early Christian commentators, such as Origen of Alexandria and Sextus Julius Africanus, knew that Susanna was a late addition to Daniel, even though in Theodotion's text it was placed at the start (this is because Daniel is presented in Susanna as a promising 'young lad', v. 45). That Hippolytus chose, however, to make sense of it not chronologically but theologically, and comments on its Jewish rejection (paragraph 8 in the excerpt), is illustrative of the different status the texts of the Apocrypha had for Christians and Jews. Broadly speaking, Christians quoted and used many of them as canonical texts, whereas Jews only did so minimally; this is implied by rabbinic discussions of the second century AD, when the limits of the Jewish canon of Hebrew books were fixed (*B. Bat.* 14b; cf. *m. Yad.* 3.2–5). Indeed, it was Christian scholars of the first few centuries of the Church who largely transmitted these texts in Greek Bibles. They were therefore quoted and used alongside the more ancient biblical texts whose status was not by and large in dispute. Among the numerous examples are the following: the Wisdom of Solomon in early Christological debates (e.g. by Origen, Irenaeus of Lyon), the Prayer of Manasseh in the admonishment by bishops of sinners (e.g. *Apostolic Constitutions*) and 1 and 2 Maccabees in homilies about martyrdom (e.g. by John Chrysostom).[4]

This major difference between ancient Judaism and Christianity is also reflected in the discussions about the texts of the Apocrypha in the early Church. The Greek word *apocrypha* (which means 'secret, hidden away') was used of texts with esoteric content (cf. 2 Esdras) or of spurious texts in the context of heresy, as in the writings of Athanasius of Alexandria, and Rufinus of Aquileia, albeit not of the texts of the Apocrypha. It was Jerome (AD c. 347–420) who first applied this word to them, distinguishing them from the more ancient canonical texts written in Hebrew, a fact of which earlier scholars had been aware. Origen's *Hexapla* (early third century AD) – six columns of Old Testament texts in Hebrew and various Greek versions – had shown that some texts already existed in Hebrew versions that were different from those in later Greek translation, and that others had never existed in Hebrew at all. It was the *Hebraica veritas* ('Hebrew truth') that Jerome used to translate the Vulgate, a translation that was commissioned by Pope Damasus (366–84) to replace the many 'Old Latin' translations (of Greek originals) in circulation from the second century AD onwards. Jerome proposed that the texts of the Apocrypha could be used for edification (cf. Hippolytus, above), but not for establishing any Christian dogma given that they are pseudonymous and contain errors – a viewpoint that proved influential in the longer term. That said, he was encouraged to translate some of them into Latin (i.e. Tobit, Judith, Additions to Daniel and Esther). The others were translated and later included in the Vulgate.

Jerome's caution and critique of them was, however, opposed by Augustine and the Latin West in general, given their undoubted early Christian use.[5] But important caveats about the latter claim nonetheless need mentioning. The canonical lists of Old Testament texts in early Church writings, East and West, indicate the variable attestation of the texts of the Apocrypha: none of them (e.g. Melito of Sardis, Cyril of Jerusalem, Gregory of Nazianzus), some of them (e.g. Epiphanius of Salamis, Hilary of Poitiers), and most of them (e.g. Augustine of Hippo, the Council of Carthage 397). The principal ancient Greek uncial manuscripts of the Old Testament (codices Vaticanus, Sinaiticus, Alexandrinus) also show their variable attestation, in both order and content (which indicates, in addition, that *apocrypha* did not simply mean texts not in the Hebrew canon).[6] Moreover, the texts of the Apocrypha were quoted much less in the doctrinal disputes of the fourth to fifth centuries AD, given the prevalence of multiple heretical texts, and the concern to deploy undisputed sacred texts in defence of orthodoxy – a concern that may be traced to earlier periods (e.g. Origen, Irenaeus).

Medieval Christianity

In the medieval period, the preferred biblical descriptors were 'canonical' and 'ecclesiastical' – 'apocrypha' tended to be a derogatory designation. But the texts, whether in Greek or Latin translation, continued to be recognized by most in the Church, East and West, even if there was significant variation in practice. There are, again, ready examples of this. The list of canonical biblical texts affirmed at the Council of Rome (382), and repeated in the list of Pope Innocent I (401–17), appears in the collection of Church laws sent to Emperor Charlemagne by Pope Adrian I (772–95) and adopted in the Frankish Empire in 802. On a quite different front, the book of Tobit was influential in wedding ceremonies. For instance, the order of matrimony used in the Diocese of Salisbury in 1085, and throughout Britain by the thirteenth century, contains a priestly blessing that evokes the book of Tobit. As well as alluding to the angel Raphael's blessing (Tob. 12.6), and other texts, it alludes to the demon Asmodeus who killed all of Sarah's seven husbands on her successive wedding nights before she met Tobias:

Sarum Missal

(eleventh century AD)

After Mass let bread and wine, or some other good liquid in a vessel be blessed, and let them partake thereof in the name of the Lord, the priest saying:

V: The Lord be with you.
R: And with thy spirit.

Let us pray.

Collect.

Bl(+)ess, O Lord, this bread and this draught and this vessel, as thou didst bless the five loaves in the wilderness, and the six water-pots in Cana of Galilee; that all they who taste of them, may be discreet, sober and undefiled, O Saviour of the world, Who livest etc.

On the following night, when the bridegroom and bride have gone to bed, the priest shall approach the bed-chamber, saying:

V: The Lord be with you.
R: And with your spirit.

Let us pray.

Collect.

Bl(+)ess, O Lord, this sleeping-chamber, who neither slumberest nor sleepest, thou who watchest over Israel watch over thy servants who rest in this bed, guarding them from all phantasies and illusions of devils; guard them waking that they may meditate on thy commandments; guard them sleeping that in

---

their slumber they may think of thee; and that here and everywhere they may ever be defended by the help of thy protection. Through etc.

Then shall this blessing be said over them in bed:

Let us pray.

Collect.

God bl(+)ess your bodies and souls; and bestow his bless(+)ing upon you, as he blessed Abraham, Isaac, and Jacob. R. Amen.[7]

On a different front again, the Maccabean martyrs were commemorated in medieval piety – although they had been celebrated as Christian martyrs since the early Church (e.g. Origen *Mart.* 22—27; Cyprian *Fort.* 11). The ancient Jewish texts do not give their names, but these were invented later. The Calendar of Martyrs in the Syrian Church calls their mother Shamuni; whereas the *Greek Menea*, ritual books of the Eastern Orthodox Church, call her Solomonis. The brothers were also given non-Jewish names, such as Abion, Antonius, and Gourias. The first day of August was their traditional feast day in the Western Church, and they continued to be commemorated on that day even when the feast of St Peter in Chains (cf. Acts 12.1–11) became the main feast for that day. The *Sarum Missal* adds the following Collect to the Collect of St Peter in Chains:

Sarum Missal

(eleventh century AD)

Memory of the Martyrs.

Collect.

Let the crown of the martyred brothers, who are thine gladden us, O Lord, and both increase and strengthen our faith, and comfort us with their manifold protection. Through etc.

Lesson. Acts, xii.12–17.

He came to the house ... out of prison.[8]

A large church, or basilica, was built in their honour in Antioch in Syria, a major centre of early Christianity during the Roman Empire. Augustine had commented that the commemoration of the scene of their martyrdom in Antioch rather than Jerusalem was ironic: it was their persecutor's city of rule. In the later medieval era, there were also legends in circulation about their bodily remains. According to one of these legends, they were taken from Antioch to Constantinople, and then on to Rome and placed in the church of St Peter Ad Vincula ('St Peter in Chains'). However, in the later medieval era a dispute arose about them between Rome and a convent in Cologne, dedicated to the Maccabees, which claimed that it had their heads in golden vases. Be that as it may, in the Divine Office of the Roman Church, and hence in its Sarum version, the scriptural readings at Matins (the night office) were taken (with some variations) from Wisdom and Sirach in the second half of August, from Tobit and Judith in the second half of September, and from 1 and 2 Maccabees throughout October.

Reformation Christianity

While Jerome's view of the texts of the Apocrypha had been a minority view, some later medieval and Reformation scholars still distinguished them from the more ancient canonical texts (e.g. Nicholas of Lyra, John Wycliffe, Cardinal Ximenes). Others distinguished between them more carefully, such as Andreas Bodenstein of Karlstadt (1520): he divided the Apocrypha into non-canonical but holy texts (e.g. the Wisdom of Solomon, Tobit), and those that deserved censorship (e.g. 1 Esdras, Bel and the Dragon). The Apocrypha also became embroiled in Reformation-era doctrinal disputes over purgatory, prayers for the dead (2 Macc. 12.39–45), and the relationship between faith and works (Tob. 12.9; Sir. 3.30; 2 Esd. 9.7). Martin Luther's influential translation of the Old Testament (1534) has a preface in which he denied their primary canonical status, yet he acknowledged their usefulness (cf. Jerome). He had the Apocrypha placed in an appendix, a practice that became standard in early Protestant Bibles (e.g. the Coverdale 1535, the Matthew 1537, the Great 1539). The following excerpt expresses this qualified perspective well:

Geneva Bible: 'Apocrypha The Argument'

(1560)

These books that follow in order after the Prophets unto the New Testament, are called the Apocrypha; that is books, which were not received by a common consent to be read and expounded publicly in the Church, neither yet served to prove any point of Christian religion, save inasmuch as they had the consent of the other Scriptures called canonical to confirm the same, or rather whereon they were grounded: but as books proceeding from godly men, were received to be read for the furtherance of the knowledge of the history, and for the instruction of godly manners: which books declare that all times God had

---

an especial care of his Church and left them not utterly destitute of teachers and means to confirm them in the hope of the promised Messiah, and also witness that those calamities that God sent to his Church, were according to his providence, who had both so threatened by his Prophets, and so brought it to pass for the destruction of their enemies, and for the trial of his children.[9]

In Reformation-era Bibles, the contents and order of the texts of the Apocrypha varied; in the Geneva Bible the Prayer of Manasseh was not placed in its appendix, but it followed 2 Chronicles. The distinction drawn in the excerpt between 'a point of Christian religion' (dogma) and 'godly manners' (edification) is also seen in other near-contemporary Church documents: for instance, Article 6, 'Of the Sufficiency of the Scriptures', of the *Thirty-Nine Articles* (1563), which, tellingly, appeals to Jerome as an ancient authority. Interestingly, Article 35, 'Of The Homilies', refers to sermons on Protestant doctrine and practice that nevertheless quote from the Apocrypha about 80 times (as well as from other sources, e.g. early Church writings). The Geneva Bible, produced in Switzerland by English churchmen, contained, as well as an apparatus of cross-references and maps, Calvinist marginal notes that, depending on ecclesiastical allegiances, made it either loved or loathed. The strong influence of the Geneva Bible was responded to with the production of other Bibles in English: the Roman Catholic Douay-Rheims (1610), and the Anglican Bishops' Bible (1568), which, subject to revisions, became the basis of the now very famous and popular Authorized Version (1611). An especially strong early Roman Catholic response to Protestant developments is seen in the following excerpt:

Council of Trent

(1545–63)

Decree Concerning the Canonical Scriptures

The sacred and holy, ecumenical, and general Synod of Trent, – lawfully assembled in the Holy Ghost, the same three legates of the Apostolic See presiding therein, – keeping this always in view, that, errors being removed, the purity itself of the Gospel be preserved in the Church; which (Gospel), before promised through the prophets in the holy Scriptures, our Lord Jesus Christ, the Son of God, first promulgated with His own mouth, and then commanded to be preached by His Apostles to every creature, as the fountain of all, both saving truth, and moral discipline; and seeing clearly that this truth and discipline are contained in the written books, and the unwritten traditions which, received by the Apostles from the mouth of Christ himself, or from the Apostles themselves, the Holy Ghost dictating, have come down even unto us, transmitted as it were from hand to hand; (the Synod) following the examples of the orthodox Fathers, receives and venerates with an equal affection of piety, and reverence, all the books both of the Old and of the New Testament – seeing that one God is the author of both – as also the said traditions, as well those appertaining to faith as to morals, as having been dictated, either by Christ's own word of mouth, or by the Holy Ghost, and preserved in the Catholic Church by a continuous succession. And it has thought it meet that a list of the sacred books be inserted in this decree, lest a doubt may arise in any one's mind, which are the books that are received by this Synod.

They are as set down here below: of the Old Testament: the five books of Moses, namely, Genesis, Exodus, Leviticus, Numbers, Deuteronomy; Joshua, Judges, Ruth, four books of Kings [= 1 and 2 Samuel, and 1 and 2 Kings], two of Paralipomenon [= 1 and 2 Chronicles], the first book of Ezra, and the second which is entitled Nehemiah; Tobit, Judith, Esther, Job, the Davidic Psalter, consisting of a hundred and fifty psalms; the Proverbs, Ecclesiastes, the Canticle of Canticles, Wisdom, Ecclesiasticus, Isaiah, Jeremiah, with Baruch; Ezekiel, Daniel; the twelve minor prophets, namely, Hosea, Joel, Amos, Obadiah, Jonah, Micah, Nahum, Habakkuk, Zephaniah, Haggai, Zacharias, Malachi; two books of the Maccabees, the first and the second.

Of the New Testament: the four Gospels, according to Matthew, Mark, Luke, and John; the Acts of the Apostles written by Luke the Evangelist; fourteen epistles of Paul the apostle, (one) to the Romans, two to the Corinthians, (one) to the Galatians, to the Ephesians, to the Philippians, to the Colossians, two to the Thessalonians, two to Timothy, (one) to Titus, to Philemon, to the Hebrews; two of Peter the apostle, three of John the apostle, one of the apostle James, one of Jude the apostle, and the Apocalypse of John the apostle.

But if any one receive not, as sacred and canonical, the said books entire with all their parts, as they have been used to be read in the Catholic Church, and as they are contained in the old Latin vulgate edition; and knowingly and deliberately condemn the traditions aforesaid; let him be anathema. Let all, therefore, understand, in what order, and in what manner, the said Synod, after having laid the foundation of the confession of faith, will proceed, and what testimonies and authorities it will mainly use in confirming dogmas, and in restoring morals in the Church.[10]

This major Church council, which sat in Trento and Bologna, Italy, expressed in a combative way the spirit of the Counter-Reformation. Its session on Scripture, on 8 April 1546, gave rise to this clear decree: it emphasized the continuity of Church tradition; it defined authoritatively, for the first time since the early Church, the limits of the canon of the Bible (identifying this as the Vulgate); and it issued an anathema (curse) on anyone who opposed any part of this decree. Moreover, the closing sentence rejects the distinction between dogma and morality, as drawn by Jerome and the later Protestant Reformers. Interestingly, the Clementine Bible – the official edition of the Vulgate published later in 1592 – had some of the texts of the Apocrypha not listed in this decree placed in an appendix after the New Testament (Prayer of Manasseh, 1 Esdras, 2 Esdras) for their preservation as sacred texts.

The Greek Orthodox Synod of Jerusalem (1672), also a response to the Protestant Reformation – especially Calvinism – also reaffirmed those decreed on at the Council of Trent; but it added 1 Esdras, 3 Maccabees, 4 Maccabees (in an appendix), the Prayer of Manasseh, and Psalm 151 – that is, books included and transmitted in ancient Greek Bibles. The Orthodox decree was, however, less dogmatic than a commendation, which explains some variation in Greek and Russian Orthodox practice since then. It is from this period, incidentally, that the more neutral and probably less troublesome title 'Deutero-canonical' was first coined, in 1666, by Sixtus of Siena, a Jewish convert to Roman Catholicism. The phrase identified the texts not found among the more ancient Hebrew canonical texts. Some Protestants of this divisive period, however, proved even more radical than their magisterial forebears, as the following excerpt shows:

John Lightfoot: 'Elias *Redivivus*'

(1643)

The words of the text are the last words of the Old Testament, there uttered by a Prophet, here expounded by an Angel: there concluding the Law, and here beginning the Gospel: *Behold,* says Malachi, *Mal. 4. 5. I will send you Elijah the Prophet:* And he says, the Angel, *shall go before him in the Spirit and power of Elias.* And *he shall turn the hearts of the Fathers to the children,* says the one; And *to turn the hearts of the fathers to the children,* says the other. Thus sweetly and nearly should the two Testaments join together, and thus divinely would they kiss each other, but that the wretched *Apocrypha* doth thrust in between: Like the two Cherubim in the Temple Oracle, as with their outer-wings, they touch the two sides of the house, from *In the beginning,* to *Come Lord Jesus,* so with their inner, they would touch each other, the end of the law with the beginning of the Gospel, did not this patchery of human invention divorce them asunder.

But it is a wonder to which I could never yet receive satisfaction, that in Churches that are Reformed, that have shaken off the yoke of superstition, and unpinned themselves from off the sleeve of former custom or doing as their ancestors have done: yet in such a thing as this, and of so great import, should do as first ignorance, and then superstition has done before them: It

> is true indeed that they have refused these books out of the *Canon,* but they
> have reserved them still in the *Bible:* as if God should have cast *Adam* out of
> the state of happiness, and yet have continued him in the place of happiness.
> Not to insist upon this, which is some digression, you know the counsel of
> *Sarah* concerning *Ishmael,* and in that she outstripped *Abraham* in the spirit
> of prophecy, *Cast out the bond-woman and her son, for the son of the bond-*
> *woman may not be heir with the son of the free.*[11]

This is from a sermon preached by John Lightfoot before the House of
Commons on 29 March 1643, when a public fast was held. Based on Luke
1.7, its title implied a call to reformation, as in John the Baptist's day,
and had as its historical setting the sharp religious polemics and political
polarities of the first English Civil War (1642–6), fuelled in part by the
Protestant Reformation. Its two targets are the imaginations of the ancient
Jews ('this patchery of human invention'; another paragraph in between
the paragraphs of the excerpt develops this) and the superstition of Roman
Catholics – against which ideas and quotations are marshalled. Lightfoot,
a scholar of Hebrew and rabbinic literature, was a member of the Westminster Assembly of Divines, which was appointed by the Long Parliament.
Strongly influenced by Puritanism, its purpose was to reform the Church of
England by aligning it more closely to the Presbyterianism of the Church of
Scotland – albeit without long-term success. Its *Confession of Faith* (1646)
states: 'The books commonly called Apocrypha, not being of divine inspiration, are no part of the Canon of Scripture; and therefore are of no authority
in the Church of God, nor to be any otherwise approved, or made use of,
than other human writings' (§3). Accordingly, while some early Protestant
Bibles had contained them, later Bibles rejected them outright. This stance
put such strain on the distinction between edification and dogma that some
Protestants hardly ever read them at all.

Modern Christianity

The three approaches outlined above – integration, appendix, omission
– have persisted ever since. Three examples from the modern period will
suffice to illustrate this. First, at the First Vatican Council (1868–70) the
decree of the Council of Trent was reaffirmed: the texts of the Apocrypha
were inspired, along with the other canonical texts. Second, the lectionaries
of the Church of England, attached to the Book of Common Prayer and,
more recently, *Common Worship,* make provision for the optional public
reading of texts from the Apocrypha. And third, the non-denominational
Christian charity, The British and Foreign Bible Society (The Bible Society),
formed to enable the global distribution of Bibles, decided in 1825, follow-

ing disputes over their status, to omit the Apocrypha from their Bibles in English altogether – although they were retained in versions on the Continent, where the use of the Apocrypha was normal.

The same three approaches are evident in modern Bible translations. The New Jerusalem Bible (NJB) illustrates the first tendency; the New Revised Standard Version (NRSV) the second; and the English Standard Version (ESV) the third. But, as with all matters concerning the Apocrypha, the reality is often more complex and interesting than the idea. The Revised Standard Version (RSV) has existed in forms that correspond to each of the three stances. An ESV with Apocrypha was commissioned and published by Oxford University Press in 2009 for use by Evangelicals and others who have adopted that translation for church use. There are also Study Bibles for each of the three stances: first, *The Catholic Study Bible* (2011), and the *Orthodox Study Bible* (based on the Septuagint); second, *The HarperCollins Study Bible: New Revised Standard Version with Apocryphal/Deuterocanonical Books* (2006); and third, the *English Standard Version Study Bible* (2008) – which contains a supplementary article that largely favours the position of Jerome, and closes by identifying areas of disagreement between the Apocrypha and the Old and New Testament texts. Various formats for resources such as these (e.g. online, software) have become increasingly popular as well.

The other important strand that needs mentioning in relation to the modern period are the features that have become characteristic of the modern interpretation of the Bible in general – such as the free use of critical reason, the impact of the natural sciences, and the posing by readers of historical, philosophical, and moral questions about the content of texts. These, too, have left their mark on the study of the Apocrypha. Here, the dominant concern has been to understand these texts in their ancient context, while not being bound by the beliefs and practices of Church tradition. The following excerpt, from a well-used though somewhat dated introductory textbook on the texts of the Apocrypha, illustrates this well:

Metzger: *An Introduction to the Apocrypha*

(1957)

[2 Esdras] ...the most difficult book in the Apocrypha for the modern reader to understand and appreciate. There is a certain element in the literary form which is tiresome and almost trivial. We do not care nowadays for such elaborate and fantastic symbolism. At the same time it must be acknowledged that a real vein of poetry runs throughout the book. Whether the writer is lamenting the sorrows of Jerusalem, or describing the wonders of God's handiwork in creation, or denouncing the wickedness of Rome (under the image of 'Babylon'), one feels the power of effective expression ... The author wrestles with

---

one of the most perplexing of all problems, the question of God's justice in dealing with his people ... His agonizing is both honourable and pathetic as he seeks 'to justify the ways of God to man'.

[Judith] The consensus, at least among Protestant and Jewish scholars, is that the story is sheer fiction. Apart from exaggerations in numbers (1:4, 16; 2:5, 15; 7:2, 17) ... the book teems with chronological, historical, and geographical improbabilities and downright errors. For example, Holofernes moves an immense army about three hundred miles in three days (2:21) ... Candor demands that we acknowledge that certain aspects of the grim story of Judith are far from being exemplary. At the same time we remember that it was written in a time of war to inspire a people who were fighting desperately for their religion as well as for their independence. The religious emphasis in the story is of the rigidly orthodox type: the observance of the Mosaic Law is the supreme test of piety. In fact, the book affords a valuable source for the study of Pharisaism and in its punctiliousness in going beyond the written Mosaic code.[12]

These comments on two books exemplify Metzger's position: the texts of the Apocrypha are not part of the Protestant canon, but they contain moral and religious insights of 'permanent value', and are important for better understanding the context of the contemporaries of Jesus Christ. Thus, 2 Esdras compares well with Romans 9—11 on difficult questions about the justice of God; and Judith is concerned with the people of God's tenacity under imperial subjugation, as was required in the early Christian experience. And yet, the more critical comments, on their literary form and content, do not match more recent scholars' approaches to, and appreciation of, these texts. 2 Esdras uses the well-attested ancient genre of Jewish apocalyptic writing, as does Judith that of the ancient Jewish novella. Moreover, that Judith's conscientious Torah observance amounts to 'legalism' is not obvious given the extreme circumstances she faced. Indeed, she was arguably a model Jewess – and a warrior Jewess at that – after the likes of Jael and Deborah, as portrayed in the more ancient canonical texts.

In addition, the more recent appreciation of these texts is no longer routinely drawn along denominational or even religious lines. Catholic, Orthodox, Protestant, Jewish, and non-religious readers are nowadays engaged in their study in universities and seminaries. This is the case whatever type of authority, if any, each of these groups might ascribe to them – not forgetting, also, the many other Jewish and Christian texts that have survived from antiquity (conventionally called 'Pseudepigrapha'). A reflection of this general trend is seen in the following excerpt, which is the concluding paragraph from an essay in a now widely used dictionary:

Loren T. Stuckenbruck: 'Apocrypha and Pseudepigrapha'

in J. J. Collins and D. C. Harlow (eds), *The Eerdmans Dictionary of Early Judaism* (2010)

The problems that beset the terms 'Apocrypha' and 'Pseudepigrapha' have not prevented scholars from applying them to discrete collections of ancient works that stand alongside other recognized collections of works such as the Dead Sea Scrolls, rabbinic literature, the Hekhalot texts, the Nag Hammadi Library, and the works of Philo and Josephus. These different, though sometimes overlapping, classifications of texts cannot hide the fact that in order to be interpreted, they need to be read together for a more comprehensive understanding of the diversities of Judaism that flourished during the centuries leading up to and after the turn of the Common Era.[13]

This conclusion builds on important points of detail. The plural term *apocrypha* ('secret, hidden away') does not describe this collection of texts accurately: the esoteric is in evidence (e.g. 2 Esdras; cf. Dan. 12.4), but most of them do not reflect that literal meaning (nor those now called *apocryphon* (singular): previously unknown traditions about a biblical book or figure, e.g. *Genesis Apocryphon*). The term is anachronistic too: even if they are largely identifiable as texts from Second Temple Judaism, they never formed a distinct or coherent collection in antiquity; and, while they are readily identifiable in the discourses of Christian tradition, they are attested in early Church writings to variable degrees. The plural term *pseudepigrapha* (singular *pseudepigraphon*) literally means writings of false attribution, for whatever reason (e.g. to honour an ancient figure). While this word better describes the texts of the Apocrypha, this term now conventionally refers to texts that are neither canonical nor in the Apocrypha – in other words, a much larger body of ancient Jewish and Christian texts. The Dead Sea Scrolls, discovered, translated, and published in the twentieth century, is the best-known example. These various points indicate that those who wish to better understand the complex world of ancient Jewish groups and the emergence of the early Church from that setting, of which the study of all of the texts of the Apocrypha is nowadays an integral part, must be attentive to the aspects and implications of nomenclature.

Global Christianity

Between the ninth and the fourteenth centuries AD the 'Church of the East', known more controversially as the 'Nestorian Church' in the West, was the world's largest Church in terms of geographical spread: from the Mediterranean to India and China. Its Christians knew the Bible in Syriac, a translation begun in the second century AD. Referred to as the Peshitta (Syriac for 'simple', given the absence in it of textual apparatus), it was translated from Hebrew biblical texts (including Sirach), and some Greek texts of the Apocrypha. They were treated as canonical by the fourth-century Syriac Church Fathers Aphrahat and Ephrem. However, they are variably attested, as in Western Greek Bibles, in the earliest complete Syriac biblical manuscripts, which might date to the sixth century. Its texts were encountered mainly in worship (i.e. liturgy, homily), much like the Bible in Latin in medieval Europe. Several modern Church denominations claim continuity, despite schisms, with this Eastern Christian tradition (e.g. St. Thomas Christians of Kerala, India).

There have also been churches whose establishment in East Asia grew out of the missionary activities of the much later colonial era, within which Christian beliefs and practices that include the Apocrypha formed a part. However, colonial activity at the time sometimes resulted in a very mixed if not very shameful history. The following excerpt provides an example. It is a discussion of the novel by the Filipino nationalist José Rizal, *Noli Me Tangere* (1887), whose title (meaning 'Touch Me Not') comes from part of a saying attributed to Jesus (John 20.27). The novel, set during the Spanish occupation of the Philippines, is an early example of literary resistance against European colonialism:

Sharada Sugirtharajah: *The Bible and Asia: From the Pre-Christian Era to the Postcolonial Age*

(2013)

The Bible, in Rizal's novel, is seen not as a book full of love, justice, and compassion but as a book of terror, torture, and torment for those who deviate from the path of God. This comes out clearly in a sermon Father Damaso, a manipulating priest, preached to his Filipino congregation, and which made most of them yawn. Speaking in a language that is totally unfamiliar to him – Tagalog – Father Damaso selects a biblical passage that comes from the Apocrypha, the second book of Esdras: 'I looked at my world and there it lay spoilt, and at my earth and it was in danger from men's wicked plans' (9:20 Revised English Bible). The passage goes on to speak about the punishment meted out to those who despise God's ways. The whole sermon portrays the

---

Filipino converts as sinners and heretics for not showing respect to the min-isters of God ... they are condemned as worse than the Protestants and the local Chinese. Father Damaso finds the solution for such disobedience in the dire words of Jesus, though this has no bearing on the Filipino context: 'If thy right arm offends thee, cut it off, and throw it into the fire.' ... directly implying that any harm done to the Catholic priests will be rewarded with grave punish-ment ... The 'little ones' in Matthew are the vulnerable who need protection. Here, the all-powerful Roman Catholic priests are in a round-about way sug-gested as the helpless 'little ones', and the inference is that any local Filipinos who are bent on harming the priests of the Catholic Church will have to face cruel consequences.[14]

In the novel, local Filipinos also use the Bible to critique the claims of the Roman Catholic Church: Tasio, the town philosopher and madman, who has a curious mind and has read widely, questions Roman Catholic teaching on purgatory, and the view that salvation is reserved for Catholics. José Rizal himself was exiled, arrested for inciting rebellion, and executed in Manila in 1896 at the age of 35. The novel is still popular. This is an example of how the Bible has been used in Asian literature, but tracing that phenomenon is difficult. The translation of the Bible into Asian languages – and even more so the Apocrypha – has been piecemeal, not only because of litur-gical traditionalism but also because the Apocrypha did not feature in the translation work of early Christian missionaries, especially Protestant. Their translation is thus relatively recent: by Roman Catholics in Japan (1954–9) and Sri Lanka (1986); and jointly by Roman Catholics and Protestants in Cambodia (1998).[15]

The texts of the Apocrypha were used also in Africa in the early Church, especially North Africa, where there had already been a literate Jewish diaspora community, with which early Christianity had strong cultural con-tinuity. The Septuagint was initially translated, and the Wisdom of Solomon probably composed, in Alexandria, Egypt; and episodes in the New Testament have African settings (e.g. Matt. 2, Acts 8). As in early Western Christianity around the Mediterranean basin and beyond, the texts of the Apocrypha were included in the Eastern Orthodox or Coptic (Egyptian) and Ethiopic canons – and preserved in their respective languages. Also popular were other pseudepigraphical texts (e.g. *Life of Adam and Eve, 1 Enoch, Sibylline Oracles, Jubilees*) that were not usually recognized in the biblical canons of Western Christianity. The following concerns Baruch, one of the texts of the conventional Apocrypha, in relation to more recent African experience:

Robert Wafawanaka: 'Baruch', in *The Africana Bible: Reading Israel's Scriptures from Africa and the African Diaspora*

(2009)

The idea of captivity and exilic existence is also pertinent to Africans. The experience of African slavery through no fault of their own is however contrary to Israel's exile as a result of self-confessed sin and disobedience. A new dimension is added by those Africans who experienced either self-imposed exile or left their homelands in search of better fortunes. Whatever way Africans found themselves in the Diaspora, like the ancient Israelites, they too can relate to the experience of colonial oppression, cultural dislocation, and identity crisis. In spite of Israel's admission of Torah disobedience as the major cause of the exile, the nation's demise may also be understood as the historical reality of its existence in an area dominated by ancient superpowers.[16]

This analysis detects both similarity and difference: the commonality is the trauma of exile, whereas the difference is where the element of choice has been present, whether out of necessity or aspiration. Wafawanaka also observes, prior to this excerpt, the prominence of the question 'why' (rather than 'how') in African philosophy: in customary propitiatory rituals and ceremonies intended to rectify offences towards the spirits or God – which, incidentally, recall the acts of confession and charity in Baruch. The authors of *The Africana Bible* consider other lines of exploration for the texts of the Apocrypha: the relationship between the range of black women's experience and the mixed portrayal of women (e.g. Judith, 1 Esdras, Sirach); similarities with African folk wisdom (e.g. Wisdom of Solomon); and the seduction and danger of power and celebrity in black church denominations and in popular culture (e.g. Prayer of Manasseh) – themes that are, of course, by no means confined to African or African diasporic experience.

The last example concerns the Apocrypha and South America. The Italian explorer Christopher Columbus is famous for his exploration, exploitation, and colonization of the Americas: the 'New World' (although the Icelander Leif Erickson had travelled to North America five centuries before). Columbus led his four transatlantic voyages under the sponsorship of the Spanish Catholic monarchs Ferdinand II and Isabella I. There were various religious, political, and personal motives for the voyages. By appeal to selected passages from Scripture, and to early and medieval theologians (e.g. Augustine of Hippo, Nicholas of Lyra, Pierre d'Ailly), Columbus became convinced of his prominent role in an apocalyptic timetable that predicted the evangelization of the nations, including distant islands to the west, thereby allying himself with the need to wrest Jerusalem from Islamic control in the east. This eschatological outlook is expressed in *The Book of*

Prophecies (perhaps taken with him on his fourth voyage), and the near-contemporary letter sent to his religious counsellor in Seville, a Carthusian friar, who assisted with the compilation of the *Prophecies*:

Christopher Columbus: *The Book of Prophecies*

(1501–2)

May Jesus and Mary go with us. Amen.

Letter from the very magnificent and most prudent Don Christopher Columbus, admiral viceroy and governor in perpetuity of the islands of the Indies and the mainland regions discovered by him, etc., to Father Gaspar Gorricio, etc.

Reverend and devoted father: When I came here, I began to collect in a book excerpts from authoritative sources that seemed to me to refer to Jerusalem; I planned to review them later and to arrange them appropriately. Then I became involved in my other activities and did not have time to proceed with my work; nor do I now. And so I am sending the book to you so that you can look at it. Perhaps your soul will motivate you to continue the project and our Lord will guide you to genuine *auctoritates*. The search for texts should be continued in the Bible, and the *Commentary* is often useful and illuminating and should be used for clarification.
Granada, 13 September 1501

[Reply from the abovementioned]

This the beginning of the book or collection of *auctoritates*, sayings, opinions, and prophecies concerning the need to recover the holy city and Mount Zion, and the discovery and conversion of the islands of the Indies and of all peoples and nations, for Ferdinand and Isabella, our Spanish rulers.[17]

The book from which the excerpt comes contains quotations from the Apocrypha (e.g. 1 Maccabees, Baruch, Wisdom of Solomon). However, one of the texts that had already influenced Columbus is 2 Esdras 6.42: 'On the third day you commanded the waters to be gathered together in a seventh part of the earth; six parts you dried up and kept so that some of them might be planted and cultivated and be of service before you.' This implied that just one-seventh of the earth's surface is covered in water, with the rest available for cultivation (an interpretation of Genesis 1.6 which has no exact parallel in antiquity). That it struck Columbus as significant is evident from his annotations of the French churchman and astronomer Pierre d'Ailly's *Imago Mundi* (1410). This was a collection of geographical essays that deploys theological and other ancient authorities (e.g. Aristotle, Pliny, Seneca) to calculate the size of landmasses. Columbus' reading and analysis led him to calculate that the Atlantic Sea was a narrow highway between Europe and Asia – although his calculations of its width were strenuously disputed by others. Columbus' interpretative framework was determinative: an intertwining of geography and eschatology, a framework that apocalyptic texts such as 2 Esdras served all too well.

Part 3: Application

Apocrypha/Deutero-Canon in ministry

Churches that nowadays have the Apocrypha read in public worship are in continuity with early and medieval tradition and practice. Accordingly, their liturgies provide plenty of examples of this. The words 'Eternal rest grant unto them' from the *Introitus* of the Roman Catholic Requiem Mass recall 2 Esdras 2.34–35. The Orthodox service of Vespers employs the Wisdom of Solomon 3.1–3 in its commemoration of major saints. The Church of England's prayer book *Common Worship* indicates that the canticle *Benedicite*, from 'The Song of the Three Jews' 35–66c, used at Lauds (the morning office) since the fourth century, is an alternative for the *Te Deum* at Matins during Lent. Preachers for whom lectionary readings from the Apocrypha are optional will most likely write quite different sermons if its texts are read publicly in church services. For example, a sermon on the raising of Jairus' daughter (Mark 5.21–43) could highlight either the precious gift of life if coupled with the birth of Samuel in 1 Samuel 1 or the unnaturalness of death if coupled with verses from the Wisdom of Solomon 1 and 2 (Fourth Sunday after Trinity, Year B). Even then, Christians who do not formally recognize the Apocrypha in public worship are sometimes unknowingly influenced by it. The popular hymn *Nun danket alle Gott*, 'Now thank we all our God' (*c.* 1636), by the Lutheran clergyman Martin Rinkart (1586–1649), was inspired by Sirach 50.22–24, from the poetic praises of Simon the High Priest.

Most Christians agree that the Apocrypha is valuable and useful for understanding early Christianity; examples were given above that showed both Christian continuity and discontinuity with this Jewish literary heritage – even if they had much less prominence for the New Testament writers than the more ancient canonical texts. And yet uncertainty about the status of the Apocrypha persists, due to the official positions taken towards them by the clergy and the scholars of different church denominations, and in consequence the varying degrees of familiarity with them in those churches. In Protestant thought, for instance, in addition to their lack of formal quotation in the New Testament, the caution about them is often explained with reference to the 'criteria of canonicity' in evidence in the early Church – as outlined in the introductory chapter. An example that draws on debates in early and later Church history, but which bears on ministry in the present, illustrates the significance of this.

What is to be made of the practice of 'prayers for the dead' (2 Macc. 12.39–45)? These prayers are intended to assist the temporary suffering of a departed loved one, in purgatory, prior to entrance into heaven. Catholic and Orthodox theologians have traditionally explained this practice by means of not only this episode in the Apocrypha, but also biblical beliefs about the community of the living and the dead ('the cloud of witnesses' in Hebrews; cf. Heb. 11.35–36), and evidence from the early Church (e.g. catacomb inscriptions, liturgies) – as well as the compassionate impulse to pray for the departed. Protestant critics, who do not accept the Apocrypha's canonicity, respond by mentioning its lack of explicit support elsewhere in the Old and New Testaments, and they argue that the practice serves no purpose: according to the New Testament writers, the departed enter either heaven or hell immediately (Luke 16.19–31; Heb. 9.27). Funeral prayers are, thereby, more about the comfort of the bereaved. The prayers of each of these traditions are, for such reasons, directed towards God with very different assumptions and expectations about both prayer and the afterlife. In this way, beliefs and practices depend in part on decisions about canonicity. It shows, in other words, that the relationship between theology and practice is a constructive task, in which views of what constitutes the Bible and its interpretation have a major role to play. This also serves as a reminder that the question of authority is never far away: who should decide on such matters, and on what basis?

Apocrypha/Deutero-Canon in mission

Christianity is a public religion whose ancient texts form part of the literary heritage of humankind. This means that the Apocrypha, canonical or otherwise, is available to anyone who wishes to make sense of the origins of the world's most populous faith. Its texts are often studied by scholars dedicated to making sense of those beginnings. Its texts help to identify the shared practices that persisted into later centuries (e.g. Tobit on almsgiving, and 4 Maccabees on the relationship between reason and faith), and to articulate the differences between Judaism and Christianity (e.g. attitudes to the Torah). Christianity has the person of Jesus Christ at its heart, and this is the most important aspect in this context. It highlights that which explains not only the gradual and eventual 'parting of the ways' between ancient Judaism and Christianity, but also the major differences with other religions (e.g. Buddhism, Hinduism), in which that ancient Jewish context is not familiar. Indeed, the prominence given to Jesus Christ is such that Christians do not identify their faith simply with its ancient texts: the ultimate focus lies in a person – the Word incarnate (John 1.1–18; cf. Sir. 24.1–12) – whose followers call and invite others to join with them as fellow disciples of their Lord, as modelled in the pages of the New Testament and beyond. In short, whatever status the Apocrypha should finally have, it is the New Testament texts that are distinctively and undoubtedly canonical for all Christians.

The role of the Apocrypha in mission may be seen elsewhere. Its texts present human beings in realistic and appealing ways. Their heroes and heroines are examples of dedicated faith and charity, even to the point of death as martyrs – examples that may take on fresh significance in view of persecution against religious groups in today's world. By stark contrast, the Apocrypha has comedy in its pages: the stench of a fish's liver and heart that make a demon flee (Tobit), royal madness and farcical reversal (3 Maccabees), and an exploding god (Bel and the Dragon). The Apocrypha has provided inspiration for the arts too: the phrase 'A Daniel come to judgement' from Susanna in Shakespeare's comedy *A Merchant of Venice* (1596–8); Judith (*Oloferno deistvo*) at Tsar Alexei Mikhailovich's court theatre in Moscow in the 1670s; Handel's oratorio *Judas Maccabaeus* (1747) – and the paintings of Cranach, Feti, and Rubens, to name but a few. More recently the film *1492: Conquest for Paradise*, directed by Ridley Scott and released in the quincentenary year 1992, has the Christopher Columbus character cite 2 Esdras to justify his calculations for a westward voyage to get to Asia and its riches, rather than travel to face different political obstacles in an eastward direction. The Apocrypha has also bequeathed practical wisdom (e.g. Sir. 38.9–15 and 42.3 on the importance of medicine and accountancy) and proverbial phrases (e.g. *Magna est veritas et praevalet*, 'Great is truth, and strongest of all', 1 Esd. 4.41).

With all that has been discussed above in view, it seems appropriate to conclude that, like the Old and New Testament texts, which have an undisputed canonical status for the vast majority of Christians, the texts of the Apocrypha should be studied and appreciated more than they currently are. This is the case whatever position any Christian takes towards them regarding the canonical contents of the Bible. The three positions outlined above – integration, appendix, omission – have never prevented these texts playing a role in helping make sense of the origins of Christianity in its ancient Jewish context. Whatever is to be made of the particular issues – such as the criteria of canonicity, and specific beliefs and practices attached to the Apocrypha in the history of Christianity – it remains the case that the Apocrypha has been, and is, a part of the large and rich fabric of Christianity: Catholic, Orthodox, and Protestant. Whether the encounter with the texts of the Apocrypha is normal, occasional, or rare, it is important to know about them, if only in terms of their legacies and effects. In the reception or 'afterlife' of these texts, it is likely that many will, at some point, come across them, and will benefit by making sense of their contribution in the history of Christianity.

Notes

1 The double title Apocrypha/Deutero-Canon is used in the headings of this chapter, and elsewhere in the book, to acknowledge both possibilities, but the first of these is used in the text for the sake of convenience.

2 This comparison of Wisdom 12—14 and Romans 1 draws, in part, on Metzger, B. M., 1967, *An Introduction to the Apocrypha*, New York: Oxford University Press, pp. 158–60.

3 Hippolytus of Rome, 'On Susannah', Intoduction, 7–8, 52, 55, 61, in Roberts, A. and Donaldson, J. (eds), 1886, *Fathers of the Third Century: Hippolytus, Cyprian, Caius, Novatian, Appendix, Ante-Nicene Fathers: The Writings of the Fathers Down to A.D. 325*, Edinburgh: T&T Clark, vol. 5, pp. 293, 294, 296–7.

4 See further, Voicu, S. J. (ed.), 2010, *Apocrypha*, ACCS OT, 15, Downers Grove, IL: Inter-Varsity Press.

5 See further, Law, T. M., 2013, *When God Spoke Greek: The Septuagint and the Making of the Christian Bible*, New York: Oxford University Press, pp. 151–66.

6 For useful charts, see the 'Lists and Catalogues of Old Testament Collections', in McDonald, L. M., 2007, *The Biblical Canon: Its Origin, Transmission and Authority*, Peabody, MA: Hendrickson, pp. 585–8.

7 Warren, F. E. (tr.), 1911, *The Sarum Missal in English*, The Library of Liturgiology and Ecclesiology for English Readers IX, London: The De La More Press, Part 2, pp. 159–60. Note: 'V' = verse; 'R' = response; and '(+)' indicates the ritual blessing of the sign of the cross.

8 Warren, *The Sarum Missal in English*, Part 2, pp. 435–6.

9 Berry, L. E. (ed.), 2007, *The Geneva Bible: 1560 Edition*, Peabody, MA: Hendrickson, p. 386.

10 Waterworth, J. (tr.), 1848, *The Canons and Decrees of the Sacred and Oecumenical Council of Trent*, London: Dolman, pp. 17–19.

11 Lightfoot, J., 1643, 'Elias *Redivivus*', in Pitman, J. R. (ed.), 1822, *The Whole Works of John Lightfoot*, London, vol. 6, pp. 131, 132.

12 Metzger, *Apocrypha*, pp. 30, 50, 52.

13 Stuckenbruck, L. T., 2010, 'Apocrypha and Pseudepigrapha', in Collins, J. J. and Harlow, D. C. (eds), *The Eerdmans Dictionary of Early Judaism*, Grand Rapids, MI; Cambridge: Eerdmans, p. 161.

14 Sugirtharajah, R. S., 2013, *The Bible and Asia: From the Pre-Christian Era to the Postcolonial Age*, Cambridge, MA; London: Harvard University Press, pp. 239–40.

15 Ogden, G., with contributions from Arimichi, E., Somaratna, G. P. V., Katoppo, P. G., Heuken, A., Hunt, R., China Group, Ponchaud, F. and Aung Than, A., 2001, 'Bible Translation', in Sunquist, S. W. (ed.), *A Dictionary of Asian Christianity*, Grand Rapids, MI: Eerdmans, pp. 84, 86.

16 Wafawanaka, R., 2009, 'Baruch', in Page, H. R. (ed.), *The Africana Bible: Reading Israel's Scriptures from Africa and the African Diaspora*, Minneapolis, MN: Fortress Press, p. 308.

17 Rusconi, R. (ed.) and Sullivan, B. (tr.), 1997, *The Book of Prophecies Edited by Christopher Columbus*, Berkeley, CA; London: University of California Press, pp. 55, 59.

7

Conclusion: Resources for Further Study

HYWEL CLIFFORD

As stated in the Introduction, there are many ways in which the Christian use of the Old Testament may be approached and articulated. The model presented in the preceding chapters is but one of them. The purpose of this concluding chapter is to recommend resources to readers who wish to pursue their interests further with this threefold model in view. But before delving into the detail some general points must be mentioned. First, it is essential to be clear about what purposes a reader has when approaching the Old Testament, whether they are concerned with introductory matters about its historical understanding, its later interpretation, or its application in ministry and mission. In this regard, each reader will most likely have quite different interests, whether or not an integrative or synthetic Christian use of the Old Testament as presented in this book is the overall aim. Second, there is huge variety in the available resources on the Old Testament: generalist and specialist, technical and devotional, Jewish and Christian, and cutting-edge studies on the latest global issues (e.g. trade, migration, violence, climate). In view of this, it is essential, again, to be clear about what type of resource is consulted: its content, its agenda, and its perspective. Third, this chapter is primarily an entrée into bibliographical resources for student and general readers of the Old Testament, including some online and electronic resources. There are many other lists of resources available, which provide significantly more detail.[1]

Part 1: Introduction

This section is a discussion of the resources that focus on understanding the Old Testament in its ancient historical context. This is often called 'the world of the Bible' because the canonical texts were composed in that setting. The literature of any period, whether ancient or modern, is made best sense of in its original context. These resources are characterized by the analysis of the Old Testament texts with respect to matters such as the relationship between Israel and its ancient Near Eastern neighbours, the religious, political, and social characteristics of a life lived in biblical lands, and the skills needed to gain detailed knowledge of the biblical texts as ancient texts. Nonetheless, their interpretation and application for the Church often feature. This section covers the following areas: Maps and media; Encyclopaedias and dictionaries; Introductions to the Old Testament; Canonical sections; Commentary; and Biblical languages.

Maps and media

Aharoni, Y., et al., 2002, *The Carta Bible Atlas*, 4th edn, Jerusalem: Carta.

Curtis, A., 2007, *Oxford Bible Atlas*, 4th edn, Oxford: Oxford University Press.

www.bibleplaces.com

www.biblicalarchaeology.org

Fant, C. E. and Reddish, M. G., 2008, *Lost Treasures of the Bible: Understanding the Bible Through Archaeological Artifacts in World Museums*, Grand Rapids, MI; Cambridge: Eerdmans.

Keel, O., 1978, *The Symbolism of the Biblical World: Ancient Near Eastern Iconography and the Book of Psalms*, London: SPCK (original 1972).

King, P. J. and Stager, L. E., 2001, *Life in Ancient Israel*, Louisville, KY; London: Westminster John Knox.

Murphy O'Connor, J., 1998, *The Holy Land: An Oxford Archaeological Guide from Earliest Times to 1700*, Oxford and New York: Oxford University Press.

Pritchard, J. B. (ed.), 1969, *Ancient Near Eastern Pictures Relating to the Old Testament*, 3rd edn, Princeton, NJ: Princeton University Press.

Pritchard, J. with Page, N. (eds), 2008, *HarperCollins Atlas of Bible History*, Grand Rapids, MI: Zondervan.

Bibles often include maps, charts, and photos to help bring the biblical texts visually to life. There are, however, resources that offer expansive detail in print and digital formats. A Bible atlas is an excellent starting point for this. *The Carta Bible Atlas*, by Jewish scholars, is, in effect, a biblical companion by means of annotated maps of biblical episodes and events; discursive text provides commentary on these, its diagrams and its drawings. The *Oxford Bible Atlas* is more discursive, and it includes colour photographs – as does the *HarperCollins Atlas of Bible History*, which was produced by an international team of scholars. To assist in the visualization of biblical places, the website www.bibleplaces.com currently advertises an impressive pictorial library of 'more than 17,500 high-resolution photographs', many of which are often reproduced in print publications. The website www.biblicalarchaeology.org is a good portal for attractive print and digital media about the latest archaeological discoveries (e.g. magazines, DVDs). There are many excellent books available with photographs, diagrams, and drawings of archaeological sites and evidence, and their implications for biblical understanding (Fant and Reddish; Keel; King and Stager; Murphy O'Connor).

Encyclopaedias and dictionaries

Alexander, T. D. et al. (eds), 2003–11, *Dictionary of the Old Testament*, 4 vols, Downers Grove, IL; Leicester: Inter-Varsity Press.

Botterweck, J. G., Fabry, H.-J. and Ringgren, H. (eds), 1974–2006, *Theological Dictionary of the Old Testament*, 15 vols, Grand Rapids, MI: Eerdmans (original 1970–1995).

Bromiley, G. W. (ed.), 1979–88, *The International Standard Bible Encyclopedia*, 4 vols, rev. edn, Grand Rapids, MI: Eerdmans.

Browning, W. R., 1996, *Dictionary of the Bible*, Oxford: Oxford University Press.

Coogan, M. D. (ed.), 2011, *The Oxford Encyclopedia of the Books of the Bible*, 2 vols, New York: Oxford University Press.

Freedman, D. N. (ed.), 1992, *Anchor Bible Dictionary*, 6 vols, New York and London: Doubleday.

Freedman, D. N. (ed.), 2000, *Eerdmans Dictionary of the Bible*, Grand Rapids, MI: Eerdmans.

Hahn, S. (ed.), 1992, *Catholic Bible Dictionary*, New York: Doubleday.

Metzger, B. M. and Coogan, M. D. (eds), 1993, *The Oxford Companion to the Bible*, Oxford: Oxford University Press.

Powell, M. A. (ed.), 2011, *HarperCollins Bible Dictionary*, rev. edn, New York: HarperCollins.

Sakenfeld, K. D. (ed.), 2006–9, *The New Interpreter's Dictionary of the Bible*, 5 vols, Nashville, TN: Abingdon Press.

VanGemeren, W. (ed.), 1992, *New International Dictionary of Old Testament Theology and Exegesis*, 5 vols, Grand Rapids, MI: Zondervan; Carlisle: Paternoster.

www.jewishencyclopedia.com

www.biblehub.com

www.bibleodyssey.org

Due to its lengthy compositional growth and development, the Old Testament refers to many people, places, beliefs, institutions, and customs: it is a treasure trove of ancient detail. This makes encyclopaedias and dictionaries on the Bible (including the New Testament) essential tools for readers who wish to comprehend the biblical world in its manifest diversity. The single-volume publications (Browning; Freedman; Hahn; Metzger; Powell) are useful for quick reference: their entries, organized alphabetically, are concise. The multi-volume publications, which are more comprehensive, are organized alphabetically by theological keywords (Botterweck, Fabry and Ringgren; VanGemeren), all kinds of topics (Bromiley; Coogan; Freedman; Sakenfeld), and topics appropriate to each canonical section (the Inter-Varsity Press dictionaries). Cross-referencing and headwords are often used to redirect the reader to other entries in these volumes. The internet's seemingly limitless storage capacity makes websites an ideal forum for encyclopaedias and dictionaries. Some websites reproduce older print material (www.jewishen-cyclopedia.com, www.biblehub.com), whereas others are solely digital, up to date, and currently expanding (www.bibleodyssey.org).

Introductions to the Old Testament

Alexander, P. and Alexander, D., 2009, *The Lion Handbook to the Bible*, 4th edn, Oxford: Lion.

Anderson, B. W., 1975, *The Living World of the Old Testament*, 4th edn, Harlow: Longman.

Arnold, B. T., 2014, *Introduction to the Old Testament*, Cambridge: Cambridge University Press.

Barton, J. (ed.), 2002, *The Biblical World*, 2 vols, Abingdon: Routledge.

Barton, J. (ed.), 2016, *The Hebrew Bible: A Critical Companion*, Princeton, NJ: Princeton University Press.

Barton, J. and Bowden, J., 2004, *The Original Story: God, Israel and the World*, London: Darton, Longman and Todd.

Boadt, L., Clifford, R. J. and Harrington, D. J., 2012, *Reading the Old Testament: An Introduction*, 2nd edn, New York: Paulist Press.

Brown, M. J., 2000, *What They Don't Tell You: A Survivor's Guide to Biblical Studies*, Louisville, KY: Westminster John Knox.

Brueggemann, W., 2003, *Introduction to the Old Testament. The Canon and Christian Imagination*, Louisville, KY: Westminster John Knox.

Chapman, S. B. and Sweeney, M. A. (eds), 2016, *The Cambridge Companion to the Hebrew Bible/Old Testament*, Cambridge: Cambridge University Press.

Charpentier, E., 1981, *How to Read the Old Testament*, London: SCM Press.

Childs, B. S., 1979, *Introduction to the Old Testament as Scripture*, Philadelphia, PA: Fortress Press.

Collins, J. J., 2004, *Introduction to the Hebrew Bible, with CD Rom*, Minneapolis, MN: Fortress Press.

Collins, J. J., 2014, *A Short Introduction to the Hebrew Bible*, 2nd edn, Lanham: Fortress Press.

Coogan, M. D., 2009, *A Brief Introduction to the Old Testament: The Hebrew Bible in Its Context*, New York and Oxford: Oxford University Press.

Dillard, R. B. and Longman, T., 1995, *An Introduction to the Old Testament*, London: Apollos.

Drane, J., 2011, *Introducing the Old Testament*, 3rd edn, Oxford: Lion.

Geertz, J. C. et al., 2012, *T&T Clark Handbook of the Old Testament: An Introduction to the Literature, Religion and History of the Old Testament*, London: T&T Clark.

Geoghegan, J., Homan, M., 2003, *The Bible for Dummies*, Hoboken, NJ: Wiley.

Harrington, D. J., 1981, *Interpreting the Old Testament: A Practical Guide*, OTM, 1, Wilmington, DE: Michael Glazier.

Jenkins, S., 2004, *The Bible from Scratch*, rev. edn, Oxford: Lion.

Rogerson, J. W. and Lieu, J. (eds), 2006, *The Oxford Handbook of Biblical Studies*, Oxford: Oxford University Press.

The genre of 'introduction' conventionally covers the areas discussed in this section of this chapter. Their appeal is that they provide sufficient generality and detail to make sense of the Old Testament in one volume – unlike publications that focus on specific information (e.g. an atlas) or an individual biblical book (e.g. a commentary). Of those listed, some have the new student and general reader in view (Alexander and Alexander; Barton; Barton and Bowden; Brown; Chapman and Sweeney; Coogan; Drane; Geoghegan and Homan; Jenkins); others are more advanced (Geertz et al.). The collections of 'state of the art' essays on both the Old and New Testaments (Barton; Rogerson and Lieu) are similarly comprehensive in scope. As with many publications on the Old Testament mentioned in this chapter, another aspect to bear in mind is their denominational leaning: some are written from a Catholic perspective (Boadt, Clifford and Harrington; Collins; Harrington), and others from a more Protestant and sometimes specifically Evangelical perspective (Arnold; Brueggemann; Childs; Dillard and Longman) – although in neither case are these denominational perspectives asserted strongly: their emphasis is on historical understanding. Some are rather dated, but still useful (Anderson; Charpentier). The inclusion of supplementary digital resources (Collins) is becoming increasingly widespread.

Canonical sections

Pentateuch

Alexander, T. D., 2002, *From Paradise to the Promised Land: An Introduction to the Main Themes of the Pentateuch*, 2nd edn, Carlisle: Paternoster.

Alexander, T. D. and Baker, D. W. (eds), 2003, *Dictionary of the Old Testament: Pentateuch*, Downers Grove, IL; Leicester: Inter-Varsity Press.

Blenkinsopp, J., 1992, *The Pentateuch: An Introduction to the First Five Books of the Bible*, London: SCM Press.

Briggs, R., Lohr, J. N. and Moberly, R. W. L. (eds), 2012, *A Theological Introduction to the Pentateuch: Interpreting the Torah as Christian Scripture*, Grand Rapids, MI: Baker.

Gooder, P., 2005, *The Pentateuch: A Story of Beginnings*, London: T&T Clark.

Houston, W., 2013, *The Pentateuch*, London: SCM Press.

Vogt, P. T., 2009, *Interpreting the Pentateuch: An Exegetical Handbook*, HOTE, Grand Rapids, MI: Kregel.

Wenham, G. J., 2003, *Exploring the Old Testament, Vol. 1: The Pentateuch*, London: SPCK.

There are a good number of solid studies on the Pentateuch, whose analysis in the modern period has most clearly represented the historical-critical approach to the Bible. Most of the books listed offer analyses of not only biblical content, structure, themes, and specific details, but they also give attention to the Pentateuch's composition, which remains a specialist topic in university faculties and departments. Some are at ease with the methods and results of the source-critical analysis of the Pentateuch (Blenkinsopp; Gooder; Houston), whereas others are more cautious about its importance (Alexander; Vogt; Wenham), an outlook that is at times evident in the dictionary (Alexander and Baker). The preference for 'final form' literary readings of the Pentateuch is often seen among the latter publications; their authors are interested in the exposition of the biblical books as Christian Scripture (Briggs, Lohr and Moberly; Vogt). Contemporary ideological readings (e.g. feminist, ecological) are also on display (Houston). But in all of these cases the emphasis is first and foremost on historical understanding. All the scholars listed have been enriched by the modern discovery of ancient Near Eastern texts and archaeology (e.g. myths, hymns, laws) that shed light on the Pentateuch (and the Old Testament in general) in its ancient historical context.

Historical Books

Arnold, B. T. and Williamson, H. G. M. (eds), 2006, *Dictionary of the Old Testament: Historical Books*, Downers Grove, IL; Leicester: Inter-Varsity Press.

Barr, J., 2000, *History and Ideology in the Old Testament: Biblical Studies at the End of the Millennium*, Oxford and New York: Oxford University Press.

Bright, J., 1981, *A History of Israel*, 3rd edn, London: SCM Press.

Campbell, A. F., 2004, *Joshua to Chronicles: An Introduction*, Louisville, KY: Westminster John Knox.

Chisholm, R., 2006, *Interpreting the Historical Books: An Exegetical Handbook*, HOTE, Grand Rapids, MI: Kregel.

Coogan, M. D. (ed.), 1998, *The Oxford History of the Biblical World*, New York and Oxford: Oxford University Press.

Davies, P. R., 2015, *In Search of 'Ancient Israel'*, 3rd edn, Sheffield: Sheffield Academic Press.

Dever, W. G., 2003, *Who Were the Early Israelites and Where Did They Come From?*, Grand Rapids, MI: Eerdmans.

Finkelstein, I. and Silberman, N. A., 2001, *The Bible Unearthed*, New York: Free Press.

Grabbe, L. L. (ed.), 1997, *Can a 'History of Israel' Be Written?*, Sheffield: Sheffield Academic Press.

Kitchen, K. A., 2003, *On the Reliability of the Old Testament*, Grand Rapids, MI: Eerdmans.

Lemche, N. P., 1998, *The Israelites in History and Tradition*, London: SPCK.

Leuchter, M. A. and Lamb, D. T., 2016, *The Historical Writings: Introducing Israel's Scriptures*, Minneapolis, MN: Fortress Press.

McConville, J. G. and Satterthwaite, P., 2007, *Exploring the Old Testament, Vol. 2: The Histories*, London: SPCK.

Noll, K. L., 2013, *Canaan and Israel in Antiquity*, 2nd edn, London: Bloomsbury.

Provan, I., Long, V. P. and Longman, T., 2015, *A Biblical History of Israel*, 2nd edn, Louisville, KY: Westminster John Knox.

Whitelam, K. W., 1996, *The Invention of Ancient Israel: The Silencing of Palestinian History*, London: Routledge.

Williamson, H. G. M. (ed.), 2007, *Understanding the History of Ancient Israel*, Oxford: Oxford University Press.

There are not many scholarly introductions to the Historical Books compared to the other canonical sections. Those that are (Campbell; Chisholm; Leuchter and Lamb; McConville and Satterthwaite) – including the dictionary (Arnold and Williamson) – are often part of a series on the canonical sections that reflect a more explicit commitment to the biblical texts as Christian Scripture, although the latter aspect is rarely dominant. Many scholarly studies are, however, much more concerned with the questions of historicity (e.g. the archaeological and textual evidence for the events as described in the Old Testament) and historiography (i.e. whether the biblical writers wrote 'history' – however that term of Greek derivation is understood with respect to the biblical texts). The former question is well represented by those who tend towards either the maximalist position (Bright; Kitchen; Provan, Long and Longman) or the minimalist position (Davies; Lemche; Whitelam), although those opposed categories are not particularly satisfactory – as mentioned in the Introduction. The posing of these questions has nonetheless opened up new vistas and critical analysis (Barr; Williamson) that have, in turn, led to fresh consideration of whether these books are best read not so much as history but as a theological narrative or even story (see also Chapter 3 by Douglas Earl). Ancient Near Eastern archaeological and textual discoveries of the modern era, once again, play a major role for all these scholars (see also Coogan; Dever; Finkelstein and Silberman; Noll).

Poetry and Wisdom

Bartholomew, C. G. and O'Dowd, R. P., 2011, *Old Testament Wisdom Literature: A Theological Introduction*, Downers Grove, IL; Nottingham: Inter-Varsity Press.

Bellinger, W. H., 2012, *Psalms: A Guide to Studying the Psalter*, 2nd edn, Grand Rapids, MI: Baker.

Bullock, C. H., 2004, *Encountering the Book of Psalms*, Grand Rapids, MI: Baker.

Clifford, R. J., 1998, *The Wisdom Books: Interpreting Biblical Texts*, Nashville, TN: Abingdon Press.

Crenshaw, J. L., 2010, *Old Testament Wisdom: An Introduction*, 3rd edn, Louisville, KY: Westminster John Knox.

Day, J., 2013, *Psalms*, London: T&T Clark.

Dell, K. J., 2000, *'Get Wisdom, Get Insight': An Introduction to Israel's Wisdom Literature*, London: Darton, Longman and Todd.

Futato, M. D., 2007, *Interpreting the Psalms: An Exegetical Handbook*, HOTE, Grand Rapids, MI: Kregel.

Gillingham, S. E., 2008, *Psalms through the Centuries*, vol. 1, Oxford: Blackwell.

Hargreaves, J. A., 2005, *Guide to the Psalms*, 2nd edn, London: SPCK.

Holladay, W. L., 1996, *The Psalms through Three Thousand Years: Prayerbook of a Cloud of Witnesses*, Minneapolis, MN: Fortress Press.

Hunter, A., 2006, *Wisdom Literature*, London: SCM Press.

Johnston, P. S. and Firth, D. G. (eds), 2005, *Interpreting the Psalms: Issues and Approaches*, Leicester: Apollos.

Longman, T. and Enns, P. (eds), 2008, *Dictionary of the Old Testament: Wisdom, Poetry and Writings*, Downers Grove, IL; Nottingham: Inter-Varsity Press.

Lucas, E., 2003, *Exploring the Old Testament: Vol. 3: The Psalms and Wisdom Literature*, London: SPCK.

Murphy, R. E., 1990, *The Tree of Life: An Exploration of Biblical Wisdom Literature*, New York and London: Doubleday.

Von Rad, G., 1972, *Wisdom in Israel*, London: SCM Press (original 1970).

Weeks, S., 2010, *An Introduction to the Study of Wisdom Literature*, London and New York: T&T Clark.

There are plenty of studies on the Psalms, whose widespread appreciation stems from their regular use in worship. Their appeal is their honest and poignant poetic expression of a rich palette of human experiences in relation to God. The books listed give particular attention to their ancient composition, meaning, and use (Bellinger; Bullock; Day; Dell; Johnston and Firth), increasingly their later reception (Gillingham; Holladay), and also their use as Christian Scripture (Futato; Hargreaves). The wisdom books are also popular due to the universal, human topics they treat with reflective insight and practical realism. This has also been enhanced by the modern discovery of other ancient Near Eastern wisdom texts (see also Chapter 4 by Ryan P. O'Dowd). That said, their concentrated study in the modern era is a relatively recent phenomenon. It is therefore pleasing that there are now many fine introductions to this Old Testament literature. Some are modern classics (Von Rad); others are widely used (Clifford; Crenshaw; Murphy); and the latest (Bartholomew and O'Dowd; Hunter; Longman and Enns; Lucas; Weeks) build on this valuable and important trend.

Prophetic Books

Barton, J., 2007, *Oracles of God: Perceptions of Ancient Prophecy in Israel After the Exile*, 2nd edn, London: Darton, Longman and Todd.

Blenkinsopp, J., 1996, *A History of Prophecy in Israel*, rev., enlarged edn, Louisville, KY: Westminster John Knox.

Boda, M. J. and McConville, J. G. (eds), 2012, *Dictionary of the Old Testament Prophets*, Downers Grove, IL; Nottingham: Inter-Varsity Press.

Davies, P. R., 1996, *The Prophets: A Sheffield Reader*, Sheffield: Sheffield Academic Press.

Eaton, J. H., 1997, *Mysterious Messengers*, London: SCM Press.

Grabbe, L. L., 1995, *Priests, Prophets, Diviners, Sages: A Socio-Historical Study of Religious Specialists in Ancient Israel*, Valley Forge, PA: Trinity Press International.

McConville, J. G., 2002, *Exploring the Old Testament: Vol. 4: The Prophets*, London: SPCK.

Moberly, R. W. L., 2006, *Prophecy and Discernment*, Cambridge: Cambridge University Press.

Nissinen, M., 2000, *Prophecy in its Ancient Near Eastern Context*, Atlanta, GA: SBL.

Petersen, D. L., 2002, *The Prophetic Literature: An Introduction*, Louisville, KY: Westminster John Knox.

Sawyer, J. F. A., 1993, *Prophecy and the Biblical Prophets*, Oxford: Oxford University Press.

Smith, G., 2014, *Interpreting the Prophetic Books: An Exegetical Handbook*, Grand Rapids, MI: Kregel.

Taylor, R. A., 2016, *Interpreting Apocalyptic Literature: An Exegetical Handbook*, Grand Rapids, MI: Kregel.

There has been a long-standing interest in the Prophetic Books among Christians, primarily because of their visionary significance as 'foretellers' for the New Testament writers and early Christianity. This is reflected, to varying extents, in recent studies, although that is not the sole reason for their appeal, given that they were first and foremost 'forthtellers' in ancient Israel and beyond (Barton; Boda and McConville; Moberly; Smith; Taylor). Accordingly, many modern introductory guides (Eaton; Blenkinsopp; Petersen; Sawyer) give particular attention to the composition of the Prophetic Books, the literary genres employed in prophecy, the prophets' relationship to other institutions such as worship and kingship, and the phenomenon of prophecy as such – especially in view of the modern discovery of ancient Near Eastern prophetic texts (see also Davies; Grabbe; Nissinen). The legacy of the prophetic texts is multi-faceted (see also Chapter 5 by Lena-Sofia Tiemeyer) – as is the case for all of the canonical sections.

Apocrypha/Deutero-Canon

DeSilva, D., 2002, *Introducing the Apocrypha: Message, Context and Significance*, Grand Rapids, MI: Baker.

Goodman, M., 2001, 'Introduction to the Apocrypha', in Barton, J. and Muddiman, J. (eds), *Oxford Bible Commentary*, Oxford: Oxford University Press, pp. 617–26.

Harrington, D. J., 1999, *Invitation to the Apocrypha*, Grand Rapids, MI: Eerdmans.

Kaiser, O., 2004, *The Old Testament Apocrypha: An Introduction*, Peabody, MA: Hendrickson.

Metzger, B. M., 1957, *An Introduction to the Apocrypha*, New York: Oxford University Press.

Wright, S., 2014, *Why Read the Apocrypha? The Books that Protestants Forgot*, Cambridge: Grove.

Xeravits, G. G., Zsengellér, J. and Szabó, X. (eds), 2014, *Canonicity, Setting, Wisdom in the Deuterocanonicals. Papers of the Jubilee Meeting of the International Conference on the Deuterocanonical Books*, Berlin, Germany; Boston, MA: de Gruyter.

The books of the Apocrypha are familiar texts in Catholic and Orthodox traditions, in which they are canonical Christian Scripture. Fine introductions to these books are written from that perspective (Harrington) – and specialist studies as well (Xeravits, Zsengellér and Szabó). But there has also been a significant and steady interest in them among modern scholars from what may be broadly labelled Protestant traditions (DeSilva; Kaiser; Metzger; Wright) – scholars who are convinced of their historical importance, even if their canonicity is rejected, or at least questioned, by them. As they are largely Jewish religious texts, their analysis is a regular part of studies in ancient Judaism (Goodman). Anyone who investigates the Jewish context from which Christianity arose must study them, as well as other ancient Jewish religious sources (e.g. the Dead Sea Scrolls).

Commentary

Biblical commentary is ordinarily concerned with the systematic explanation of the text: word by word, verse by verse, chapter by chapter – and the implications of this analysis for interpretation and for application. This long-standing practice can be traced to the biblical period, as well to all subsequent periods (see below under Part 2: Interpretation). What follows are some comments about recent publications: single-volume commentaries on the Bible as a whole, commentary series, and an exegetical checklist whose questions typically form the basis of biblical commentary. It is essential, as ever, to attend to the overall purpose of any given commentary in question, and to observe how the emphasis and focus of each specialist commentator serve that aim. Given the variety of commentaries available today, and since biblical commentary is always capable of improvement, it is an important rule of thumb to consult at least two commentaries on any given biblical text.[2]

Single-volume commentaries

Barton, J. and Muddiman, J. (eds), 2001, *The Oxford Bible Commentary*, Oxford: Oxford University Press.

Brown, R. E., Fitzmyer, J. A. and Murphy, R. E. (eds), 1999, *The New Jerome Biblical Commentary*, Upper Saddle River, NJ: Prentice-Hall.

Carson, D. A. (ed.), 1994, *New Bible Commentary*, 4th edn, Downers Grove, IL; Leicester: Inter-Varsity Press.

Dunn, D. G. and Rogerson, J. W. (eds), 2003, *Eerdmans Commentary on the Bible*, Grand Rapids, MI; Cambridge: Eerdmans.

Mays, J. L. and Blenkinsopp, J. (eds), 2000, *The HarperCollins Bible Commentary*, rev. edn, San Francisco: HarperSanFrancisco.

Attridge, H. W. (ed.), 2006, *The HarperCollins Study Bible: New Revised Standard Version with Apocryphal/Deuterocanonical Books*, rev. and updated edn, New York: HarperCollins.

Berlin, A. and Brettler, M. Z. (eds), 2004, *The Jewish Study Bible*, Oxford: Oxford University Press.

Carson, D. A. (ed.), 2015, *NIV Zondervan Study Bible*, Grand Rapids, MI: Zondervan.

Grudem, W. A. (ed.), 2008, *English Standard Version Study Bible*, Wheaton, IL: Crossway.

Jack Suggs, M., Sakenfeld, K. D. and Mueller, J. R. (eds), 1992, *The Oxford Study Bible: Revised English Bible with the Apocrypha*, New York: Oxford University Press.

St Athanasius Orthodox Academy, 2008, *Orthodox Study Bible*, Nashville, TN: Thomas Nelson.

> Senior, D. and Collins, J. J. (eds), 2011, *The Catholic Study Bible*, 3rd edn, Oxford and New York: Oxford University Press.

Single-volume commentaries on the whole Bible are a useful first port of call when seeking to understand a biblical text. By convention, they offer brief snapshots of books, chapters, and verses; but while their weakness might be their brevity, their corresponding strength is the convenience they offer in helping the reader to make quick sense of a text without getting lost in too much potentially confusing detail. This type of commentary is usually written by a team of scholars. Those listed also have denominational leanings – that is, Catholic (Brown, Fitzmyer and Murphy), Evangelical (Carson), or an ecumenical and inter-religious range (Barton and Muddiman; Dunn and Rogerson; Mays and Blenkinsopp). The latter point also applies to the Study Bibles (of selected translations) listed above, which typically present marginal comments on the biblical text. The use of this format is a practice that can be traced to antiquity and beyond: the *Glossae Ordinariae* of the medieval period is a fine example. These publications often feature introductory essays for the reader's orientation into the biblical world.

Commentary series

AB	Anchor Bible
AOTC	Apollos Old Testament Commentary
BBC	Blackwell Bible Commentaries
BCOT	Biblical Commentary on the Old Testament
BKAT	Biblischer Kommentar Altes Testament
BST	Bible Speaks Today
CBC	Cambridge Bible Commentary
CC	Continental Commentaries
CCSS	Catholic Commentary on Sacred Scripture
DSB	Daily Study Bible
EBC	Expositor's Bible Commentary
ECC	Eerdmans Critical Commentary
Herm	Hermeneia
IB	Interpreter's Bible
ICC	International Critical Commentary
Int	Interpretation
ITC	International Theological Commentary
JPSBC	Jewish Publication Society Bible Commentary
JPSTC	Jewish Publication Society Torah Commentary

NAC	New American Commentary
NCB	New Century Bible
NCBC	New Cambridge Bible Commentary
NIB	New Interpreter's Bible
NIBCOT	New International Biblical Commentary on the Old Testament
NICOT	New International Commentary on the Old Testament
NIVAC	New International Version Application Commentary
OTG	Old Testament Guide
OTL	Old Testament Library
SHBC	Smyth and Helwys Bible Commentary
TOCT	Tyndale Old Testament Commentaries
TPC	The Preacher's Commentary
WBC	Word Biblical Commentary

There is a huge array of commentary series available. Many more could have been listed! There are two broad tendencies in their emphasis and focus: ancient language, composition, and context (e.g. AB, BKAT, ECC, Herm, ICC, OTL); and exposition and application for ministry and mission (e.g. BST, DSB, EBC, IB, Int, NIB, TPC). These broad tendencies are not, however, mutually exclusive: many combine both in various creative ways. Other factors to bear in mind are their religious standpoint, whether Jewish (JPSBC, JPSTC) or Christian (most in the list); and that selected Bible translations are used in some series (e.g. NIBCOT). There are modern 'classics' and widely respected examples in all of the series: e.g. B. S. Childs on Exodus (OTL), M. Cogan and H. Tadmor on Kings (AB), H. G. M. Williamson on Ezra, Nehemiah (WBC), and W. Zimmerli on Ezekiel (Herm). While they are not listed here, there are also valuable commentaries that are not part of a commentary series as such (e.g. P. M. Joyce on Ezekiel). There are also introductions that are not commentaries, but that nevertheless provide helpful starting points for each book – such as the Old Testament Guides (e.g. J. Day on the Psalms; J. Barton on Isaiah 1—39; K. J. A. Larkin on Ruth and Esther), and the newer series T&T Clark Approach to Biblical Studies (e.g. M. E. Mills on Joshua to Kings; J. Stromberg on Isaiah). A recent and attractive development in Old Testament commentary is an emphasis and focus on Reception History (e.g. BBC).

Exegetical checklist

Literature	
Canon	• In what canonical section of the Bible is the text and its book located? • What does its canonical position indicate about the text's subject matter? • What is the text's place in the biblical narrative (Old and New Testaments) as a whole?
Composition	• Are there any indicators of authorship in the text or its book? • How does modern Biblical Criticism (e.g. Source, Form, Redaction) help in answering this? • What are the text's literary genre, structure, style, and techniques?
Content	• Are there any important debates over the translation of specific words or phrases? • What are the text's principal themes, phrases, and words? • What contribution does the text make to the book generally?
History	
Setting	• What are the text's time, place, and setting as presented in the text? • How does this fit into the chronology and geography of ancient Israelite history? • Does the text indicate a broader awareness of the ancient Near Eastern setting?
Audience	• Who is addressed within the text itself? • Who was the likely original audience of the text? • Who else might have been the intended addressees?
Historicity	• What kind of historical information does this text present? • Is there any evidence (e.g. archaeological, textual) that illuminates what it describes? • How does this text relate to the question of historicity?
Theology	
God	• How is the divine realm presented in the text? • Which of the following are mentioned: divine names, titles, actions, characteristics? • What is the relationship between God and others in the text?
Humanity	• How are human beings presented in the text? • What actions or characteristics do the human beings display? • How do human beings relate to God, or as individuals in community, in the text?

Activities	• Which of the following (or any other activity) is mentioned in the text: sacrifice, priesthood, temple, law, kingship, praise, prayer, wisdom, prophecy? • What does the activity convey in general about religious life in ancient Israel? • Does the message of the text commend or critique that activity?
Interpretation	
OT/HB	• Is the text quoted, paraphrased, or alluded to elsewhere in the Old Testament? • Do any of its motifs or themes recur or echo elsewhere in the Old Testament? • How did ancient Jewish interpreters understand this text?
Christianity	• Is the text quoted, paraphrased, or alluded to in the New Testament? • What have been the traditional interpretations of the text in the history of Christianity? • How has the text informed specific practices (e.g. worship, doctrine)?
Application	• How might the text inform Christian ministry and mission generally? • How might the text apply specifically (e.g. pastoral care, society)? • What local, national, or international issues do interpretations of the text address?

This checklist covers key areas of exegesis as an aspect of biblical commentary. They are the kind of questions that are typically asked to enable an effective grasp of the various ways in which a biblical text has been understood, interpreted, and applied. The checklist is deliberately weighted towards understanding a biblical text in its ancient context. Questions about how it might be later interpreted and applied in the modern world are included. But the following of the checklist in sequence will indicate more clearly how traditional, and then modern, interpretations and applications of a text have emerged organically out of that ancient context. This checklist also covers the main areas that require comment in university and college examinations, although in that scenario – as with sermons, Bible Studies, or meditations on Scripture – not all of the categories will be of equal value and importance all of the time.[3]

Biblical languages

Cook, J. A. and Holmstedt, R. D., 2013, *Beginning Biblical Hebrew: A Grammar and Illustrated Reader*, Grand Rapids, MI: Baker.

Futato, M. D., 2003, *Beginning Biblical Hebrew*, Winona Lake, IN: Eisenbrauns.

Hackett, J. A., 2010, *A Basic Introduction to Biblical Hebrew*, Peabody, MA: Hendrickson.

Lambdin, T. O., 1973, *Introduction to Biblical Hebrew*, London: Darton, Longman and Todd.

Seow, C. L., 1995, *A Grammar for Biblical Hebrew*, rev. edn, Nashville, TN: Abingdon Press.

Weingreen, J., 1959, *A Practical Grammar for Classical Hebrew*, 2nd edn, Oxford: Clarendon.

Andreas, S., 2012, *An Introduction to Biblical Aramaic*, Louisville, KY: Westminster John Knox.

Greenspahn, F. E., 2007, *An Introduction to Aramaic*, Atlanta, GA: SBL.

Van Pelt, M. V., 2011, *Basics of Biblical Aramaic: Complete Grammar, Lexicon, and Annotated Text*, Grand Rapids, MI: Zondervan.

Conybeare, F. C. and Stock, G. St, 2001, *Grammar of Septuagint Greek: With Selected Readings, Vocabularies, and Updated Indexes*, Grand Rapids, MI: Baker (original 1905).

Thackeray, H. St J., 1909, *A Grammar of the Old Testament in Greek: According to the Septuagint, Vol. 1: Introduction, Orthography, Accidence*, Cambridge: Cambridge University Press (reprint G. Olms, 1978).

www.accordancebible.com

www.bibleworks.com

www.cadrebible.com

www.logos.com

www.mechon-mamre.org

www.olivetree.com

www.stepbible.org

Danker, F. W., 2003, *Multipurpose Tools for Bible Study with CD-ROM*, 3rd edn, Minneapolis, MN: Fortress Press.

Kaltner, J. and McKenzie, S. L. (eds), 2002, *Beyond Babel: A Handbook for Biblical Hebrew and Related Languages*, SBL, Leiden: Brill.

Kelley, P. H., Mynatt, D. S. and Crawford, T. G., 1998, *The Masorah of Biblia Hebraica Stuttgartensia: Introduction and Annotated Glossary*, Grand Rapids, MI: Eerdmans.

Tov, E., 2012, *Textual Criticism of the Hebrew Bible*, 3rd edn, rev. and expanded, Minneapolis, MN: Fortress Press.

Würthwein, E., 2014, rev. and expanded by Fischer, A. A., *The Text of the Old Testament: An Introduction to the Biblia Hebraica*, 2nd edn, Grand Rapids, MI: Eerdmans (original 1988).

The Old Testament was largely written in ancient Hebrew. Most students will need a tutor to learn this language. There are many good textbooks available (Cook and Holmstedt; Futato; Hackett; Seow); the older ones are still very valuable (Lambdin; Weingreen). Each of these needs enrichment, whether that is by listening to Hebrew online (www.mechon-mamre.org) or visiting a local synagogue to hear biblical Hebrew read and sung. There are good textbooks on biblical Aramaic (Andreas; Greenspahn; Van Pelt), which is best learnt after Hebrew (and, in turn, Syriac). Having knowledge of Greek is important for reading the Old Testament translated into that language. There are textbooks for this (Conybeare and Stock; Thackeray), but it is usually approached through New Testament or Classical Greek – as is biblical Latin via its other ancient forms. The study of other languages from the ancient Near Eastern setting of the Bible (e.g. Egyptian, Akkadian, Ugaritic; see Kaltner and McKenzie) is usually only possible at certain universities and colleges. There are now excellent digital tools for biblical language study: websites (www.stepbible.org), powerful and sophisticated software (BibleWorks for Windows, Accordance for Macintosh), bumper packages (logos.com), and phone Apps (Olive Tree, Cadre Bible). These can be used on multiple electronic devices. Some of the tools and packages, given their quality and size, are expensive, although institutional licences make them available to matriculated students. As with all things digital, this is a fast-moving area of development. There are, nonetheless, relatively up-to-date guides in print to the study of the biblical languages as an aspect of biblical study in general (e.g. Danker). With the acquisition of knowledge and skills in biblical languages also comes the opportunity to get to grips with the technicalities of Textual Criticism (Kelley et al.; Tov; Würthwein).

Part 2: Interpretation

The aspect of interpretation was not absent in the discussion above. After all, giving due attention to the ancient historical context of a biblical text carries with it certain reasonable assumptions about interpretation. Above all, the authors aimed to convey messages that were themselves acts of interpretation; and composing a religious text that communicates required theological reflection and literary skill. Moreover, the exegetical checklist on pp. 209–10 posed questions that indicate the biblical writers were already in an organic and dynamic world of interpretation: the biblical texts show the reinterpretation of pre-existing traditions taking place. This is all an important reminder that interpretation is not only a post-biblical phenomenon. It was also evident in the preceding chapters, especially regarding later books that built on earlier biblical traditions (i.e. the Apocrypha). Indeed, this is a specialist area of study in itself. Expressions such as 'inner-biblical exegesis' and 'intertextuality' are commonplace in contemporary scholarly literature, in addition to conventional terms such as quotation, paraphrase, and allusion.[4] That said, the second section of each of the preceding core chapters has nonetheless been largely concerned with interpretation as a post-biblical phenomenon. The following comments are, accordingly, concerned with that.

Dictionaries, encyclopaedias, histories

Bray, G. L., 1996, *Biblical Interpretation: Past and Present*, Downers Grove, IL; Leicester: Inter-Varsity Press.

Coggins, R. J. and Houlden, J. L. (eds), 1990, *A Dictionary of Biblical Interpretation*, London: SCM Press.

Grant, R. M. and Tracy, D., 1984, *A Short History of the Interpretation of the Bible*, 2nd edn, Philadelphia, PA: Fortress Press.

Hauser, A. J. and Watson, D. F. A., 2001–3, *History of Biblical Interpretation, Vol. 1 The Ancient Period, Vol. 2 The Medieval Through the Reformation Periods*, Grand Rapids, MI; Cambridge: Eerdmans.

Hayes, J. H. (ed.), 1990, *Dictionary of Biblical Interpretation*, 2 vols, Nashville, TN: The Abingdon Press.

McKenzie, S. L. (ed.), 2013, *The Oxford Encyclopedia of Biblical Interpretation*, 2 vols, New York: Oxford University Press.

McKim, D. K. (ed.), 1998, *Historical Handbook of Major Biblical Interpreters*, Downers Grove, IL; Leicester: Inter-Varsity Press.

Paget, J. C. and Schaper, J. (eds), 2012–15, *The New Cambridge History of the Bible*, 4 vols, Cambridge: Cambridge University Press.

Saebo, M. (ed.), 1996–2014, *Hebrew Bible/Old Testament: The History of its Interpretation*, 3 vols, Göttingen: Vandenhoeck & Ruprecht.

Yarchin, W., 2004, *History of Biblical Interpretation: A Reader*, Peabody, MA: Hendrickson.

There are many excellent books about biblical interpretation. Given the generality of the phrase 'biblical interpretation', dictionaries, encyclopaedias, and histories treat a large range of topics, both the core and the associated. Dictionaries and encyclopaedias (Coggins and Houlden; Hayes; McKenzie) typically contain articles about books and topics within the

Bible, as well as the major interpreters, stages, and concepts in the history of its interpretation. The histories (Bray; Grant and Tracy; Hauser and Watson; McKim; Saebo; Yarchin) give fuller and specific attention to the later contexts in which biblical interpretation has occurred; in so doing they generate or imply a story about interpretation – much like the chapters in this book – since there are identifiable trends and patterns in that history. The *New Cambridge History of the Bible* is a different publication: it treats both the history of the formation of the Bible as such, as well as its later interpretation in multiple historical contexts – and much more (e.g. translation, the arts). The profusion of these resources about interpretation is the result of many factors, but above all this is due to a heightened awareness of the complex pluralism of both the history of interpretation and the contemporary world itself.

History of interpretation

The following comments about the Christian interpretation of the Old Testament, with reference to the categories used in the preceding chapters (Early, Medieval, Reformation, Modern, Global), draw out some of the patterns and trends that have emerged. As a result, this privileges a specific history. But this is done neither in a vacuum nor without an acknowledgement of the porous complexity of that history. And it is not meant presumptuously, as was indicated in the Introduction to this book. The biblical texts are public documents, available to one and all – as their constant echo in wider society indicates. It is nonetheless up to Christian interpreters to make the case for their viewpoints, as all kinds of interpreters of texts must do for theirs, the religious and the non-religious. But religiously committed biblical interpretation is arguably the most valuable and interesting, because it takes most seriously the biblical texts, including the life and death matters of which the ancient biblical writers wrote. Christian biblical interpretation is not, therefore, merely a colourful carnival, even though it might easily appear like that at times. Rather, Christian biblical interpretation is a series of acts of contextualization, done in faith.

Early Christianity

Beale, G. K. and Carson, D. A. (eds), 2007, *Commentary on the New Testament Use of the Old Testament*, Grand Rapids, MI: Baker; Nottingham: Apollos.
Carson, D. A. and Williamson, H. G. M. (eds), 1992, *It is Written: Scripture Citing Scripture. Essays in Honour of Barnabas Lindars*, Cambridge: Cambridge University Press.

Heine, R. E., 2007, *Reading the Old Testament with the Ancient Church: Exploring the Formation of Early Christian Thought*, Grand Rapids, MI: Baker.

Kannengiesser, C., 2006, *Handbook of Patristic Exegesis*, BAC, 1, Leiden; Boston: Brill.

Kugel, J. L., 1997, *The Bible As It Was*, Cambridge, MA; London: Belknap Press of Harvard University Press.

Kugel, J. L., 1998, *Traditions of the Bible: A Guide to the Bible As It Was at the Start of the Common Era*, Cambridge, MA; London: Harvard University Press.

Longenecker, R., 1999, *Biblical Exegesis in the Apostolic Period*, rev. edn, Grand Rapids, MI: Eerdmans.

Moyise, S., 2001, *The Old Testament in the New*, London: Continuum.

Oden, T. C. (ed.), 1998–, *Ancient Christian Commentary on Scripture*, 29 vols, Downers Grove, IL: Inter-Varsity Press.

Wilken, R. (ed.), 2003–, *The Church's Bible*, 4 vols, Grand Rapids, MI: Eerdmans.

Young, F. M., 1997, *Biblical Exegesis and the Formation of Christian Culture*, Cambridge: Cambridge University Press.

The early Christians understood the Jewish Jesus to be the divine figure who had transformed the interpretation of biblical texts. Many ancient methods of Jewish exegesis, such as Midrash, are evident in the New Testament (Beale and Carson; Carson and Williamson; Kugel; Moyise). This heritage continued in the Patristic period (e.g. Origen, Jerome), although this period also attests sharp exchanges, between Jews and Christians over the inheritance and ownership of the biblical texts (cf. John 8; Acts 7), and among those in the early Church given its own emergent orthodoxy and heresies. The multi-ethnic character of early Christianity meant that biblical texts were often interpreted figuratively – their ideas and patterns recontextualized for new audiences, with didactic and moral teaching also drawn from them for both Jew and Gentile. The literal (historical) and figurative (typological, allegorical) dimensions of ancient interpretation led to two tendencies or 'schools', the Antiochene and the Alexandrian, respectively, which both interacted with currents in late antique Roman society (e.g. rhetoric, philosophy). Augustine's *De Doctrina Christiana*, which prioritizes charity as the key to interpretation, was meant as a guide to scriptural exegesis for those teachers who had not had a sophisticated 'secular' education. A distinctive culture of Christian interpretation thereby emerged, embedded in Church practices (e.g. liturgy, homily). Its hallmarks were various: the translation of the biblical texts into different languages (Greek, Latin, Syriac etc.), a larger canon (i.e. with the New Testament, and the Apocrypha), the use of the book-like 'codex' (rather than continue with the scroll, as in Judaism), and a new discourse represented by the titles Old Testament and New Testament. The books listed above contain samples of early Christian texts (Oden; Wilken) and descriptions and analyses of that new culture (Heine; Kannengiesser; Longenecker; Young).

Medieval Christianity

Evans, G. R., 1984–5, *The Language and Logic of the Bible*, 2 vols, New York and Cambridge: Cambridge University Press.

Lawrence Bond, H., Krey, P. D. W. and Ryan, T. (eds), 2015, *The Bible in Medieval Tradition*, Grand Rapids, MI: Eerdmans.

Liere, F. A. van, 2014, *An Introduction to the Medieval Bible*, Cambridge: Cambridge University Press.

Lubac, H. de, *1998–2009, Medieval Exegesis*, 3 vols, Grand Rapids, MI: Eerdmans; Edinburgh: T&T Clark (original 1959–64).

McNally, R. E., 1959, *The Bible in the Early Middle Ages*, Westminster, MD: Newman.

The doctrines and practices of medieval Christianity concerning the Old Testament were in large measure in continuity with those of early Christianity: the biblical texts were read for their prefigurations of Christ, the Church, and the spiritual and moral life. The ancient centres of Christianity bequeathed traditions about beliefs, worship, and living, in which the Old Testament texts were already fully integrated within a Christian framework and view of history. The medieval period is known for particular developments and achievements: early missions, monastic orders, the papacy, universities, cathedrals, hospitals, and pilgrimage – to name some of the best known. As for developments and achievements in the interpretation of the Old Testament, the following are noteworthy: the copying and preservation of biblical manuscripts, the translation of biblical texts into vernacular languages, the widespread use of the Quadriga (the four senses of Scripture), and the quotation of authoritative Patristic interpretations (e.g. in the *Glossa Ordinariae* – much like early rabbinic interpretations in medieval Judaism). Old Testament scenes and characters were elaborately portrayed in illuminated manuscripts, and in stained-glass windows. Developments in doctrine and practice also left their mark on the interpretation and application of the Old Testament: within the Church (e.g. Marian devotion), and on a larger international canvas (e.g. the Crusades, anti-Judaism) – developments that both then and later proved highly controversial. The books listed (Evans; Lawrence Bond, Krey and Ryan; Liere; Lubac; McNally) provide analyses and examples of these features and trends.

Reformation Christianity

Bornkamm, H., 1969, *Luther and the Old Testament*, Philadelphia, PA: Fortress Press.

McGrath, A. E., 2012, *Reformation Thought: An Introduction*, 4th edn, Malden, MA; Oxford: Wiley-Blackwell.

Muller, R. A. and Thompson, J. L. (eds), 1996, *Biblical Interpretation in the Era of the Reformation: Essays Presented to David C. Steinmetz in Honor of his 60th Birthday*, Grand Rapids, MI; Cambridge: Eerdmans.

Pelikan, J., 1996, *The Reformation of the Bible: The Bible of the Reformation*, New Haven, CT; London: Yale University Press.

Puckett, D. L., 1995, *John Calvin's Exegesis of the Old Testament*, Louisville, KY: Westminster John Knox.

Reardon, B., 1995, *Religious Thought in the Reformation*, 2nd edn, London: Longman.

Steinmetz, D. C., 1990, *The Bible in the Sixteenth Century*, Durham, NC; London: Duke University Press.

The European Renaissance was a humanistic cultural movement inspired by the renewal of Classical Studies: a return to the texts of Greek and Roman antiquity, the critical study of ancient texts in their original languages, and developments in the fine arts. Many Reformation-era theologians (e.g. Erasmus, More, Luther, Calvin) were trained in its outlook and skills. Accordingly, the Renaissance attention to ancient texts had its counterpart in the Reformation renewal of doctrine and practice via the study of the Bible. The corruption and complexity of some late-medieval Christianity had already led to calls for reform, and biblical exegesis in all its forms (e.g. homily, treatise, tract) became a lever for critique and polemic, as well as serving the on-going life of the Church. This is seen in various ways regarding the interpretation of the Old Testament. Rather than read its texts solely in Latin, their on-going translation into vernacular languages became occasions for questioning the biblical bases of medieval theology and practice. This also encouraged popular Bible reading, enabled by the mass production of Bibles, due to the introduction in Europe of a movable-type printing press by Johannes Gutenberg (c. 1440). While early Protestant Bibles included the Apocrypha, if only in an appendix, some later translations did not, given their seeming support for contested beliefs and practices (e.g. prayers for the dead, purgatory, faith and works). The traditional Christian interpretation of the Old Testament continued, but in reaction to the excesses of medieval allegory, Luther focused more directly on the Christ of faith in relation to the Old Testament (Bornkamm), and Calvin on the literal or 'plain sense' (Puckett). The latter went hand in hand with the increased study of Hebrew and consideration of Jewish interpretations (even if anti-Judaism continued).

This was also the period of the establishment of the Regius professorships in Hebrew at major universities across Europe (Cambridge 1540, Oxford 1546). There are many fine guides to this period of theological revolution and change (McGrath; Reardon), some with a particular focus on the Bible (Muller and Thompson; Pelikan; Steinmetz).

Modern Christianity

Barton, J., 2007, *The Nature of Biblical Criticism*, Louisville, KY; London: Westminster John Knox.

Barton, J. and Morgan, R., 1988, *Biblical Interpretation*, Oxford: Oxford University Press.

Frei, H. W., 1974, *The Eclipse of Biblical Narrative: A Study in Eighteenth and Nineteenth Century Hermeneutics*, New Haven, CT: Yale University Press.

Kraeling, E. G. H., 1955, *The Old Testament since the Reformation*, New York: Harper.

Legaspi, M. C., 2010, *The Death of Scripture and the Rise of Biblical Studies*, Oxford: Oxford University Press.

Rogerson, J. W., 1984, *Old Testament Criticism in the Nineteenth Century: England and Germany*, London: SPCK.

The Renaissance and Reformation focus on the literary and the linguistic, coupled with the radical renewal of Church doctrine and practice, were watershed episodes in European Christianity. But it was the freedom to critique Christianity and religion as such, in view of the immediately preceding centuries of religious strife and warfare, as well as significant discoveries and developments in the natural and social sciences, that led to 'historical criticism' becoming the hallmark of an increasingly secularized modernity. This had obvious effects in the study of the Old Testament. Scholars no longer automatically deferred to traditional views, but they applied their reason to analyse the biblical texts as ancient literature: their authorship, composition, historical truth, and ethics (Barton and Morgan; Frei; Kraeling; Legaspi; Rogerson). The modern task has thereby been largely that of the reconstruction of the historical development of ancient Israelite religion and society, without assuming that this equates to what the biblical texts present. The discovery since the nineteenth century of ancient Near Eastern texts, languages, and archaeology – which might either confirm or contradict the biblical texts – has often served this overall aim. There are now well-established 'learned societies' – the Society of Biblical Literature (founded 1880), the Society for Old Testament Studies (founded 1917), and more recently the European Association of Biblical Studies (1996) – in which reconstruction is the predominant activity. The analysis of the biblical texts is typically approached as critical studies in antique religion, with ancient Israelite religion seen as a variant, albeit a significant and influential variant, of widespread patterns of the ancient Near East.

Global Christianity

Adeyamo, T. (ed.), 2006, *Africa Bible Commentary*, Grand Rapids, MI: Zondervan.

Boer, R. and Segovia, F. F. (eds), 2012, *The Future of the Biblical Past: Envisioning Biblical Studies on a Global Key*, Atlanta, GA: SBL.

Ceresko, A. R., 2001, *Introduction to the Old Testament: A Liberation Perspective*, rev. and expanded edn, Maryknoll, NY: Orbis.

Patte, D. and Croatto, J. Severino (eds), *Global Bible Commentary*, Nashville, TN: Abingdon Press.

Roncace, M. and Weaver, K. (eds), 2013, *Global Perspectives on the Bible*, Upper Saddle River, NJ: Pearson.

Rowland, C. and Corner, M., 1990, *Liberating Exegesis: The Challenge of Liberation Theology to Biblical Studies*, London: SPCK.

Starr, C. (ed.), 2008, *Reading Christian Scriptures in China*, London and New York: T&T Clark.

Sugirtharajah, R. S., 2001, *The Bible and the Third World: Precolonial, Colonial and Postcolonial Encounters*, Cambridge: Cambridge University Press.

Sugirtharajah, R. S., 2006, *The Postcolonial Biblical Reader*, Malden, MA: Oxford: Blackwell.

Sugirtharajah, R. S., 2013, *The Bible and Asia: From the Pre-Christian Era to the Postcolonial Age*, Cambridge, MA; London: Harvard University Press.

West, G, O. and Dube, M. W. (eds), 2010, *The Bible in Africa: Transactions, Trajectories and Trends*, Leiden: Brill.

Global Christianity can easily signify post-colonial Christianity – that is, forms of faith different from those of Western Christianity and its mixed colonial legacies. Moreover, since the centres of Christian growth are now not in the West, but in Asia and Africa, there is a real danger of using the term 'global' in solely oppositional terms (e.g. white vs non-white, rich vs poor, individualist vs communal). Some perspectives are framed in this way – and rightly so, where oppressive interpretations need exposing (Rowland and Corner; Sugirtharajah). That said, 'global' may also be used constructively. An attention to the spread of Christianity, from its inception until now, shows that biblical interpretation has always been global (i.e. geographically expansive), as well as contextually specific. This does not warrant the *reductio ad absurdum* that all interpretation, removed from the original biblical context, is wrong. But it highlights the potential for either better or worse interpretation, given the particularities of each context, biblical and subsequent. In other words, no interpretation can fully exhaust the reservoir of biblical meaning, as any Old Testament canonical section can be used to illustrate. Put more constructively, if 'non-Western' interpretations are insightful (Adeyamo; Ceresko; Starr; West), and more so than some kinds of 'Western' interpretation, then their enrichment of the Christian story is essential. The term 'global' is also a reminder that there are issues of global significance (e.g. trade, migration, violence, climate) about which we are increasingly aware, via the internet and the media. These might not always be, in principle, new issues, but the call to be a responsible global citizen confronts us more than ever. There are now, as a result, scholars whose publications hold the horizon high so that biblical interpretation, while locally applied, remains part of a truly global Christian story (Boer and Segovia; Patte and Croatto; Roncace and Weaver). This is, not surprisingly, a major growth area in Biblical Studies.

Method, hermeneutics, theology

Barton, J., 1996, *Reading the Old Testament. Method in Biblical Study*, 2nd edn, London: Darton, Longman and Todd.

Barton, J. (ed.), 1998, *The Cambridge Companion to Biblical Interpretation*, Cambridge: Cambridge University Press.

Fitzmyer, J. A., 2008, *The Interpretation of Scripture: In Defence of the Historical-Critical Method*, New York: Paulist Press.

Gillingham, S. E., 1998, *One Bible, Many Voices: Different Approaches to Biblical Studies*, London: SPCK.

Law, D. R., 2012, *Historical Critical Method: A Guide for the Perplexed*, London: T&T Clark.

McKenzie, S. L. and Haynes, S. R. (eds), 1993, *To Each Its Own Meaning: An Introduction to Biblical Criticisms and Their Applications*, Louisville, KY: Westminster John Knox.

Soulen, R. N. and Kendall Soulen, R., 2011, *Handbook of Biblical Criticism*, 4th edn, Louisville, KY: Westminster John Knox.

Briggs, R., 2003, *Reading the Bible Wisely*, London: SPCK.

Collins, J. J., 2005, *The Bible after Babel: Historical Criticism in a Postmodern Age*, Grand Rapids, MI: Eerdmans.

Davies, E. W., 2013, *Biblical Criticism: A Guide for the Perplexed*, London: Bloomsbury.

Holgate, D. and Starr, R., 2006, *SCM Studyguide to Biblical Hermeneutics*, London: SCM Press.

Jobling, D., Pippin, T. and Schleifer, R. (eds), 2001, *The Postmodern Bible Reader*, Oxford: Blackwell.

Osborne, G. R., 2006, *The Hermeneutical Spiral: A Comprehensive Intro-duction to Biblical Interpretation*, 2nd edn, Downers Grove, IL: Inter-Varsity Press.

Parris, D., 2009, *Reception Theory and Biblical Hermeneutics*, Princeton, NJ: Pickwick.

Thiselton, A., 2009, *Hermeneutics: An Introduction*, Grand Rapids, MI; Cambridge: Eerdmans.

Vanhoozer, K. J., 1998, *Is There a Meaning in this Text? The Bible, the Reader, and the Morality of Literary Knowledge*, Leicester: Apollos.

Baker, D. L., 2010, *Two Testaments, One Bible*, 4th edn; Nottingham: Inter-Varsity Press.

Balentine, S. E. (ed.), 2015, *The Oxford Encyclopedia of the Bible and Theol-ogy*, 2 vols, New York: Oxford University Press.

Bartholomew, C. G., 2015, *Introducing Biblical Hermeneutics: A Comprehensive Framework for Hearing God in Scripture*, Grand Rapids, MI: Eerdmans.

Carl, S. (ed.), 2015, *Verbum Domini and the Complementarity of Exegesis and Theology*, Grand Rapids, MI: Eerdmans.

Childs, B. S., 1979, *Introduction to the Old Testament as Scripture*, Phila-delphia, PA: Fortress Press.

Fowl, S. (ed.), 1997, *The Theological Interpretation of Scripture: Classic and Contemporary Readings*, Cambridge, MA; Oxford: Blackwell.

Goldingay, J., 1995, *Models for Interpretation of Scripture*, Grand Rapids, MI: Eerdmans; Carlisle: Paternoster.

Vanhoozer, K. J. (ed.), 2005, *Dictionary for Theological Interpretation of the Bible*, Grand Rapids, MI: Baker; London: SPCK.

The close study of biblical texts has always required skill, be it concerned with translation (i.e. Textual Criticism) or interpretation (i.e. Hermeneutics) – to give two examples that can be traced to antiquity and all subsequent periods. In the modern period in particular, however, a set of methods developed that are 'genetic' in focus – that is, they are concerned with what is known about the original circumstances of a text's composition, so as to establish its most likely original meaning. These are explained in guides to method as kinds of 'criticism': Source, Form, and Redaction Criticism are the standard set of three (Barton; Fitzmyer; Gillingham; Law; McKen-zie and Haynes; Soulen and Kendall Soulen). The term 'criticism' has since broadened out to include other kinds: Literary, Rhetorical, and Canonical Criticism are usually concerned with the 'final form' of the text (often as Sacred Scripture). Moreover, the disciplines of the human sciences have been applied: Psychological, Sociological, and Anthropological Criticism are another standard set of three. These many methods are often presented as a 'tool-kit' to assist the student and general reader in probing a text's meaning at its various stages of emergence.

But in postmodernity, philosophical questions have been posed about authors, texts, and interpreters, such that 'method' now includes any ideological standpoint that clearly has a significant role to play in the act of interpretation (Briggs; Collins; Davies; Holgate; Jobling, Pippin and Schleifer; Osborne; Parris; Thiselton; Vanhoozer). The various interests represented are many: gender, race, and sexuality are yet another set of three. This development has been in part a reaction to some of the over-confident and, it turns out, ideologically laden, reconstructions of Historical Criticism. For instance, just as modern Western thinkers see themselves as progressive, they often suppose the same was true of ancient Israelite thinkers. Whether or not the latter was the case, the suspicion is that some modern historical critics tend to see what they wish to see. The current state of affairs is, as a result, a radically pluralistic and open field, given that all interpreters are ideologically committed. Not surprisingly, this field now increasingly includes – of necessity – the Christian theological interpretation of biblical texts (Baker; Balentine; Bartholomew; Carl; Childs; Fowl; Goldingay; Vanhoozer).

Canon, authority, tradition

Barton, J., 1997, *The Spirit and the Letter: Studies in the Biblical Canon*, London: SPCK.

Beckwith, R., 1985, *The Old Testament Canon of the New Testament Church*, London: SPCK; Grand Rapids, MI: Eerdmans.

Bruce, F. F., 1988, *The Canon of Scripture*, Glasgow: Chapter House.

Lim, T. H., 2014, *The Formation of the Jewish Canon*, New Haven, CT: Yale University Press.

McDonald, L. M., 2007, *The Biblical Canon: Its Origin, Transmission and Authority*, Peabody, MA: Hendrickson.

McDonald, L. M., 2011, *The Origin of the Bible: A Guide for the Perplexed*, London: T&T Clark.

Abraham, W. J., 1981, *The Divine Inspiration of Holy Scripture*, Oxford: Oxford University Press.

Barr, J., 1983, *Holy Scripture: Canon, Authority, Criticism*, Oxford: Clarendon.

Barton, J., 1993, *People of the Book? The Authority of the Bible in Christianity*, rev. edn, London: SPCK.

Brueggemann, W., 2005, *The Book that Breathes New Life: Scriptural Authority and Biblical Theology*, Minneapolis, MN: Fortress Press.

Marshall, I. H., 1995, *Biblical Inspiration*, new edn, Carlisle: Paternoster.

O'Neill, J. C., 1991, *The Bible's Authority: A Portrait Gallery of Thinkers from Lessing to Bultmann*, Edinburgh: T&T Clark.

Thompson, M. D., 2006, *A Clear and Present Word: The Clarity of Scripture*, Downers Grove, IL: Inter-Varsity Press.

Bacote, V., Miguelez, L. C. and Okholm, D. L. (eds), 2004, *Evangelicals and Scripture: Tradition, Authority and Hermeneutics*, Downers Grove, IL: Inter-Varsity Press.

Bechard, D. P. (ed., tr.), 2002, *The Scripture Documents: An Anthology of Official Catholic Teachings*, Collegeville, MN: Liturgical Press.

Brettler, M. Z., Enns, P. and Harrington, D. J., 2013, *The Bible and the Believer: How to Read the Bible Critically and Religiously*, New York and Oxford: Oxford University Press.

Levenson, J. D., 1993, *The Hebrew Bible, the Old Testament, and Historical Criticism: Jews and Christians in Biblical Studies*, Louisville, KY: Westminster John Knox.

Noll, M. A., 1991, *Between Faith and Criticism: Evangelicals, Scholarship and the Bible in America*, 2nd edn, Leicester: Apollos.

Okoye, J. C., 2011, *Scripture in the Church: The Synod on the Word of God and the Post-Synodal Exhortation Verbum Domini*, Collegeville, MN: Liturgical Press.

Pentiuc, E. J., 2014, *The Old Testament in Eastern Orthodox Tradition*, Oxford: Oxford University Press.

There has been, since postmodernity, a retrieval of theological interpretations of Scripture. This is not only to do with pluralism, in which traditional religious voices also gain a seat at the biblical table. It is also to do with recognizing that the biblical texts are religious texts, and that is how they have mostly been interpreted and applied: as sacred canon, however much the investigation of canonization poses tricky historical questions (Barton; Beckwith; Bruce; Lim; McDonald). Moreover, the almost exclusively genetic focus in modern criticism on a text's original circumstances has its limits: quite often, such details cannot be known for certain. Furthermore, the biblical texts are rich and multi-layered: they are part of an organic and dynamic world of interpretation, in which they already transcended their original circumstances, due to their ancient role in inter-generational religious instruction. This recognition has been a fruit of studies in ancient biblical interpretation. In addition, analyses of their divine quality as sacred texts – a standard belief in Jewish and Christian antiquity – has often taken place against the backdrop of Historical Criticism, as well as this being a traditional doctrinal topic (Abraham; Barr; Barton; Brueggemann; Marshall; O'Neill; Thompson). A number of scholars, Christian and Jewish, in this current period of retrieval, have therefore sought to marry the critical and the theological, although this continues to have variable contours, depending on the religious and denominational tradition in question

(Bacote, Miguelez and Okholm; Bechard; Brettler, Enns and Harrington; Levenson; Noll; Okoye; Pentiuc).

Part 3: Application

What, then, does the Old Testament provide for the Christian Church in its ministry and mission? This question cannot, of course, be answered fully, not only because of the limited space available here, but above all because the tapestry is too expansive and rich to be captured in sufficient breadth and detail. But it may be helpful to highlight some of the ways in which the Old Testament, as a whole and via each canonical section, has this role in the Christian Church. The following comments recapitulate some of the proposals made in the third and final sections of each of the preceding chapters, while reframing them in a general way. It is as this juncture that not only the interpretation, but also the application, of the Old Testament becomes most distinctive and committed in practice, in comparison with both other religions in which these texts are also sacred (i.e. Judaism, Islam) and non-religious interpretation where they need not be. This is, in short, about reading the Old Testament in the light of the action of God through the person of Jesus Christ in the Holy Spirit. According to the Christian worldview, this co-operative divine activity explains and guides the drama of salvation, which is at the centre of the purposes of God for the world.

Ministry

Theological understanding

Alexander, T. D. and Rosner, B. S. (eds), 2000, *New Dictionary of Biblical Theology*, Leicester: Inter-Varsity Press.

Brueggemann, W., 2002, *Reverberations of Faith: A Theological Handbook of Old Testament Themes*, Louisville, KY; London: Westminster John Knox.

Brueggemann, W., 2008, *Old Testament Theology: An Introduction*, Nashville, TN: Abingdon Press.

Goldingay, J., 2003–9, *Old Testament Theology: Israel's Gospel, Israel's Faith, Israel's Life*, 3 vols, Downers Grove, IL: Inter-Varsity Press.

Moberly, R. W. L., 2013, *Old Testament Theology: Reading the Hebrew Bible as Christian Scripture*, Grand Rapids, MI: Baker.

Preuss, H. D., 1995–6, *Old Testament Theology*, 2 vols, Edinburgh: T&T Clark (original 1991–2).

Léon-Dufour, X. (ed.), 1995, *Dictionary of Biblical Theology*, 2nd edn, London: Chapman (original 1962).

The ministry of the Church is rooted in the action of the one God of the Old Testament. God's gifts to humankind are understood through overarching biblical themes such as creation, covenant, promise, redemption, glory, purity, justice, and messianic hope. In other words, God is passionately and compassionately involved with the world and its inhabitants, a relationship largely modelled through the many and varied experiences of ancient Israel (Alexander and Rosner; Brueggemann; Goldingay; Moberly; Preuss; Xavier-Dufour). It is here that the Church's ministry begins, instructed and inspired by an ancient relationship that illustrates how the people of God were provided for by God, and how they, in turn, were to serve society and the world. The Christian understanding of this relationship is one in which the human condition, as presented in the Old Testament, is viewed afresh through the person of Jesus Christ. Accordingly, through Christ the image of God in humankind is renewed; human journeying through life's highs and lows has Christ as the shepherd and guide; through him is promised both victory over all spiritual enemies and eternal rest; his full embracing of our humanity makes him the ideal spiritual companion in life; and his messianic Kingdom redeems the relationships with God and one another that mere human beings cannot achieve. This is a theological view of relationships that is ministerial: service is at its heart.

Worship

Adam, P., 2004, *Hearing God's Words: Exploring Biblical Spirituality*, Downers Grove, IL; Leicester: Inter-Varsity Press.

Bechtel, C. M. (ed.), 2008, *Touching the Altar: The Old Testament For Christian Worship*, Grand Rapids, MI: Eerdmans.

De la Croix, Paul-Marie, OCD, 1961–3, *Spirituality of the Old Testament*, 3 vols, St Louis, MO: B. Herder.

Goldingay, J., 1993, *Praying the Psalms*, Bramcote: Grove.

Lombaard, C., 2012, *The Old Testament and Christian Spirituality: Theoretical and Practical Essays from a South African Perspective*, Atlanta, GA: SBL.

Bos, R., 2008, *We Have Heard that God is With You: Preaching the Old Testament*, Grand Rapids, MI; Cambridge: Eerdmans.

Greidanus, S., 1999, *Preaching Christ from the Old Testament*, Grand Rapids, MI; Cambridge: Eerdmans.

Kent, J. G. R., Kissling, P. J. and Turner, L. A. (eds), 2010, *'He Began with Moses': Preaching the Old Testament Today*, Nottingham: Inter-Varsity Press.

Rutledge, F., 2011, *And God Spoke to Abraham: Preaching from the Old Testament*, Grand Rapids, MI; Cambridge: Eerdmans.

Best, T. F. (ed.), 2008, *Baptism Today: Understanding, Practice, Ecumenical Implications*, Collegeville, MN: Liturgical Press.

Boland, V. and McCarthy, T. (eds), 2012, *The Word is Flesh and Blood: The Eucharist and Sacred Scripture*, Dublin: Dominican Publications.

Bromiley, G. W., 1957, *Sacramental Teaching and Practice in the Reformation Churches*, Grand Rapids, MI: Eerdmans.

Daniélou, J., 1960, *The Bible and the Liturgy*, London: Darton, Longman and Todd (original 1951).

Gooder, P. and Perham, M., 2013, *Echoing the Word: the Bible in the Eucharist*, London: SPCK.

Ministry is expressed first and foremost in the worship of God, and the spirituality that feeds that relationship. In the Old Testament, the principles and practices of holiness and justice are the necessary hallmarks of a life lived before God in a covenant relationship of promise and warning. Here is a God who is to be honoured and feared respectfully, who is revealed through the wonder of creation, or in holy and overwhelming grandeur, but who can also be mysterious and unapproachable. Christian worship and spirituality has always been in continuity with this rich portrayal, across all major Church denominations (Adam; Bechtel; De la Croix; Goldingay; Lombaard). Specific liturgical practices are nourished by the use of the Old Testament, both in 'word' (Bos; Greidanus; Kent, Kissling and Turner; Rutledge) and in 'sacrament' (Best; Boland and McCarthy; Bromiley; Gooder and Perham). The times and seasons of the various calendars that shape the Church's year are also patterned after the Old Testament, but with new versions of the Sabbath, Passover, and the Day of Atonement – the Lord's Day, the Eucharistic meal, and Easter – to name three examples (Daniélou). Christian prayer and praise continue to draw heavily on the Psalms. The Church also has a rich hymnody that – as any hymnbook illustrates – often deploys Old Testament ideas in recounting the drama of Christian salvation.

Pastoralia

Ballard, P. H., Holmes, S. R. and Elkins, W. (eds), 2005, *The Bible in Pastoral Practice: Readings in the Place and Function of Scripture in the Church*, London: Darton, Longman and Todd.

Challis, W., 1997, *The Word of Life: Using the Bible in Pastoral Care*, London: Marshall Pickering.

Collicutt McGrath, J., 2015, *The Psychology of Christian Character Formation*, London: SCM Press.

Hoare, L., 2015, *Using the Bible in Spiritual Direction*, London: SPCK.

Pattison, S., Cooling, M. and Cooling, T., 2007, *Using the Bible in Christian Ministry*, London: Darton, Longman and Todd.

Whipp, M., 2013, *Study Guide to Pastoral Theology*, London: SCM Press.

Bennett, D. W., 1993, *Metaphors of Ministry: Biblical Images for Leaders and Followers*, Grand Rapids, MI: Baker; Carlisle: Paternoster.

Heywood, D., 2011, *Reimagining Ministry*, London: SCM Press.

Laniak, T. S., 2006, *Shepherds After My Own Heart: Pastoral Traditions and Leadership in the Bible*, Leicester: Apollos.

Runcorn, D., 2011, *Fear and Trust: God-Centred Leadership*, London: SPCK.

Stevens, M. E., 2012, *Leadership Roles of the Old Testament: King, Prophet, Priest, Sage*, Eugene, OR: Cascade Books.

Effective pastoral care, given the responsibility that comes with its applied nature and consequential effects, requires a high level of discernment in the use of biblical texts (Ballard, Holmes and Elkins; Challis; Collicutt McGrath; Hoare; Pattison, Cooling and Cooling; Whipp). It is in relationship with God that people find transformation, renewal, and healing. The narratives and the poetry of the Old Testament speak, in their different ways, to the remoulding of often strained human affections, whether that is towards God or one another, or within ourselves as individuals. Be it the time-framed journeying of the narrative of God's people, or the momentary poignancy of a poetic image, the pastoral care of individuals in community is frequently nourished by these sacred texts. The Old Testament reflects a strong communal focus, of mutual obligations, as well as many examples of individuals – the noble, the nasty, and the normal – that are both instructive in the life of the Church. That Jesus spent time apart as an individual with God, as well as living his life in community with his disciples, models this dual focus perfectly; his ministerial practice was, in other words, collaborative (Heywood). His example encourages recognition of another important theme: leadership. The Old Testament highlights the necessity of leadership to organize and shepherd communities; whether that is through priests, kings, sages, prophets, or others (Laniak; Runcorn; Stevens). Each of these, despite their own particularities, provides instruction about leadership as an aspect of ministry, even though in the Church each of these roles tends to be seen through later New Testament perspectives.

Mission

Theological understanding

Bauckham, R., 2003, *Bible and Mission*, Carlisle: Paternoster; Grand Rapids, MI: Baker.

Hoggarth, P. et al., 2013, *Bible in Mission*, Oxford: Regnum Books International.

Okoye, J. C., 2006, *Israel and the Nations: A Mission Theology of the Old Testament*, Maryknoll, NY: Orbis.

Senior, D. and Stuhlmueller, C., 1983, *The Biblical Foundations for Mission*, London: SCM Press.

Williamson, H. G. M., 1988, *Variations on a Theme: King, Messiah and Servant in the Book of Isaiah*, Carlisle: Paternoster.

Wright, C. J. H., 2006, *The Mission of God: Unlocking the Bible's Grand Narrative*, Nottingham: Inter-Varsity Press.

The mission of the Church is, likewise, rooted in the action of the one God of the Old Testament. It would be easy to suppose that much of the Old Testament is concerned primarily with the society of ancient Israel. However, that would be to lower its horizons too much. There are many points at which the reader is prompted to lift the horizon higher to see a larger divine purpose for the world. This is evident from its opening sentences about creation in the Pentateuch, and in the forward-looking visions in the Prophetic Books that anticipate the inclusion of the Gentiles among the people of God. With an eye to this, the mission of God for the world, according to the Old Testament, becomes easier to see elsewhere: the promise that the ancestors of Israel would be a blessing to the nations; Israel's vocation to be a 'kingdom of priests' in the world; and that the nations would bring tribute to the messianic (anointed) king in Jerusalem. Given that the Church has, since its inception, been an ethnically diverse community, inspired by this worldwide vision, this interpretation of the Old Testament is firmly established in the life and work of the Church around the world. However, mission is not only concerned with ethnic identity, as it impacts all aspects of the human experience – gender, language, social status – including experiences that threaten life itself: the cosmic foe of death. Mission is thus all-encompassing, and the Church's vocation, led and inspired by the ideal example of Jesus Christ as the Son and the Servant of God, is to embody and proclaim the message of salvation to all humankind (Bauckham; Hoggarth et al.; Okoye; Senior and Stuhlmueller; Williamson; Wright).

Society

Barton, J., 2002, *Ethics and the Old Testament*, 2nd edn, London: SCM Press.

Barton, J., 2014, *Ethics in Ancient Israel*, Oxford: Oxford University Press.

Brawley, R. L. (ed.), 2014, *The Oxford Encyclopedia of the Bible and Ethics*, 2 vols, Oxford: Oxford University Press.

Green, J. B. and Lapsley, J. E. (eds), 2013, *The Old Testament and Ethics: A Book-By-Book Survey*, Grand Rapids, MI: Baker.

Strawn, B. A. (ed.), 2015, *The Oxford Encyclopedia of the Bible and Law*, Oxford: Oxford University Press.

Williamson, H. G. M., 2012, *He Has Shown You what is Good: Old Testament Justice Then and Now: the Trinity Lectures, Singapore, 2011*, Cambridge: Lutterworth Press.

The Church's role in society is thus one of witness: to be a beacon of hope in an often dark world. Its vocation in this respect is to proclaim a unique message of salvation from all that is opposed to the living God, and from that which oppresses and enslaves people (e.g. sin, death, evil powers). This is worked out in various ways in the Old Testament: priestly laws, royal edicts, wisdom sayings, and prophetic oracles. These facets of proclamation are later developed in the pages of the New Testament, in the examples of Jesus and then of Paul whom he commissioned, with both of them following after Old Testament patterns. The Old Testament anticipates the fruitfulness of this mission in examples of conversion and participation in the purposes of God, including the non-Israelite (e.g. Balaam, Rahab, Naaman). The Church's witness is not confined, however, to proclamation. At its best, the Christian Church community models the love of God and neighbour in society: to show how the principles and practices of holiness and justice comfort the downtrodden and challenge the oppressor. The Old Testament texts are extremely valuable in this regard, not only because they proclaim such hopeful and transformative ideals, but also because ancient Israel's own narratives are shot through with both success and failure. The texts that address life in all its bewildering fragmentation – including the shocking and the brutal – may be turned from a curse into a blessing. By engaging with them, they have the capacity to mould our sensibilities and practical responses to suffering. A fresh appreciation of the richness of the Old Testament for ethical reflection is currently a growth area in Biblical Studies (Barton; Brawley; Green and Lapsley; Strawn; Williamson). This is important in an age in which the ethical contributions of religion in general is contested in the public square.

Culture

Allison, D. C. et al. (eds), 2009–, *Encyclopedia of the Bible and Its Reception Online*, 30 vols (projected), Berlin; Boston: De Gruyter.

Beavis, M. A. and Gilmour, M. J. (eds), 2012, *Dictionary of the Bible and Western Culture*, Sheffield: Sheffield Phoenix Press.

Lieb, M., Mason, E. and Roberts, J. (eds), 2011, *The Oxford Handbook of the Reception History of the Bible*, Oxford: Oxford University Press.

Beal, T. K. (ed.), 2015, *The Oxford Encyclopaedia of the Bible and the Arts*, New York: Oxford University Press.

Campbell, R. H., 1981, *The Bible on Film: A Checklist, 1897–1980*, Metuchen, NJ: Scarecrow Press.

Debray, R., 2004, *The Old Testament through 100 Masterpieces of Art*, London and New York: Merrell.

Long, S. S. and Sawyer, J. F. A., 2015, *The Bible in Music: A Dictionary of Songs, Works, and More*, Lanham, MA: Rowman & Littlefield Publishers.

Louvish, S., 2007, *Cecil B. DeMille and the Golden Calf*, London: Faber and Faber.

Shepherd, D., 2013, *The Bible on Silent Film: Spectacle, Story and Scripture in the Early Cinema*, Cambridge: Cambridge University Press.

Stern, M., 2011, *Bible and Music: Influences of the Old Testament on Western Music*, Jersey City, NJ: Ktav.

Becker, K. J. et al., 2010, *Catholic Engagement with World Religions: A Comprehensive Study*, Maryknoll, NY: Orbis.

Ford, D. F. and Pecknold, C. C. (eds), 2006, *The Promise of Scriptural Reasoning*, Malden, MA; Oxford: Blackwell.

Glaser, I., 2012, *The Bible and Other Faiths: What Does the LORD Require of Us?*, Carlisle: Global Christian Library.

The Old Testament texts have exercised an incalculable influence in the history of human society and culture. This is evident in many ways across the world: institutions, laws, education, figures of speech, literature, music, poetry, and the fine arts – in addition to public monuments to the Christian faith such as cathedrals and their stained-glass windows (Allison et al.; Beavis and Gilmour; Lieb, Mason and Roberts). The arts are an especially rich seam in this respect (Beal; Campbell; Debray; Long and Sawyer; Louvish; Shepherd; Stern). While the forces of secularization and rival worldviews appear strong, this influence is still very much alive. Some might point to the historical examples of G. F. Handel's oratorio *Messiah* (1741), Lord Byron's poem *The Destruction of Sennacherib* (1815), or Cecil B. DeMille's biblical epic film *The Ten Commandments* (1956), but this influence is on-going. The widespread use of imagery about Eve in the advertising of women's luxury products is but one contemporary example.[5] The phenomenon of globalization has, however, shaken the Church out its comfortable, cultural slumbers. For instance, the increasingly widespread practice of interfaith dialogue, whereby Christians share both the similarities and the differences that they have with those of other religions – and not only Judaism and Islam – has brought fresh perspectives to the Christian application of the Old Testament (Becker et al.; Ford and Pecknold; Glaser). That there are issues of global significance that affect everyone (e.g. trade, migration, violence, climate), with which the Old Testament texts resonate, is another aspect of this. To fulfil its calling and vocation – to participate in the divine healing of the world and the nations – it is incumbent upon the Christian Church to be attentive to these and all of the diverse dimensions of mission.

Notes

1 The following are examples: the bibliographical sections at the end of each biblical book in a single-volume Bible commentary, such as Barton, J. and Muddiman, J. (eds), 2001, *The Oxford Bible Commentary*, Oxford: Oxford University Press, which includes a 'Bibliographical Guide to Biblical Studies', pp. 1331–45; bibliographies for Old Testament canonical sections, such as Sparks, K. L., 2002, *The Pentateuch: An Annotated Bibliography*, Grand Rapids, MI: Baker; and the *Society for Old Testament Studies Book List*, which is an annual review of the latest scholarly publications. There are also many good websites with large amounts of information, whether put together by individual scholars or through scholarly collaboration; some require external user subscription (e.g. www.oxfordbiblicalstudies.com).

2 See, again, Barton and Muddiman, *Oxford Bible Commentary* (note 1 above). Certain publications catalogue, analyse, and evaluate the available commentaries: see Longman, T., 2013, *Old Testament Commentary Survey*, 5th edn, Grand Rapids, MI: Baker; Leicester: Inter-Varsity Press; and not only commentaries but also other theological resources: Glynn, J., 2007, *Commentary and Reference Survey: A Comprehensive Guide to Biblical and Theological Studies*, 10th edn, Grand Rapids, MI: Kregel.

3 See further, for instance, Douglas, S. K., 1984, *Old Testament Exegesis: A Primer for Students and Pastors*, 2nd rev., enlarged edn, Philadelphia, PA: Westminster John Knox; Gorman, M. J., 2009, *Elements of Biblical Exegesis: A Basic Guide for Students and Minsters*, rev. and expanded, Peabody, MA: Hendrickson. For an example of how various methods can apply to one biblical book, see Hendel, R., 2010, *Reading Genesis: Ten Methods*, Cambridge: Cambridge University Press. A widely respected primer on method is Barton, J., 1996, *Reading the Old Testament. Method in Biblical Study*, 2nd edn, London: Darton, Longman and Todd. See further, under the heading 'Method, hermeneutics, theology' (p. 220) in the present volume.

4 The following provide fine starting points: Carson, D. A. and Williamson, H. G. M. (eds), 1992, *It is Written: Scripture Citing Scripture. Essays in Honour of Barnabas Lindars*, Cambridge: Cambridge University Press; Collins, J. J. and Harlow, D. C. (eds), 2010, *The Eerdmans Dictionary of Early Judaism*, Grand Rapids, MI; Cambridge: Eerdmans; Fishbane, M., 1985, *Interpretation in Ancient Israel*, Oxford: Clarendon; Henze,

M. (ed.), 2012, *A Companion to Biblical Interpretation in Early Judaism*, Grand Rapids, MI: Eerdmans; Kugel, J. L., 1997, *The Bible As It Was*, Cambridge, MA; London: Belknap Press of Harvard University Press; Kugel, J. L., 1998, *Traditions of the Bible: A Guide to the Bible As It Was at the Start of the Common Era*, Cambridge, MA; London: Harvard University Press.

5 See further, Edwards, K. B., 2012, *Admen and Eve: The Bible in Contemporary Advertising*, Sheffield: Sheffield Phoenix Press.

Index of Biblical References

Poetry and Wisdom

Prophetic Books

New Testament

Index of Sources

Ancient Near East

Ancient Judaism

Poetry and Wisdom

Prophetic Books

Index of Names

Index of Subjects